ZAPPA

OMNIBUS PRESS
LONDON · NEW YORK · PARIS · SYDNEY

Copyright © 1993 Omnibus Press
(A Division of Book Sales Limited)

Edited by Chris Charlesworth.
Cover & book designed by Michael Bell Design.
Picture research by Miles & David Brolan.

ISBN 0.7119.3099.6
Order No. OP 47102

Exclusive Distributors:
Book Sales Limited
8/9 Frith Street,
London W1V 5TZ, UK.

Music Sales Corporation
225 Park Avenue South,
New York, NY 10003, USA.

Music Sales Pty Limited
120 Rothschild Avenue,
Rosebery, NSW 2018, Australia.

To the Music Trade only:
Music Sales Limited
8/9 Frith Street,
London W1V 5TZ, UK.

Photo credits: Front cover: Mark Hanauer / Retna.
Back cover: Mark Hanauer / Retna; Barry Plummer /
LFI; Giovanni Canitano / Retna; Rex Features &
Bonnie Schiffman / Retna. Paul Campbell: 36; Dagmar /
Starfile: 53; Anne Fishbein / Retna: 92; Mark Harlan /
Starfile: 97b; London Features International: 10b, 11,
17, 20b, 21t&b, 24, 27, 29, 30, 46, 50, 61t, 64 / 65,
69t&b, 72, 76, 79, 80, 89, 88, 89, 90, 97t, 99, 102,
104, 106, 108, 112; Malcolm Lubliner / Michael Ochs
Archives: 18 / 19; Alice Ochs / Michael Ochs Archives:
27r, 28r; Michael Ochs Archives: 4, 16, 26, 28t, 28r,
35t&b, 37, 39, 40, 43, 48, 55, 56 / 57, 63, 91;
Pictorial Press: 7b, 32/33; Barry Plummer: 25;
Chuck Pulin / Starfile: 9t, 45, 52, 66, 70, 74, 75, 83r,
86, 87, 94, 100; Mike Putland / Retna: 54, 60, 62, 93;
David Redfern / Redferns: 41, 42; Relay: 15, 31, 34, 44,
47, 61b, 71, 73, 101; Rex Features: 3, 9b, 10t, 38, 49,
51, 58, 67, 77, 78, 81, 85, 95, 96, 98, 103, 107, 109;
John Roca / LGI: 82 / 83; Daniel Root / Retna: 12;
Starfile: 20t; Scott Weiner / Retna: 105.

A catalogue record for this book is available from
the British Library.

Printed by Singapore National Printers
Limited, Singapore.

—INTRODUCTION—

A catalogue of everything that Frank Zappa has ever produced would fill
an encyclopedia. It would be hard to find anyone in the music business (outside
the world of jazz) who has released so much material - more than fifty albums -
or who has toured so much - literally thousands of concerts. In fact it took the
"Torchum" gang in Germany four volumes of their *The Torchum Never Stops* to list
his records and appearances and even that did not include biographical material
or printed interviews, of which there are probably more than a thousand.

Since I feel that biographical details are of prime importance in this case I have
restricted the record listing to UK and US releases only, and to albums only except
for singles released before the formation of the Mothers of Invention.

Singles have never been an important medium for Zappa and in many cases were
pulled off albums by the record company A&R people without Zappa's involvement.
The gig list is by no means complete, but it is of great importance because so many
of Zappa's records are in fact live recordings, sometimes collaged together,
sometimes with new material overdubbed on top.

I have tried to include all the many changes in line-up for both the recordings
and the tours. Sometimes I have included material from my own journals describing
Zappa's home, recording sessions I have attended, concerts or fragments from
interviews. These are always identified. I hope Frank's many fans will find
something of value here.

Miles

-1940-0-54-

—1940–1950—

21 DECEMBER

Frank Vincent Zappa, born in Baltimore, Maryland, the eldest son of Italian-American parents. His father was born in Partinico, a small town near the north coast of Sicily to the west of Palermo and arrived in the United States as a child. It is from his father that Frank claims Arab and Greek blood. His mother was first generation American of Neapolitan and Franco-Italian stock. Frank's parents often spoke Italian around the house and his maternal grandmother spoke no English.

He was the first of four children. After him came Bobby, then Carl and finally a daughter called Candy. Frank's father was an aspiring immigrant who had worked his way through college at the University of North Carolina at Chapel Hill by cutting hair, a trade he learned from his own father who worked as a barber on the Maryland waterfront. Frank grew up in the close-knit Baltimore Italian Catholic immigrant community surrounded by relatives.

During the war, his father worked as a meteorologist at the Edgewood Arsenal where the US military manufact-ured mustard gas. The Zappa family lived in a nearby army housing project at 15 Dexter Street, Edgewood, and because of their proximity to the lethal gas storage tanks, the entire family was issued with gas masks. Frank used his as a space helmet when he played in the back yard. Dexter Street ended in open countryside with a creek and small woods – ideal for the Zappa children to play in.

Frank's father had ambitions for him to become a scientist and though he was initially interested in chemistry, his parents were reluctant to buy him proper equipment because he was obsessed with explosives. He could make gunpowder by the time he was six and by the age of 12 he had already been involved in several explosive accidents.

He finally gave up chemistry when he was 15 but maintains that…
"Chemical combinatorial theories persist however in the process of composition." [Zappa: 1981]

Frank was a frail child who suffered from asthma, sinus trouble and earaches. The winters in Maryland were severe and his parents were so concerned for his health that his father took a job in Florida as a military ballistics engineer, calculating shell trajectories, in order to move his family to a warmer climate. The war was still on and there was plenty of military work. Living in the Everglades, Frank's health improved and he grew rapidly, gaining a foot in height, but his mother was homesick for her family so in the end they returned to Maryland.

This time they lived in a rowhouse in Baltimore, but after the freedom of the countryside, both in Edgewood and in Florida, Frank hated it and his health again began to suffer.

His parents were also unhappy with their situation and eventually Frank's father landed a job teaching metallurgy at the Naval Post-Graduate School in Monterey, California.

—1951—

JANUARY

The Zappas moved to Monterey, California, best known as the setting for John Steinbeck's novel *Cannery Row*. Though Monterey has a very pleasant climate in the summer, in the winter it suffers from rain and fog and when the Zappa family arrived, exhausted after driving across the country, it was freezing cold.

—1953—

By 1953 the family had moved to Pacific Grove on the peninsula just south of Monterey. Here twelve year old Frank went to summer school where he took a basic training course in drumming for kids who were going to be in the drum and bugle corps back in school. His teacher was Keith McKillip, something of a local hero in drumming circles.

"They had all these little kids about eleven or twelve years old lined up in this room. You didn't have drums, you had these boards – not pads, but a plank laid across some chairs – and everybody stood in front of this plank and went rattlety-tat on it." [Zappa: 1977]

Later that year the Zappa family moved to Pomona, California where his father took a job with Convair working as a metallurgist. This was Frank's first experience of living in the scattered suburban communities east of Los Angeles where he was later to begin his recording career.

—1954—

Still working for the defence industry, Frank's father next moved his family to El Cajon, just outside San Diego, where he had a job working on the Atlas guided missile system. It was here that Frank first heard of Edgard Varèse.

He was flipping through *Look Magazine* and found an article about Sam Goody's record store in New York. They claimed that Goody could sell anything, even a record called *Ionizations* by Edgard Varèse which consisted of nothing but drums and sirens. Nobody would want to own this record said *Look* and yet Sam Goody was actually selling it. Frank liked the sound of it very much but it was about a year before he found a copy.

El Cajon was basically a cowboy town, not the sort of place to stock Varèse, but one day Frank stayed over with a friend of his who lived in La Mesa, a more genteel community to the north of El Cajon and there in the hi-fi store he found

The Complete Works of Edgard Varèse, Volume 1. **Look** magazine had even got the title wrong. The album was Elaine Music Stores EMS 401 conducted by Frederic Waldman, under the supervision of the composer and "Ionization" was on it.

Frank had never bought an album before…

"The guy wanted six dollars for it and I said 'Six dollars for a record!' He said, 'How much money you got?'"

Frank paid him $3.75. The store had been using it to demonstrate hi-fi but had never managed to sell anything with it.

The family had a small Decca record player next to his mother's ironing board. It stood on little wrought iron legs because the speaker was on the bottom, so the sound reflected off the table. You had to put a quarter on the tone arm to weigh it down. The record had sirens and bass drums and a lion roaring and Frank was delighted with it. His parents forbade him to play it in their presence because the sirens made his mother neurotic while she was ironing and soon the record player was banished to Frank's bedroom.

– 1955 –

By now the Zappas were living in San Diego proper and Frank was attending Mission Bay High School near the University of San Diego. One day in 1955, Frank was riding in the car with his parents and happened to turn on the radio. The song which came on was "Gee" by The Crows [Rama 5, 1953], followed by "I" by The Velvets. [Red Robin 122, December 1953]. To 14-year old Frank they sounded fabulous and he knew he was on to something when his parents insisted on turning off the radio.

His parents were not music lovers and the only music Frank heard at home was the background music to soap-operas and swing bands on the radio. Now he began to seriously collect rhythm and blues records. He discovered a store on the ground floor of the Maryland Hotel in San Diego which even stocked Lightnin' Slim and Slim Harpo sides which were very rare because Excello, who released them, would only supply R&B records if the store took their gospel records as well.

Frank became something of an R&B expert and spent hours listening to Johnny 'Guitar' Watson, Clarence 'Gatemouth' Brown, The Orchids, The Nutmegs, The Gladiolas and all the great doo-wop groups of the period. His favourite record was "Angel In My Life" by The Jewels [Imperial 5351, April 1955]. He took it to his high school music teacher, Mr. Kavelman, and asked him why he liked it so much. "Parallel fourths", Mr Kavelman told him.

In his early teens Frank used to build models and sew clothes for puppets and marionettes. He gave puppet shows for his family acting out Stan Frieberg records. His first move into the world of show business was at the Los Angeles County Fair when he convinced his little brother Carl to pretend he was his ventriloquist dummy, sit on his lap and lip-sync "Riot In Cell Block Number 9" by The Robins [Spark 103, 1954] .

When Frank was living in San Diego he fell in with a fast crowd who listened to a lot of rhythm and blues…

"I used to know a lot of vicious teenage hoodlum type characters who identified very strongly with that sort of music because not only did the lyric content match their lifestyle, but the overall timbre of the music seemed to express the way they felt." [Zappa: 1970]

All this time Frank had continued his drum practice – even though he didn't own a drum. In his bedroom he had a bureau which had once been a rather elegant piece of furniture until one of his Italian relatives painted it green. Frank proceeded to flake all the paint off it by beating it with his drum-sticks. Eventually his mother hired a snare drum for him but insisted that he practise out in the garage.

At the age of fourteen Frank joined a high school rhythm and blues band called The Ramblers, led by Elwood 'Junior' Madeo. They played covers of Little Richard's early releases such as "Directly From Heart To You". The piano player's name was Stuart Congdon and The Ramblers would rehearse in his living room. Stuart's father was a preacher, and he would not allow a drum set in the house even if Frank had owned one, but he did allow Frank to beat on a pair of pots held between his legs like bongos…

"I'm sitting there trying to play shuffles on these two pots between my legs! I was really hurting for an instrument in those days." [Zappa: 1977]

Frank finally talked his parents into buying him a $50 drum set from a neighbour. It consisted of a kick drum, a little Zyn high-hat, a snare, one floor tom, and one 15" Zyn ride cymbal. One week after obtaining a complete kit, he played his first professional gig. The Ramblers were booked to play the Uptown Hall in San Diego, in the Hillcrest district at 48th and Mead.

The Zappa family in the mid-fifties

"I remember it well, going to my first gig, I got over there, set up my drums, and noticed I had forgotten my only pair of sticks. And I lived way on the other side of town." [Zappa: 1977]

They had to drive all the way back to get them. The band received $7.00 between them for the night's work. In the end Elwood 'Junior' Madeo fired Frank because he couldn't keep a good beat and played the cymbals too much.

At 14, Frank still retained an interest in scientific matters and at the high school Open House Night he and several friends started a number of fires using a combination of solid rocket fuel and stink bomb powder. In his autobiography Zappa wrote...

"They threw me out of school and were going to put me on probation, but my mother pleaded with the probation guy (who happened to be Italian) and explained that my Dad was about to be transferred out of San Diego to Lancaster – and they let me go."

Lancaster is in the Antelope Valley to the north of the San Gabriel Mountains which separate it from the Los Angeles conurbation 40 miles away. It had a population of about a hundred thousand spread out over 200 square miles of high desert on the edge of the Mojave Desert, near Edwards Airforce Base. After mid-morning it was too hot to go outside. Frank lived in a tract of little stucco houses at 45438 Third Street East, near the Antelope Valley Fair Grounds...

"Okies with cars dying in their yards. You know how you always have to pull up a Chevrolet and let it croak on your lawn... [Zappa: 1970]

Frank's 15th birthday came around not long after the family arrived in Lancaster and his mother said that she would spend $5.00 on him. Since he was still playing *The Complete Works of Edgard Varèse, Volume 1* to everyone who came to visit and studying its lengthy sleeve notes, he decided that he would spend the money on a phone call to Edgard Varèse. He naturally assumed that Varèse lived in Greenwich Village because that was where all the composers and artists lived and sure enough, directory assistance informed him that Mr. Varèse lived on Sullivan Street and gave him the number.

Frank got through to Varèse's wife who said that the composer was in Brussels, working on a score but that Frank should call back in a few weeks. This time he actually spoke to the great man, who, among other things informed his young fan that he was working on a piece entitled "Déserts". Since he was living in the desert, Frank found this pretty exciting and has always thought of the piece as being about the Mojave.

The second album that Frank bought was a cheap issue of Stravinsky's *The Rite of Spring*...

"I listened to those albums for about two years before I owned any others. And I liked them equally as well as Rhythm and Blues, so my whole background is just those elements." [Zappa: 1970]

One problem with Lancaster was that nobody knew who Johnny 'Guitar'

Watson was and there was nowhere he could buy his rhythm and blues records. Frank's solution was to work at the local record store during lunch times and after school. He became the buyer for the store and ran...

"a campaign to upgrade the musical taste of the community."

He brought in records like "Tell Me Darling" by The Gaylarks and "Oh What A Night" by The Dells.

Then he discovered a local source of ex-jukebox records where he could pick up Excello releases and rural blues for a song, though he would still periodically make trips down to San Diego to the Maryland Hotel for really rare stuff.

Frank went to Antelope Valley Joint Union High School which was the kind of high school where the cheerleaders were so important that they didn't stick to boola boola but ran the student government as well. One of the first things Frank did there was to organise a band. They were called The Blackouts... because several members had the tendency to go face-down after drinking peppermint schnapps (the beverage of choice at that time).

It was an eight-piece mixed group: Terry Wimberly was half Sicilian and half Indian, the Salazar brothers were Mexican, Johnny Franklin, Carter Franklin and Wayne Lyles were black and Frank was Greek-Italian. Frank played drums, Motorhead Sherwood used to dance "the Bug" in front of the group. An integrated group in 1956 was not appreciated by certain sections of the population and The Blackouts had some trouble because of their line-up.

In those days you had to have a band uniform, that was one of the main reasons for having a band in the first place. The Blackouts wore white peggers with metal belts which could be used as weapons in case of a rumble. Their shirts were either brown plaid or dark blue lamé. Most of the money they made went to buy uniforms.

They had ten songs that they could play really well, half of which were covers of rhythm and blues classics that were already five or six years old in 1956: "Behind the Sun", "Pocky Docky Stomp", "Bacon Fat" which was fairly recent, "Kansas City", Little Richard's "Directly From My Heart To You" and for the rest of the evening they took requests.

To the south east of Lancaster there was a mainly black community called Sun

Village and it was people from there who supported the group...

"We had these huge Negro dances and this upset the people in the town." [Zappa: 1968]

The police arrested Frank for vagrancy the night before one show and kept him in jail overnight. His parents bailed him out.

None of the big acts from Los Angeles ever came up to play Lancaster so The Blackouts had the r&b and rock'n'roll market cornered...

"The band stayed together until everybody got to hate each other's guts." [Zappa: 1968]

After Frank left the group it turned into The Omens, some of whom later joined The Mothers and some joined Captain Beefheart's Magic Band.

Frank met Don van Vliet, later known as Captain Beefheart, at high school in 1956. Don was the only person Frank knew in Lancaster who had an interest in rhythm and blues records and they quickly became best friends. They would get together after school and listen to records for three or four hours...

"We'd start off at my house, and then we'd get something to eat and ride around in his old Oldsmobile looking for pussy – in Lancaster! Then we'd go to his house and raid his old man's bread truck and we would sit and eat pineapple buns and listen to these records until five in the morning and maybe not go to school the next day. It was the only thing that seemed to matter at the time." [Zappa: 1968]

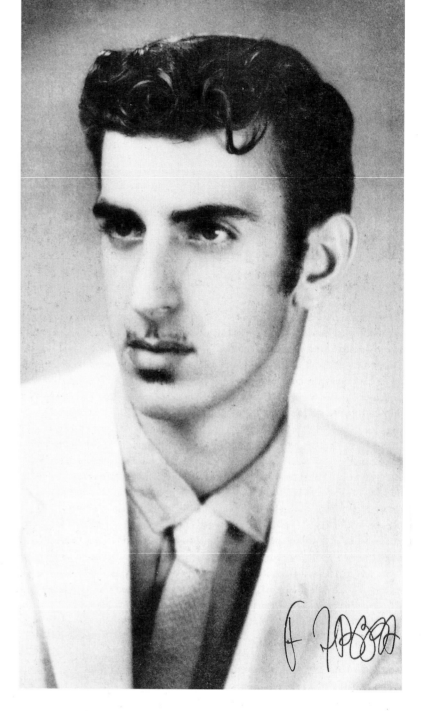

Frank's High School graduation portrait

They would quiz each other on record lore: record numbers, number of records released, flip sides.

Don spent most of his time driving around the desert in a powder blue Oldsmobile with a terracotta werewolf head that he had modelled himself mounted on the dashboard and was always dressed in the latest pachuco fashion – Mexican hip. He dropped out of school in his senior year to take over his father's Helms Bread truck route to Mohave after his father had a heart attack. He got himself a girlfriend who came to live with him at his parents' house but he still found plenty of time to see Frank.

Frank` was often suspended from high school...

"I was a jerk in high school and got thrown out quite frequently."

He actually had several teachers who helped him in his future career. Frank would spend hours sitting talking with the vice-principal Ernie Tossi in his office and even invited Tossi back to meet his folks. Don Cerveris, his English teacher, quit his job while Frank was at high school and moved to Hollywood but Frank kept in touch and it was through him that Frank wrote his first film score. His music instructor was Mr. Ballard who let him conduct the school orchestra and on

several occasions allowed Frank to write his compositions up on the blackboard for the orchestra to play – invaluable for a composer who has no other way of knowing what his work sounds like. Ballard and Tossi both received name-checks on Frank's first album.

Frank had first heard about serial music and the work of Anton von Webern from his music teacher in San Diego, Mr. Kavelman, and since then had been studying music composition. He bought a copy of *Counterpoint: Strict and Free* by H.A.Clarke, published in Philadelphia in 1929. The second page of the text read: "Never write any of the following successions:

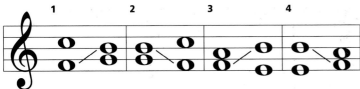

Numbers 1 and 2 are very harsh. Numbers 3 and 4 not so harsh and of common occurrence in modern usage."

Frank played them, said "Great" and never read any further. These successions are also used frequently by Stravinsky whom Frank thinks also probably saw them in a counterpoint book.

Frank began writing his own early serial music scores. When he finally heard them performed he didn't like them…
"I didn't like it. I knew the serial integrity was there but nobody else was going to hear the mathematics that went into it."

He continued playing with The Blackouts.

Frank spent the summer of 1957 with his Aunt Mary back in Baltimore and wrote to Edgard Varèse asking if he could come up to New York and visit. He received a handwritten reply which read:

VII 12th/57

Dear Mr. Zappa,
I am sorry not to be able to grant you your request. I am leaving for Europe next week and will be gone until next spring. I am hoping however to see you on my return.
With best wishes.
Sincerely
Edgard Varèse.

It was a visit never to be. Varèse died on 6 November 1965. Frank had the letter framed and it hangs in a prominent position in his workroom.

By late 1957, it had become obvious to Frank that he was not cut out to be a drummer. The main instrument used in rhythm and blues and doo-wop was the saxophone, but when someone was allowed to play a brief guitar solo, Frank's ears always pricked up. He couldn't get enough of it. This was the attraction of Johnny 'Guitar' Watson and the rural

blues players whose records he collected.

Frank's brother Carl had a guitar that he wasn't using that he had paid $1.50 for at an auction. Soon it was Frank's. It had an arch-top, f-holes and a cracked base. You couldn't tell the make because the whole finish had been sanded off. It had very high action, the strings were so high off the fingerboard that playing chords was virtually impossible. Frank started playing lines right away…
"In four weeks I was playing shitty teenage leads." [Zappa: 1968]

It was obvious that he needed to know chords so he got a Mickey Baker chord book and began to figure them out, though playing them was not as easy as playing lead. When he left The Blackouts, a few months later, his much loved drum set was part hired out and part sold off to The Bluenotes, a rival r&b band.

During his senior year in high school Frank took a special harmony course with Mr. Russell, which entailed going over to the Antelope Valley Junior College Campus on the outskirts of town. At the same time, his father began pressuring him to go on and study music at the Curtis Institute but Frank was determined not to go on to college; he had already

Below: Dweezil Zappa and Frank

had enough of education. He graduated from Antelope Valley Joint Union High School on Friday, June 13th 1958, with 20 units less than he was supposed to have, but since they didn't want to see him back again for another year they let it pass.

The problem was, the only way to meet girls was at college…

"I figured I wanted to get laid but when I went to find somebody to stuff it up, they were all going to school", Frank told biographer David Walley.

Frank enrolled at the Antelope Valley Junior College. He was there long enough to make the earliest recordings of Don van Vliet…

"I had conned him into doing a parody of a rhythm and blues vocal in one of the class rooms at the junior college. We borrowed a tape recorder from school and recorded a song called 'Lost In A Whirlpool' about a guy who has been flushed down the toilet by his girlfriend and is confronted by a blind brown fish." [Zappa: 1970]

In the spring of 1959, the ever restless Francis Zappa Sr. moved his family on to Claremont, not far from Pomona where they had lived in 1953. Instead of going with them, Frank tried his luck in Hollywood. He was 18. He moved into a cheap neighbourhood called Echo Park, between Downtown and Hollywood, to the north of the Hollywood Freeway near Elysian Park which now houses the Dodgers Baseball Stadium. By the late Sixties it had become a student area but when Frank first moved there it was a mostly Mexican neighbourhood.

His old English teacher and friend, Don Ceveris, was trying to make it as a screen writer and had written a low-budget Western called *Run Home Slow*. The producer, Tim Sullivan, hired Frank to write the score but as usual there

Captain Beefheart

were a few problems, notably with the leading lady who had a miscarriage on the third day of shooting. The production was shelved for a few years for Sullivan to raise more money.

Meanwhile Frank's health began to deteriorate again; he was not eating properly and the stomach ulcers he developed when he was 16 began to give him pain. He did the sensible thing and moved home where he enrolled in Chaffee Junior College in Ontario. Here he took a harmony course with Miss Holly which required him to do keyboard practice. Though he wasn't enrolled, he also sat in on a composition course taught by Mr. Kohn at nearby Pomona College.

At Chaffee he met Kay Sherman and pretty soon they were living together. Frank completed one semester at school, then came the summer vacation and though he went back in the Fall, he only stayed a few weeks. That was the end of his formal education.

Frank and Kay got married and moved into a house at 314 West G Street, Ontario. Kay worked as a secretary at the First National Bank of Ontario and Frank worked in the silk-screen department of Nile Running Greeting Cards. After that he did part-time copy-writing and designing advertisements for local businesses, worked as a window dresser, a jewellery salesman and for one week he even sold Collier's Encyclopedias door-to-door.

In 1960 Frank formed The Boogie Men with himself on lead guitar and vocals, Al Surratt on drums, Kenny Burgan on saxophone and Doug Rost playing rhythm guitar. They were literally a "garage band". A press clip from the period includes a photograph of the band captioned. *"The Boogie Men rehearse 'Nite Owl' for high school weekend job, Frank Zappa's garage, Ontario, California."* The Boogie Men had no bass player because they couldn't afford one.

Naturally the Boogie Men made no money and folded. Frank brought in some much needed cash by playing cocktail music on weekends with a four-piece lounge band called Joe Perrino and The Mellotones at Tommy Sandi's Club Sahara on E Street in San Bernardino and at some of the clubs around West Covina.

By this time Frank was playing electric guitar. When he was 21 he hired a Telecaster from a music store and found that he had to start over in order to learn to play it. Then he bought a Jazzmaster which he used for about a year and a half. Though he had some cards printed which read: "F.V. Zappa. Composer – Master Blues Guitarist" with his G Street address and phone number on them, most of the time he wound up playing with Joe Perrino and The Mellotones. He wore a white dinner jacket, bow tie, black pants, black patent leather shoes, his hair slicked back and strummed four

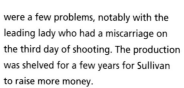

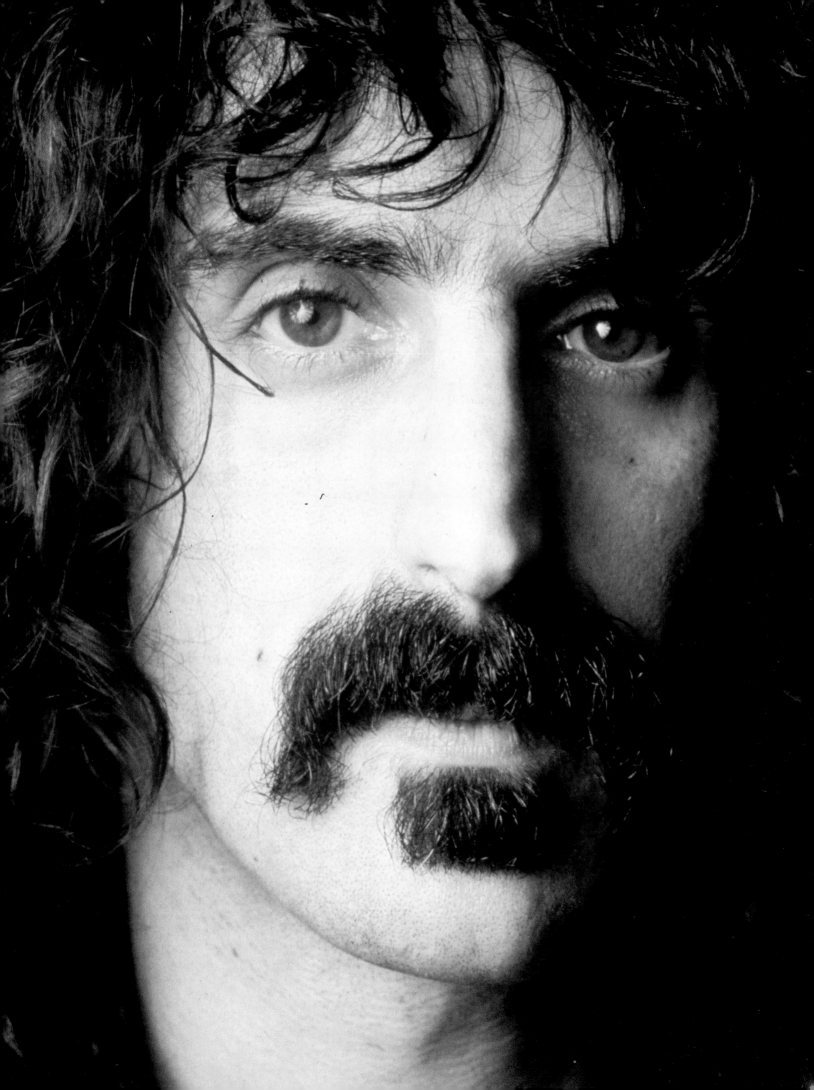

chords to a bar while sitting on a bar stool: "Anniversary Waltz", "Happy Birthday", "Green Dolphin Street" and one twist number per night with strict instructions not to turn the volume up. He got so sick of it that after he quit he put his guitar in its case and hid it behind the sofa for eight months.

The best thing to come out of this period was another film score. In June 1961, Frank began work on the score for a movie called *The World's Greatest Sinner*, written, directed and produced by Tim Carey… "Hollywood's ugliest, meanest" character actor.

Carey also played the main lead as an insurance salesman, dissatisfied with his life, who turns first to music, then religion and finally politics. He eventually repents after an unsuccessful attempt to prove himself God. Since the film had only a $90,000 budget, 80% of the filming was done in Carey's garage in El Monte.

Frank told the *Pomona Progress-Bulletin*…

"The score is unique in that it uses every type of music."

In November 1961 an eight-piece rock and roll combo, line-up unknown, recorded part of the score. In early December a 20-piece chamber ensemble recorded it and finally, on 17 December 1961, the 55-piece Pomona Valley Symphony Orchestra, under the direction of Fred E. Graff, augmented by other musicians from Pomona High School and Chaffey Junior College, played Frank's orchestral score, in a 12-hour stint at the Chaffey Auditorium using a couple of microphones and a direct mix to mono.

Frank never got paid and later described the music as "rancid." He did however salvage something from the project, as the theme from *The World's Greatest Sinner* appeared first as the

"B" side of a Baby Ray and Ferns single in 1963 and later as "Holiday In Berlin" on the 1970 *Burnt Weenie Sandwich* album.

A few miles to the north-east of Ontario is the small town of Cucamonga. Originally a stop on the AT & SF Railroad, the centre of town gradually migrated north to Route 66 where it crossed Archibald Avenue. Just north of the crossing, at 8040 North Archibald Avenue was Studio PAL, owned by Paul Buff. Frank was introduced to Buff by Ronnie Williams, a guitar player who features in "Let's Make The Water Turn Black".

Studio PAL had some very advanced features. At a time when the industry standard was mono, Studio PAL had five tracks, using an ingenious system of Paul Buff's own invention which enabled him to overdub tracks. Buff had lived in Cucamonga before serving in the US Marines where he learned electronics. When he got out he rented the rambling, three-room building on Archibald and with virtually no money set about building a state of the art studio.

The room was L-shaped and the equipment in the control room included an eight-input Presto board with its own low-budget compressor and a Rec-O-Cut lathe to cut discs. There was a Hammond spring echo and basic EQ. It was a remarkably complete and flexible system to find in a place like Cucamonga. Buff got a reasonable sound out of it; he had earlier cut "Wipeout" by The Safaris and "Flashin' Red" by The Esquires there.

Now with Frank hanging around, Buff proceeded to record a whole string of completed singles which he would then attempt to lease to record companies in Los Angeles such as Original Sound, Del-Fi, Capitol and Dot. The names of the groups changed from record to record but the same small group of musicians was on most of them. Sometimes he just could not find anyone to take the tapes, so early in 1963 he started his own label, Vigah! to release the rejected sides. The first record Frank ever made was:

The Masters [Frank Zappa, Paul Buff and Ronnie Williams]: *"Break Time"* / *"16 Tons"*. Emmy 10082. Released 1962. "A" side written by The Masters. Both sides played by them. Produced by Paul Buff at Studio PAL. Ronnie Williams overdubbed drums and bass.

Bobby Jameson: *"Gotta Find My Roogalator!"* / [*"Gotta Find My Roogalator!"*] Penthouse 503. Advance press label copies with same track on each side are the only copies that seem to have been issued sometime in late 1962. Zappa wrote the song and arranged the rhythm track. Zappa on guitar and possibly overdubbed drums and bass. Produced by Paul Buff at Studio PAL .

—1963—

Ron Roman: *"Love Of My Life"* / *"Tell Me"*. Daani 101. Released 1963. "A" side written by Frank Zappa, Ron Roman and Dave Aerni. Zappa on drums, bass and guitar. Produced by Paul Buff at Studio PAL.

Baby Ray & The Ferns: [Frank Zappa, Paul Buff, Dick Barber and Ray Collins] *"How's Your Bird?"* / *"The World's Greatest Sinner"*. Donna 1378. Released March 1963. Produced by Paul Buff at Studio PAL. Both sides written by Frank Zappa. Ray Collins sings lead on both sides.

Collins was later a founder member of The Mothers and Dick Barber became their road manager. This was the first collaboration between Collins and Zappa. Collins: "I was drinking in a bar, The Sportsman, in Pomona. Frank and his friends were playing. There wasn't even a stage. I figured that any band that played 'Work With Me Annie' was all right. They either asked me to sing with them, or I simply became too drunk and wandered up there and asked to sing with them. In any event, Frank and I got together. "I told him about an idea I had for a song. 'How's Your Bird?' was an expression that Steve Allen used to do on his TV show. One day Frank called me up and said…

'I wrote it. Let's record it.'
So we did!"

Bob Guy: *"Dear Jeepers"* / *"Letter From Jeepers"*. Donna 1380. Released April 1963. Both sides written by Frank Zappa for a monster movie as a parody of "Dinner With Drac" by John Zacherle [Cameo Parkway 130, 1958]. Frank Zappa over-dubbing the instruments / Dick Barber on percussion and back-up vocals. Bob Guy introduced horror movies at a local TV station and wanted to make a humorous monster record. He showed up wearing horn-rimmed spectacles, in a business suit, driving a white Cadillac.

Brian Lord & The Midnighters [Brian Lord with Frank Zappa, Paul Buff, Dave Aerni with Ray Collins on backing vocals]: *"The Big Surfer"* / *"Not Another One"* Vigah! 001. Released May, 1963. "A" side written by Zappa. Produced by Paul Buff at Studio PAL. Brian Lord was a local San Bernardino disc jockey who did a passable Jack Kennedy imitation. Here he imitates JFK judging a surfer dance contest using JFK's accent and referring to members of the First Family.

Paul Buff made it the first release on his Vigah! label and it received a lot of play in San Bernardino because Lord was known there as a disc jockey. Buff offered it to Capitol Records and on the strength of the airplay they bought the master right away, paying $800 in front for it. However, the record was never released because the punch line was 'As the winners of our dance contest you'll receive an all expense paid trip as the first members of the Peace Corps to be sent to Alabama.' About a week after Capitol bought the master, Peace Corps worker Medgar Evers was shot in Alabama. [Proposed release number

Capitol 4981, June 1963]

Ned and Nelda [Frank Zappa and Ray Collins]: *"Ned and Nelda"*/ *"Surf Along With Ned and Nelda"*. Vigah! 002. Released June 1963. Both sides written by Frank Zappa and Ray Collins as a parody of "Paul and Paula."

The Penguins: *"Memories of El Monte"*/ *"Be Mine"*. Original Sound 27. Released 1963. "A" side written by Frank Zappa and Ray Collins.

The Hollywood Persuaders [Frank Zappa and Paul Buff]: *"Tijuana Surf"* / *"Grunion Run"* Original Sound 39. Released 1963. *"Grunion Run"* written by Zappa, who played guitar. *"Tijuana Surf"* written by Paul Buff who multi-tracked all the instruments himself…

**"The 'A' side of 'Grunion Run' which was 'Tijuana Surf' became the number one record in Mexico for about 10 months straight and sold volumes down there."
[Zappa: 1970]**

The Heartbreakers: *"Cradle Rock"* / *"Everytime I See You"*. Donna 1381. Released April 1963. "B" side written by Frank Zappa and Ray Collins. Zappa plays guitar on "B" side. Produced at Cucamonga…

**"It was a group called The Heartbreakers, it was two 14 year old Mexican kids who sang."
[Zappa: 1970]**

Mr Clean [Frank Zappa and Paul Buff] *"Mr. Clean"* / *"Jessie Lee"*. Original Sound 40. Released July 1963. A master lease deal to Art Laboe at Original Sound. Zappa wrote, produced and played guitar on both sides.

Jim Musil Combo: *"Grunion Run"* / *"North Beach"* Jay Emm 423. Released 1963. "A" side written by Frank Zappa. Conrad & The Hurricane Strings: *"Hurricane"* / *"Sweet Love"*. Dayton 6401 [re-issued as Era 3130] Released December 1963. Produced by Frank Zappa.

The Rotations: *"Heavies"* / *"The Cruncher"*. Original Sound 41. Released early 1964? Produced by Frank Zappa. It is very likely Jim Motorhead Sherwood on baritone saxophone.

Frank got more and more involved with the recording industry and with making records. In the summer of 1963, Frank put together a little band called The Soots, featuring himself on guitar and vocals, Alex St. Clair on guitar, Vic Mortensen on drums and on lead vocals Don Van Vliet whom Frank re-named Captain Beefheart (after a complicated story about Don's uncle flashing his "beef heart" at Don's girlfriend Laurie). Among the songs recorded were "Metal Man Has Won His Wings", "Cheryl's Canon" and Little Richard's "Slippin' and Slidin'." Frank went to Milt Rogers at Dot Records in Hollywood to whom Paul Buff had introduced him and gave him the Soots masters, Dot rejected them on the grounds that "the guitar is distorted."

Next he formed a three-piece power trio called The Muthers, with Les Papp on drums and Paul Woods on bass. Frank played guitar and sang – something he has never been entirely happy to do. They had a residency at a local Ontario go-go bar, The Saints & Sinners on Holt Boulevard which catered mostly for Mexican labourers. It was a beer joint with four go-go girls in black net stockings who would boogie on stage as Frank and boys ground their way through "In The Midnight Hour." Sometimes a waitress would jump on a table. There was always a policeman in the audience and two at weekends to keep an eye on the Mexicans.

Late in 1963, Frank finally made money. The Western movie *Run Home*

Slow, which he had worked on in 1959, was suddenly revitalised. The producer Tim Sullivan paid all his debts and began shooting again. The star was Mercedes McCambridge who had played next to James Dean in *Giant*. Frank was to get two thousand dollars for writing the music.

One of the first things Frank did with the money was buy a Gibson ES-5 Switchmaster which he used for about five years. It features on his first three albums.

By this time, Paul Buff was in financial trouble. Studio PAL was deep in debt and he was in danger of losing it. He went to work as a sound engineer for Art Laboe at Original Sound. (Laboe used to put on the big dances at the El Monte Legion Stadium and issued the first *Oldies But Goodies* series of compilations.)

Frank arranged to record his soundtrack for *Run Home Slow* at Original Sound. In the course of recording Paul Buff and Frank got talking about how much money Frank had made for scoring the film music and together they arrived at a deal where Frank would take over Buff's debts and give him a thousand dollars. In return Frank would become the owner of Studio PAL. He would take over the lease, receive two pianos, one of them a baby grand, the other one a Steinway upright, and all the physical improvements on the premises including the electronic and sound equipment. The deal was signed on 1 August 1964.

Frank renamed the place Studio Z and Ray Collins, Jim Motorhead Sherwood and Don Van Vliet all came to the opening

night. Frank put up a big sign saying "Record Your Band – $15.50 per Hour" but nobody in Cucamonga had a band that they wanted to record. In the beginning this was fine – Frank had plenty of things he wanted to do himself. As he described it in his autobiography he was…

"beginning a life of obsessive overdubbage – nonstop, twelve hours a day."

Most of the tapes were either overdubs that he made himself, or tracks involving his friend Ray Collins who had co-written songs and sung with Frank on the Paul Buff productions. Following in Paul Buff's footsteps, Frank took the masters to town and shopped them around, but nobody picked up on them.

Another thing that Frank's film money went on was to pay for a divorce. He and Kay had not been getting along for some time. She particularly disliked the lifestyle that went with late night bars filled with go-go girls in black net stockings. Frank left the house at 314 West G Street and moved into Studio Z.

The studio was not exactly set up for living accommodation: there was no shower or bathtub, though there was a large industrial sink with which Frank made do. Frank's friend from Lancaster, Jim Motorhead Sherwood was in need of a place to stay so Frank invited him to move in. Motorhead was a genius at fixing cars – thus his name – and also a pretty good saxophone player. Just the

sort of person to have around. A couple of girls also moved in, including 18 year old Lorraine Belcher.

Studio Z was located across the street from a holy roller church and the local courtroom, not an ideal location. San Bernardino County is notoriously conservative and Cucamonga had only about 7,500 people in it. It was very small and close-minded. Frank's hair had been growing longer and he was a little weird. He had bought a job lot of Hollywood movie sets which he stored out back and had announced to the press that he was making a film called *Captain Beefheart Meets The Grunt People* prompting the *Ontario Daily Report* to dub him "The Movie King of Cucamonga." The local press and radio had run news items on the studio, not that the local bigots needed reminding of its existence because, as Frank described it…

"There was music coming out of that place 36 hours a day."
The inevitable happened in late 1964:
"They sent this guy in there to entrap me." [Zappa: 1970]

One evening The Muthers were playing The Saints and Sinners when a local policeman gave Frank his card and asked if he would be interested in making training films for the San Bernardino Vice Squad. Frank thought this would be a great opportunity to educate the police and show them that the weirdos they were arresting were real people. He told the cop that he would like to make a film using actual prostitutes, pimps, dope fiends and perverts.

A few weeks later a seedy looking character who said he was a used car salesman showed up at the studio. He'd heard that Frank was the "movie king of Cucamonga" and asked if Frank could provide him with a special film for a stag night. Frank quickly estimated that a sex film would cost at least $300 to make but that he could knock up a sex tape for virtually nothing. He offered a *special* tape recording for $100.

Frank and Lorraine bounced around on the bed and made a few suggestive noises. Frank edited out all the giggling and added some sleazy sex-movie music. The used car salesman showed up the next morning and asked for his tape. He told Frank he only had $50. Forget it said Frank but, stylised as a ballet dancer, the man turned to leave, twisted around again and flashed a badge. He was

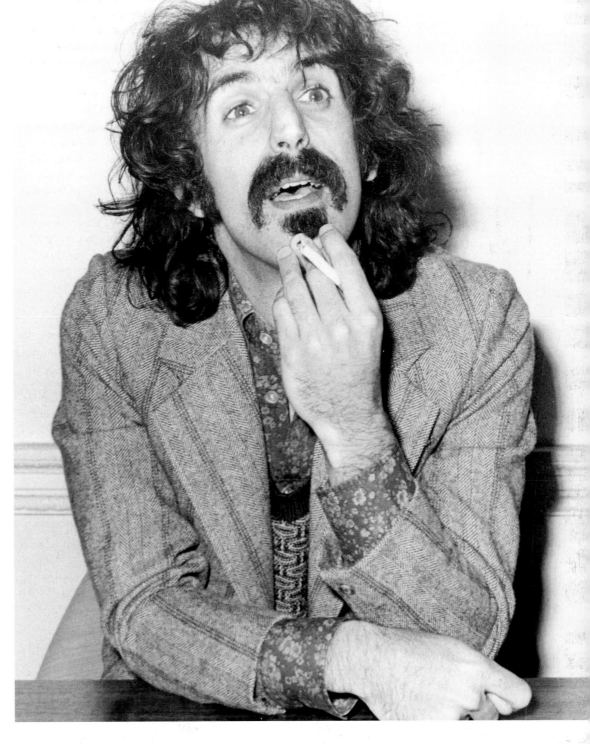

Detective Willis of the San Bernardino Vice Squad and he had not come to offer Frank a job making training films.

Just like the Dick Tracy comic strip, Willis had transmitted his conversation with Frank to a truck parked across the street via a wrist-watch transmitter. Frank and Lorraine were booked for conspiracy to commit pornography. Luckily Motorhead was out buying hamburgers and avoided arrest. The reason for the transmitter was that under California law, Frank's crime was only classed as a misdemeanour but if you talk about committing a misdemeanour

with some-one else, then it becomes a conspiracy which is a felony.

Frank's father took out a bank loan to bail him out and Frank managed to extract the royalties he was due as the author (with Ray Collins) of "Memories of El Monte" from Art Laboe in order to get Lorraine out.

In court the 27 year old district attorney got Frank ten days in jail by using evidence obtained from the hidden microphone…

"There were 45 men in the jail cell, the toilet and shower had never been cleaned, the temperature was

110 degrees so you couldn't sleep by night or day, there were roaches in the oatmeal, sadistic guards, and everything that was nice."
[Zappa: 1969]

As a convicted felon he avoided the draft; he was not of a high enough moral calibre to maim and kill people in Vietnam.

When Frank got out he had to give up the studio because the street was going to be widened and the studio was scheduled to be torn down. Besides which he had fallen behind with the rent. The Cucamonga days were over.

–1964–

"So I was looking for something to get into and I received a call from Ray [Collins], who had been working with a group called *The Soul Giants* in a local bar in Pomona called the Broadside. And he had just had a fight with the guitar player in the group and he was out and they were looking for a replacement, so I went down there and I joined the band."

The Soul Giants line-up: Frank Zappa – guitar, vocals / Ray Collins –

vocals / Roy Estrada – bass, vocals / Jimmy Carl Black – drums / Dave Coronado – saxophone.

Ray Hunt, the original guitarist with the band had a disagreement with Ray Collins and persisted in playing the wrong chords while Ray was singing. After an argument, Hunt left the group causing Ray Collins to call Frank. As their name suggests, The Soul Giants were a soul and r&b band, playing "In The Midnight Hour", "Louie Louie" and "Gloria." Frank thought they were a "spiffy little group" but quickly tired of playing soul covers. For some time he had been toying with the idea of a popular group which would combine modern original experimental music with popular material, and somehow convinced the band that the way to riches and success was to play original material.

"I talked them into getting weird. And we practised in what was left of the studio for about a week before I abandoned it completely. And then we went searching all over the countryside for places to work and it was really a difficult situation."
[Zappa: 1970]

Since they were no longer a soul band, and in order to show how new and original they were, they changed their name to Captain Glasspack and the Magic Mufflers. It didn't help.

"Davy, who was the wise one of the band, knew the actual truth of the matter, which was if you play original material you cannot work in a bar. He was afraid of being out of work so he quit the band. And he was right, we couldn't get a fucking job anyplace."
[Zappa: 1970]

Dave Coronado, however, had a secure job in a bowling alley.

"When you're scuffling in bars for zero to seven dollars per night per man, you think about money first. There's always the hope held out that if you stick together long enough you'll make money and you'll get a record contract. It all sounded like science fiction then, because this was during the so-called British Invasion and if you didn't sound like The Beatles or the Stones, you didn't get hired. We weren't going about it that way. We'd play something weird and we'd get fired. I'd say hang on and we'd move to another go-go bar – the Red Flame in Pomona, the Shack in Fontana, the Tom Cat in Torrance.

"While all this was going on we were called Captain Glasspack and His Magic Mufflers. It was a strange time. We even got thrown out of after-hours jam sessions. Eventually we went back to the Broadside in Pomona and we called ourselves The Mothers. It just happened by sheer accident, to be Mother's Day, [May] although we weren't aware of it at the time. When you are nearly starving to death, you don't keep track of holidays."
[Zappa: 1968]

The Mothers 1964 – 1965 line–up: Frank Zappa – guitar, vocals / Ray Collins – vocals / Roy Estrada – bass, vocals / Jimmy Carl Black – drums.

They were playing the right music, but in the wrong place and the band starved for about ten months before moving to Los Angeles.

The early Mothers, left to right: Frank, Roy Estrada, Ray Collins, Jimmy Carl Black, Billy Mundi

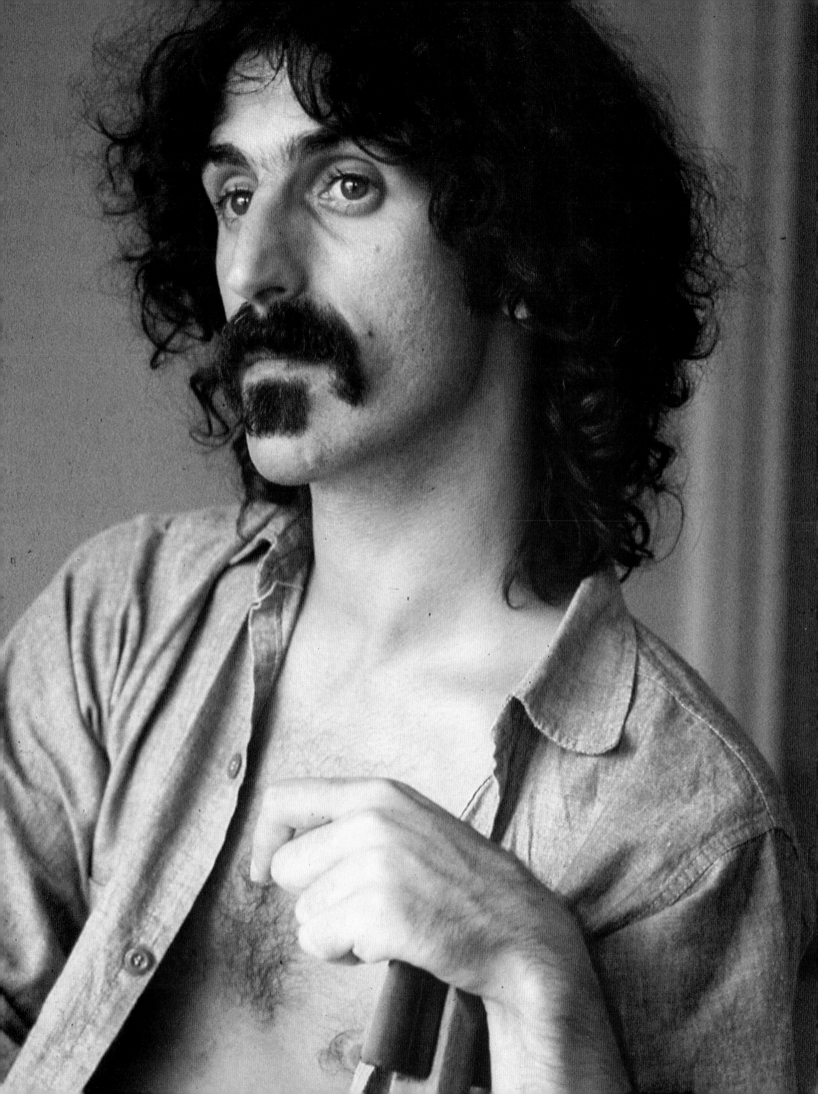

–1965–

In Los Angeles they added Alice Stuart, a folk guitarist…
"I had an idea for combining certain modal influences into our basically country blues sound. Alice played very good finger-style guitar and sang well – but she just couldn't play "Louie Louie" so I fired her." [Zappa: 1968]

Alice was replaced by Henry Vestine who was good, but again problems arose…

"As our music became progress-ively stranger, he found that he couldn't identify with what was happening, so he went into Canned Heat." [Zappa: 1968]

Frank moved to a two room apartment at 1819 Bellevue Avenue, parallel to the Hollywood Freeway in Echo Park, Los Angeles…
"a grubby little place on the side of a hill."

In 1965, psychedelia hit Los Angeles in a big way. All down the Strip, young kids were hanging out in clubs and on street corners. One popular place was Cantor's deli, at the top of Fairfax. The police over-reacted, closed clubs, tear gassed the kids and imposed a curfew. One time they arrested every single person in Cantor's.

Frank was heavily involved in the scene and used what was happening as the subject for a number of songs…
"In that house I wrote 'Brain Police', 'Oh No, I Don't Believe It', 'Hungry Freaks', 'Bowtie Daddy', and five or six other ones. About fifty percent of the songs were concerned with the events of 1965. Los Angeles, at that time, in the kiddie community that I was hanging out in, they were seeing God in colours and flaking out all over the place. You had plenty of that and meanwhile there was all that racial tension building up in Watts."

It became obvious that The Mothers needed a manager and approached a friend of theirs called Mark Cheka. He got them a job playing at a party for the man who shot *Mondo Hollywood*. There they met a friend of Cheka's named Herbie Cohen. Cheka already thought that he needed help and Herb was already booking groups.

Herb got them an audition at the Action in Hollywood, where six or seven months earlier they had been turned away because their hair wasn't long enough. It still wasn't very long but they went in wearing purple shirts and black hats…
"We looked like Mafia undertakers. The management of this establish-ment responded on a visceral level to this packaging and hired us for a four-week tour of duty. That was the start of the Big Time."

After the Action came The Whisky A Go-Go, and then the Trip. The Whisky

Above: Flo and Eddie (Mark Volman and Howard Kaylan) front The Mothers

was so cheap that they didn't even put a sign out saying they were playing inside until their last three days - and then they had to play for it. At the Trip they had lots of requests for "Help, I'm a Rock" and "Memories of El Monte" but no one danced during these songs because the audience wanted to listen…

"Elmer (Valentine) wanted people to dance in his club because if someone looked in the door and saw an empty dance floor, they wouldn't come in. At least this is what he said. So one night we played both those tunes together for an hour! For a solid hour nobody danced. Immediately after that we were selling pop bottles to get money for cigarettes and bologna." [Zappa: 1968]

It was while The Mothers were playing The Trip that Frank met Pamela Zarubica, an 18 year old student who hung out at Cantor's. Frank called her Suzy Creamcheese and began to spend a lot of time at her Laurel Canyon apartment at 8404 Kirkwood Drive. It was not long before he moved in. Pamela's flat Los Angeles monotone was a contributing factor to the popularity of The Mothers' first few albums. (Frank had a tendency to call all girls Suzy Creamcheese and when Susan Ziegler, the daughter of the owner of the Ziegler Ballrooms in Los Angeles where The Mothers often played moved to London, everyone thought that *she* was the Suzy Creamcheese on the records. The London Suzy Creamcheese was much loved by the English tabloids during the summer of love, both for her name and her very short dresses.)

Tom Wilson, house producer for MGM, was at the Trip while The Mothers were playing down the Strip at the Whisky a Go-Go. Herbie Cohen knew him well enough to be able to drag him away from his table and down the street to see The Mothers.

When Wilson walked in they were playing the "Watts Riot Song", about the only blues number in their repertoire. Wilson heard the group on stage and thought they were a blues band. He said "OK, we'll sign 'em," and went back to join his party at the Trip. The Mothers received a $2500 advance.

NOVEMBER – JANUARY 1966

The Mothers record *Freak Out!* at Sunset Highland Studios, Los Angeles and TT&G Studios, Los Angeles.

It was several months between the signing of the contract and the band entering the studio. During that time Frank discussed the plans for the album with Wilson and told him he wanted to do some orchestrations. Surprisingly Wilson agreed. In the studio the first tune they recorded was "Any Way The Wind Blows". The second tune was "Who Are The Brain Police?" and as soon as that was on the tape the people from Verve began muttering, "What is this?" and "What did we buy?" There was a series of excited phone calls from Los Angeles TTG studios back to New York, but it was too late. The Mothers laid down five tracks in the first day.

"The studio was opened at 1 a.m. on a Friday, and it was soon filled with a couple of hundred kids from the Sunset Strip, the Mothers of Invention, 'chorus leader' Kim Fowley, and various guests like Paul Butterfield and Les McCann. It went on for hours and everybody participated – some singing, some moaning, others popping gum into speakers – I don't think there has ever been anything like it!" [Michael Vosse writing in *Teen Set*, December 1966.]

MGM had little choice but to go along with the project. Frank was working so fast that they quickly spent $21,000 on this album, and had more material than they could possibly use on a single album. Frank offered them a deal. He would take a cut rate on the publishing if they would release a double album of this unknown group. They went for it.

The Mothers 1969

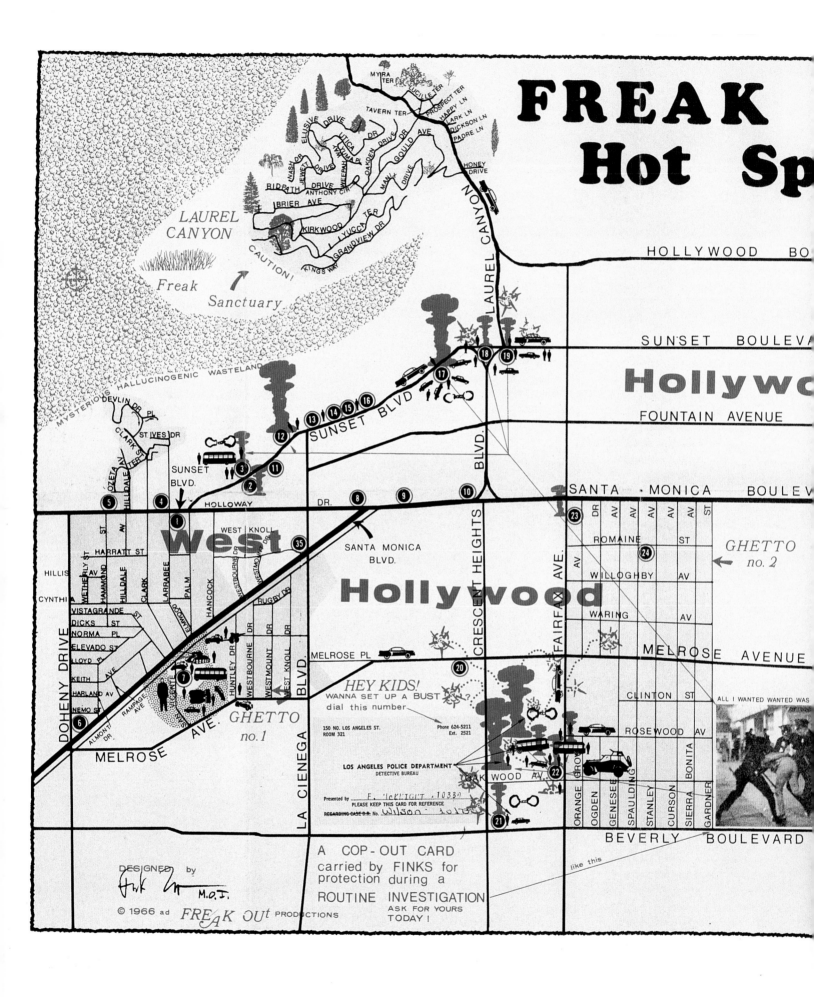

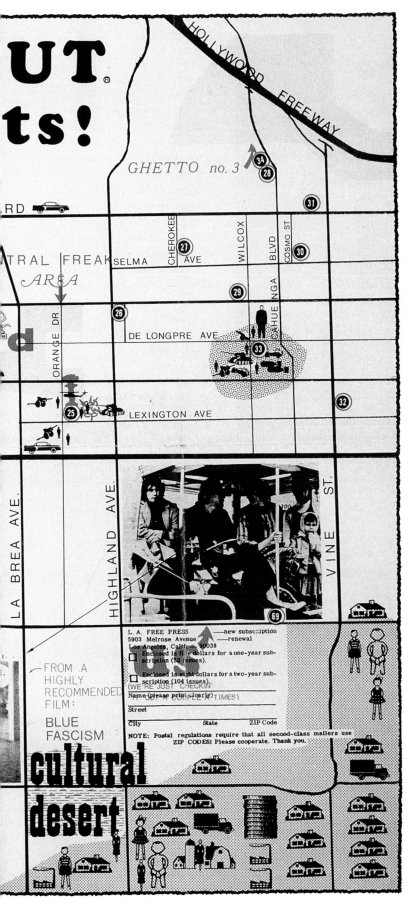

UT.
ts!

GHETTO no. 3

CENTRAL FREAK AREA

HOLLYWOOD FREEWAY

SELMA
DE LONGPRE AVE
LEXINGTON AVE

CHEROKEE AVE
WILCOX BLVD
COSMO ST
CAHUENGA
VINE ST.
ORANGE DR
HIGHLAND AVE.
LA BREA AVE.

L.A. FREE PRESS
5903 Melrose Avenue
Los Angeles, Calif. 90038
new subscription
renewal
☐ Enclosed is five dollars for a one-year sub-
scription (52 issues).
☐ Enclosed is eight dollars for a two-year sub-
scription (104 issues).
(WE'RE JUST CHECKIN' TIMES)
Name (please print clearly)
Street
City   State   ZIP Code
NOTE: Postal regulations require that all second-class mailers use
ZIP CODES! Please cooperate. Thank you.

FROM A HIGHLY RECOMMENDED FILM: BLUE FASCISM

cultural desert

1. The Cinematheque 16 still happens on a psychedelic level with rare and interesting films from the Great Underground. Located at 8815-1/2 Sunset Blvd. (phone 657-6815)

2. The Trip used to be the center of the Freak Scene See it now: 8572 Sunset Blvd.

3. Ben Franks used to be the place to go after the dancing stopped. The atomic blast denotes a bust (overall) by the L.A. heat, 8585 Sunset Blvd. (phone 655-7410)

4. Whisky a Go-Go still happens every night with top Pop Music Acts (and occasionally, lesser known fill-in groups like us). Yay, gang! Lotsa fun! 8901 Sunset Blvd. (phone 652-4202)

5. Gazzarri' s still happens on a hard rock custom pompadour sport coat level. Don't miss it at 9039 W, Sunset Blvd. (phone 273-6606)

6. The Troubadour gives you not only folk music, but folk-rock music, rock music itself, and other hybrid's, all IN CONCERT. Stunning in its concept at 9083 Santa Monica Blvd. (phone 276-6168)

7. West L A Sheriff's Station nestled in the heart of the outskirts of the fringe of where everything is happening, this moral arsenal provides shelter and sanctuary for that proud and magnificent beast we call THE WEST L.A. SHERIFF'S DEPUTY / servant & protector OR, more commonly, THE MAN. See the hapless trustees in their stenciled shirts washing HIS cars. Hear bold Aryan operatives rave about long hair freakcos and the last John Birch meeting at 720 N. San Vincente Blvd. (phone... only as a last resort if you have long hair or a beard 652-3525)

8. Barney s Beanery is still there, it is a matter of opinion whether it is still (or ever was) HAPPENING. Fun to visit: 8447 W Santa Monica Blvd. (phone 654-9240)

9. The Chez which used to be The Action which was the first place we worked when we emerged from the sticks and came to Hollywood is now High Class. A must: 8265 Santa Monica Blvd. (phone 656-3576)

10. P J.' s is now, as it was, and always (most likely but I'll check it out for you a coupla times) will be, the greatest place in town to see Trini Lopez in action. Located at 8151 W. Santa Monica Blvd. (phone 656-8000)

11. The Sea Witch is one of the teenie- bopper (no offense, gang) IN SPOTS featuring the new local bands in performances of psychedelic music b/w Cokes and Coffee... 8514 Sunset Blvd. (phone 652-9160)

12. FRED C. DOBBS Memorial Shrine... it used to be the best place to go to meet friends and dig the juke box until the heat blew it for us... or was it that bunch of outside idiots that started hanging around towards the end there, unable to maintain their coolness? The ruins are located a 8537 Sunset Blvd.

13. IT'S BOSS is teenie-bopper heaven. You only have to be 15 to get in. Located at 8433 Sunset Blvd. (phone 654-9900)

14. NIkki's Too is a day-time spot with an outdoor thing where you can ingest surprisingly good hamburgers in the company of a lot of really creepy people who sit there next to you while you're eating and hope that somebody driving by owes them money so they can scream and yell at them and make a scene so the people walking by will notice that they're sitting there and how groovy their sunglasses are... 8355 Sunset Blvd. (phone 656-9244)

15. The Colonial West Motel is a nice place to visit, but I wouldn't want to live there. My views, however, were not shared by The Paul Butterfield Blues Band, Sammy Davls Jr., or any of the other 18 million hippies who have made this their place to crash over the past few years. Conveniently located next to Nikki's Too at 8351 Sunset Blvd. (phone for reservations 656-4120)

16. The Stripcombers is HAPPENING for black leather jackets and motorcycle boots if that is your bag. Keen fun at 8301 Sunset Blvd. (for pertinent information phone the West Hollywood Sheriff's Station)

17. The Fifth Estate is one of those places that refuses to quit... even after a whole series of scenes with the heat, bravely situated at 8226 Sunset Blvd. (phone 656-7673)

18. PANDORA'S BOX is another teenie-bop underground strong-hold... a defiant little island at the top of the strip, with a picket fence around it and cops and ingenue freakos and lots of atmosphere, but tiny. Try sitting at Frascati's across the street and watching the heat surround the place, while the kids scramble for cover. Keen fun. Located at 8118 Sunset Blvd. (phone 656-9192)

19. GEE GEE'S was a scene until it was mysteriously forced out of business. It is at this moment, for rent... 8100 Sunset Blvd., next to Schwab's drugstore across the street from Ah Fong's and Greenblatts

20. The Ash Grove features ETHNIC ETHNICAL ETHNOCENT-RIC Folque Musique... I remember when Bud & Travis used to work there and Ed Pearl used to do Ethnopolitical GreasIng for the newly founded cabaret at the Idyllwild Folk Freak Sanctuary in 1958, Before Hal Zeiger invented the HOOTENANNY. Check it out at 8162 Melrose Ave (phone 653-2070)

21. VITO'S STUDIO & store & cult HQ & sanctuary & genetic laboratory which is REALLY THE PLACE TO SEE: is located at 303 N. Laurel (the bomb blast tells us that the status quo agents have made it known that they are checking Vito out)

22. CANTERS Fairfax Restaurant is THE TOP FREAKO WATERING HOLE AND SOCIAL HQ, scene of more blatant Gestapo practices than the peaceful natives care to recollect, it is a good place to go as soon as you arrive in town. If a black bus (or two) pulls up in front and you see your fellows, brethren and kinfolk being loaded into them (as if it were off to Auschwitz), do not flip out. Do something constructive: something positive... unfortun-ately, I'm not allowed to offer any suggestions, except to say, perhaps, that the silverware is cheap and easy to replace. You may cautiously approach it at 419 N. Fairfax (safer to phone 651-2030) Canters is across the street from the Kazoo (See 9.)

23. The Blue Grotto coffee house used to be nice and quiet until it got busted in the middle of the night. Meet and talk with the survivors at 1010 N. Fairfax

24. CARL'S HOUSE is where Carl lives. It wouldn't be right to give EVERYBODY the address... he would never get any sleep, poor fella

25. SITE OF A GIGANTIC & EFFECTIVE BUST where in much brutality and authoritarian B S was perpetrated with the result that all parties involved served a lot of DEAD TIME (time before trial) and got acquitted (causing then great physical and mental discomfort & status loss)

26. TTG RECORDING STUDIOS where we cut our album

27. THE BRAVE NEW WORLD is a very IN sort of late-teen Freak spot. Visit 1644 N Cherokee near M'Goos on Hollywood Blvd.

28. The Omnibus is a coffee house next door to the WILD THING at 1835 Cahuenga (phone 462-0473)

29. The Red Velvet is HQ for the plastic & pompadour set with lotsa hard rock & blue eyed soul to TURN YOU ON, BABY Located at 6507 Sunset Blvd. (phone 466-0861)

30. BIDO LIDO'S (formerly Cosmo Alley, one of our beloved manager's old coffee houses) is another underground teen-freako hot spot that launched the group LOVE "into orbit in the top pop hit charts with many smash numbers" (some of them performed on their employers) The Bido Lido's ain't quite the same... but still sort of happening & atmospheric at 1608 N. Cosmo St.

31. The Haunted House is fulla go-go & snappy ensembles & hair-dos & a genuine fire-breathing bandstand. Must be seen to be believed at 6315 Hollywood Blvd.

32. The Hollywood Ranch Market never closes and is a good place to see some REAL FREAKS. 1248 N. Vine (phone 464-0156)

33. The Hollywood Police Station, a masterpiece of Etruscan archi-tecture in the heart of primitive Hollywood

34. WILD THING is a dance place I never been to yet which is next door to the Omnibus on Cahuenga near Yucca, which has featured such groups as The West Coast Experimental Pop Art Band, The Knack and The Eastside Kids (who, I am led to believe, are funky)

35. THE TROPICANA MOTEL is groupies' paradise... that's where most of the touring groups who play the Whisky a Go-Go stay when they hit town as well as many members of active local groups like The Doors and The Byrds. Located at 8585 Santa Monica Blvd. (phone 652-5720)

69. (by request) THE LOS ANGELES FREE PRESS OFFICE, cognoscenti HQ, beacon of truth, champion of teen & otherwise justice, nice people, and more at 5903 Melrose Avenue. You would be wise to subscribe immediately upon arrival to town or you will never really know what's going on... socially or politically. THEY SELL, BOOKS. MAGAZINES, STATUS at 424-1/2 Fairfax, across from Canter's, 22. Behold the enclosed subscription blank

Above: Frank with his wife Gail

1966

JANUARY
Recording *Freak Out!*

MARCH [OR FEBRUARY]
Da-Smak, Waikiki, Hawaii.
Ten day residency. Texas.

MARCH
Recording "The Return Of The Son of Monster Magnet" using $500 worth of rented percussion equipment.

3 – 29 MAY
Double bill opening for Andy Warhol's Exploding Plastic Inevitable with the Velvet Underground and Nico at The Trip, Los Angeles. The hometown crowd naturally cheered The Mothers and booed the Velvets whose sombre black New York outfits didn't fit in with the garish Californian Freaks. The Byrds, Jim Morrison (still at UCLA Film School at the time) Sonny & Cher and Mama Cass were all in the audience for the opening night. Lou Reed developed a seething hatred for Zappa: *"He's probably the single most untalented person I've heard in my life. He's two-bit, pretentious, academic, and he can't play rock 'n' roll, because he's a loser. And that's why he dresses up funny. He's not happy with himself and I think he's right."* [Reed] This is because Zappa would make fun of the Velvets as part of his stage rap… **"These guys really suck!"**

It's hard to imagine how the Velvets and The Mothers could have shared the bill for the whole month without violence occurring. It was perhaps fortunate that the Sheriff's office closed down the club on the third day of the engagement. However, the Warhol gang and The Mothers played one more gig together:

28 – 29 MAY
Fillmore Auditorium, San Francisco. The opening audition band (who didn't get paid) was The Jefferson Airplane.

First tour:
DATE UNKNOWN
Washington DC.
Detroit, Mi.
Dallas, Tx.

24 – 25 JUNE
Fillmore Auditorium, San Francisco [opening for Lenny Bruce].

JULY
FREAK OUT [Album 1] (double album) released.

"Another thing… the interior of the "Freak Out" album made me vomit. The exterior packaging was pretty much under our control. That was all very carefully planned merchandising there. At the same time the packaging was being completed on that record I was in Hawaii. I didn't give it to an expert.
    "The result was a really ugly piece of graphic art. Some of the worst reproduction work I have ever seen. The picture in the lower right hand corner – it is a great panorama of all those people. They shrank it down and stuck it in the corner. I screamed all over the place. [Zappa: 1968]

"That whole Freak Out! album is to be as accessible as possible to the people who wanted to take the time to make it accessible. That list of names in there, if any-body were to research it, it would probably help them a great deal.
    "The Mothers were packaged two years before we actually put the band together, because I had been doing motivational research in the field, watching successes and failures of other people in the industry." [Zappa: 1968]

Among the huge quantity of material printed on the album was Zappa's statement of purpose: WHAT IS "FREAKING OUT": On a personal level *Freaking Out* is a process whereby an individual casts off outmoded and restricting standards of thinking, dress and social etiquette in order to express CREATIVELY his relationship to his immediate environment and the social structure as a whole. Less perceptive individuals have referred to us who have chosen this way of thinking and FEELING as "Freaks", hence the term: *Freaking Out*. On a collective level, when any number of "Freaks" gather and express themselves creatively through music or dance, for example, it is generally referred to as a FREAK OUT. The participants, already

emancipated from our national *social slavery*, dressed in their most inspired apparel, realise as a group whatever potential they possess for *free expression*. We would like to encourage everyone who HEARS this music to join us... become a member of *The United Mutations... FREAK OUT*.

Though the *Freak Out* album had a purposely wide appeal, like The Beatles' *Sgt Pepper*, it was also emblematic of a particular scene. *Sgt Pepper* was the soundtrack to the 1969 London hippie scene and *Freak Out* was the quintessence of the Los Angeles freak scene which centred around Cantor's deli on N. Fairfax at Oakwood, on the Strip and in Echo Park. The unofficial leader of this scene was Clay Vito, a member of "The Mothers' Auxiliary" on the album.

In October 1966, Kim Fowley described Vito: "Clay Vito was an artist who lived in California. When rock 'n' roll came along about 1954, him and his crowd began to get interested. There were different stages of rock you know, the British Sound, and Clay had this reputation as a patron.

"Groups started coming to him for guidance. One day, five guys came along and were broke - they asked if they could sleep at his studio. They were The Byrds. He also discovered groups like Love and The Leaves who made 'Hey Joe'. Nowadays if anybody opens a new club on the West Coast they have to invite Vito and his crowd. They all wait there eagerly to see if Clay turns up. If he does, everything's OK, it makes the place. You see, Vito's been with this Freak Out movement for years." It was a sensible move on Zappa's part to invite Vito and his crowd to appear on the album.

"The initial promotion on *Freak Out* consisted of bumper stickers that said, "Suzie Creamcheese" – I mean, they were lacking in charm as far as a bumper sticker would go because the logo of the company was so big. It wasn't 'in' at all, it was all really shlocky. It had 'Burp' in a big circle and all that shit, it just looked like an ad, and who wants to stick an ad on the back of your car. If they would have done it right it would have been a good campaign.

"The other thing they did, they sent out a puzzle, piece by piece, which was a puzzle made out of the cover of the *Freak Out* album that was sent out to disk jockeys, as if that would really motivate 'em, you know. A guy gets one piece in the mail every day for a week, what's he going to do? Just foam at the mouth until he's got 'em all and put 'em together? And they also had buttons which said "Suzie Creamcheese" and "Mothers of Invention" or something."

Summer: Zappa did various other work with Tom Wilson and his engineers Ami Hadani and Dave Greene, including work with The Animals and with Burt Ward.

23 JULY
Danish Center, Western Ave. Los Angeles, Ca. [*LA Free Press* Masked Ball].

29 JULY
NYC "GUAMBO": [Great Underground Arts Masked Ball and Orgy].

3 AUGUST
Lenny Bruce died of drug overdose. Frank and Pam went to his funeral.

13 AUGUST
Shrine Exposition Hall, Los Angeles, Ca.

17 SEPTEMBER
Shrine Exposition Hall, Los Angeles, Ca. "Freak Out" show.

SEPTEMBER
By this time Zappa had met and fallen in love with Gail Sloatman, a friend of Pamela's, who worked as a secretary at the Whisky A-Go-Go. When Pamela moved to Europe in late 1966, Gail moved into the 8404 Kirkwood apartment (joining Frank and three other girls). Frank and Gail are still together, more than a quarter of a century later!

The Mothers of Invention November 1966 – August 1967 line-up / Frank Zappa – guitar / Ray Collins – vocals / Jim Black – trumpet, drums, vocals / Roy Estrada – bass, vocals / Billy Mundi – drums / Don Preston – keyboards, mini-moog / Bunk Gardner – wind instruments.

NOVEMBER
Absolutely Free sessions recorded at TT&G Studios in Los Angeles in four double sessions totalling 25 hours, and mixed at MGM Studios in NYC.

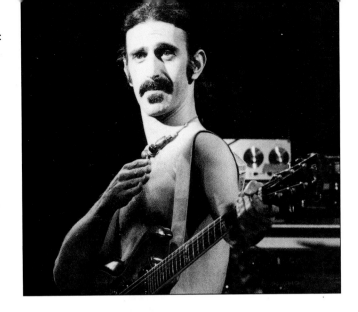

FREAK OUT
(double album)
US Verve V 5005 (mono)
US Verve V6 5005 (stereo)
Released July 1966
US CD Rykodisc RCD 40062
Released 1987

UK single album
UK Verve VLP 9154 (mono)
UK Verve SVLP 9154 (stereo)
Released March 1967
UK CD Zappa CDZAP 1
Released October 1987
(contains the double album)

Side 1:
1. Hungry Freaks, Daddy /
2. Ain't Got No Heart / 3. Who Are The Brain Police? / 4. Go Cry On Somebody Else's Shoulder /
5. Motherly Love / 6. How Could I Be Such A Fool

Side 2:
1. Wowie Zowie / 2. You Didn't Try To Call Me / 3. Any Way The Wind Blows / 4. I'm Not Satisfied / 5. You're Probably Wondering Why I'm Here

Side 3:
1. Trouble Every Day / 2. Help I'm A Rock

Side 4:
The Return Of The Son Of Monster Magnet

Line-up:
Frank Zappa - guitar, vocals / Ray Collins - lead vocals, harmonica, percussion / Jimmy Carl Black - drums / Roy Estrada - bass guitar / Elliot Ingber - lead guitar, rhythm guitar

The Mothers' Auxiliary:
Gene Estes / Eugene di Novi /

Neil le Vang / John Rotella / Kurt Reher / Raymond Kelley / Paul Bergstrom / Emmet Sargeant / Joseph Saxon / Edwin V. Beach / Arthur Maebe / George Price / John Johnson / Carol Kaye / Virgil Evans / David Wells / Kenneth Watson / Plas Johnson / Roy Caton / Carl Franzoni / Vito / Kim Fowley (featured on hypophone) (i.e.: voice) / Benjamin Barrett / David Anderle

Producer: Tom Wilson
Engineer: Ami Hadani
Recorded at Sunset Highland Studios, Los Angeles:
November 1965 - January 1966
One session, March 1966

THE ANIMALS: ANIMALISM.
US MGM E/SE 4414.
UK Decca LK 4797.
Produced by Tom Wilson.
Engineer: [on Zappa's tracks] Ami Hadani, remix engineer Dave Greene. Recorded [Zappa's tracks] at TT&G, Hollywood.

Zappa arranged Side one track one: "All Night Long" and Side one track three: "The Other Side Of This Life." The experience was not one that Eric Burdon enjoyed; he found him autocratic and commented that it was like working with Hitler.

BURT WARD: BOY WONDER I LOVE YOU / ORANGE COLORED SKY
MGM 13632 released 1967.
"A" side written by Frank Zappa. Both sides arranged, conducted and produced by Frank Zappa.

Above: The Mothers in 1967

Facing page: Frank and Gail

26 NOVEMBER:
THANKSGIVING DAY

The Mothers began a week's residency at the Garrick Theater, NYC, but were so successful that they were held over until New Year's Day.

–1967–

JANUARY

Two weeks' residency in Montreal, Quebec.

LATE JANUARY

Los Angeles. Zappa wrote *Lumpy Gravy* in eleven days. Preliminary sessions for *Lumpy Gravy* at the Capitol studios in Los Angeles.

FEBRUARY

Recording sessions for *Lumpy Gravy* continue at Apostolic studio, NYC on a block booking.

APRIL

Easter weekend: Garrick Theater, 152 Bleeker Street, NYC.

24 MAY – 5 SEPTEMBER

Garrick Theater, "Pigs and Repugnant: Absolutely Free" shows. After Los Angeles, where the police had closed virtually all the clubs, New York looked good. Easter week was so successful that the theatre management asked them to stay on through the summer…

"The gross for the five months was $103,000 and that sounds terrific, but overhead was high. Rent for the building was $1,000 a month. Electricity was another $500, so when it came to the final count, we got maybe two bills a week apiece."

Frank and Gail and the other members of the group moved to New York where they would live for 18 months.

It was at the Garrick that they began performing "atrocities"…

"We did everything. We performed a couple of marriages on stage. We pulled people out of the audience and made them make speeches. One time we brought 30 people up on stage and some of them took our instruments and the rest of them sang 'Louie, Louie', as we left.

"We had a system rigged with a wire running from the light booth at the back of the theatre to the stage and the lighting guy would send stuff down the wire. First, maybe, a spread-eagled baby doll... followed by a salami, that would ram the baby doll in the ass. It was all carefully planned and we played the right music for this sort of thing. Sometimes the lighting guy would surprise us, and send eggs or something really messy down the wire. Our big attraction was the soft giraffe. We had this big stuffed giraffe on stage, with a hose running up to a spot between the rear legs. Ray Collins would go up to the giraffe and massage it with a frog hand puppet... and then the giraffe's tail would stiffen and the first three rows of the audience would get sprayed with whipped cream shooting out of the hose. All with musicial accompaniment, of course. It was the most popular feature of our show. People would request it all the time.

"Music always is a commentary on society, and certainly the atrocities on stage are quite mild compared to those conducted on our behalf by our government. You can't write a chord ugly enough to say what you want to say sometimes so you have to rely on a giraffe filled with whipped cream. Also, they didn't know how to listen.

1967

Interest spans wane and they need something to help them re-focus.

"Actually, the way the atrocities started was accidental. Somebody had given one of the guys a big doll and one night we pulled some Marines out of the audience. Just to break the monotony. We hadn't started the atrocities yet. So we had this idea we could show the audience what Marines were really like. I threw the doll to the Marines and said, 'This is a gook baby... show us how we treat gooks in Vietnam.' And they tore that baby apart. After that we included props in all our shows. I call them visual aids.
[Zappa: 1968]

26 MAY
ABSOLUTELY FREE [Album 2]
released.

"Zappa, without exception, is the biggest talent I have ever come across. Despite his slow start in Britain, he is going to be enormously big – mark my words. I've just flown back from Copenhagen, where The 'Mothers' have *been appearing – and already they are causing a sensation over there."*
[Absolutely Free producer Tom Wilson, November 1967]

Zappa gave a track by track commentary on the album to the English underground newspaper *International Times* (IT) published August 31, 1967...
"Plastic People": The insincere ass holes who run almost everybody's country are plastic people. References to Sunset Boulevard, Pandora's Box, CIA, and Laurel Canyon, all relate to the first youth riots in Los Angeles last year.

"The Duke Of Prunes": The Duke of Prunes is a surrealistic love song. Euphemistic sexual imagery popular in country blues with which many of you might already be familiar, is transmuted in this particular piece from the basic "Fuck me, suck me, till my eyes roll back baby" to "prune me, cheese me, go-kart... " or something like that. This song, is very strange.

"Call Any Vegetable": The best clue to this song might lie in the fact that people who are inactive in a society... people who do not live up to their responsibilities are vegetables. I feel that these people, even if they are inactive, apathetic or unconcerned at this point can be motivated toward a more useful sort of existence. I believe that if you call any vegetable then it will respond to you.

"America Drinks": On this side of the album there are two versions of this set of lyrics. This version which opens side two, is in effect an abstraction (in advance of) the set of lyrics which close side two. The opening lines of "One, two, buckle my shoe" and "doopie, doopie" are derived from a tune called "My Little Red Book."

"Status Back Baby": Status Back Baby is a song about young acne America and their daily trials and tribulations. It is unfortunate that many young Americans really do worry about losing status at their high school. De Molay is a religious youth organisation in the United States. A Pom Pom Girl is a young lady who cuts strips of crêpe paper all week long after school to make an object known as a pom pom, which is a puffy ball composed of strips of crepe paper. After she has manufactured her own pom pom, she will go to the football game and jump high in the air with her pom

Above: Frank in New York

Below: Frank and Gail anticipate parenthood

ABSOLUTELY FREE
US Verve V 5013 (mono)
US Verve V6 5013 (stereo)
Released 26 May 1967
US CD Rykodisc RCD 10093
Released 1988

UK Verve VLP 9174 (mono)
UK Verve SVLP 9174 (stereo)
Released July 1967
UK CD Zappa CDZAP 12
Released January 1989

Side 1:
1. Plastic People / 2a. The
Duke of Prunes / 2b. Amnesia
Vivace / 2c. The Duke Regains
His Chops / 3a. Call Any
Vegetable / 3b. Invocation &
Ritual Dance of the Young
Pumpkin / 3c. Soft-Sell
Conclusion & Ending of Side 1

Side 2:
1. America Drinks / 2. Status
Back Baby / 3. Uncle Bernie's
Farm / 4. Son of Suzy Cream-
cheese / 5. Brown Shoes Don't
Make It / 6. America Drinks &
Goes Home

CD release adds 'Big Leg Emma'
and 'Why Don'tcha Do Me Right'
before 'America Drinks'

Line-up:
Frank Zappa - guitar /
Ray Collins - vocals / Jim Black -
trumpet, drums, vocals / Roy
Estrada - bass, vocals /
Billy Mundi - drums / Don
Preston - keyboards, mini-moog /
Bunk Gardner - wind
instruments / Jim Sherwood -
saxophone, vocals

'Brown Shoes Don't Make It'
add 2 violins, 1 viola, 1 cello,
1 trumpet and 1 contra-bass
clarinet. The little girl asking,
'What would you do Daddy?' is
Herb Cohen's daughter Lisa

'America Drinks & Goes Home'
add Herb Cohen on cash register
Suzie Creamcheese played by
Pamela Zarubica

Producer: Tom Wilson
Recorded at the Sunset
Highland Studios, Los Angeles,
during four double recording
sessions, (six hours each)
during November 1966
Engineer: Ami Hadani
Re-mix engineer: David Greene
Composed, arranged and
conducted: Frank Zappa

The Mothers in 1967

pom in her hand shouting, as she does so, these immortal words: "We've got a team that's on the beam, that's really hep to the jive. Come on tigers, let's skin 'em alive." Or, "Push 'em back, push 'em back. We like it, sissboombah." Then they drink beer and get pregnant in the back of somebody's car.

"Uncle Bernie's Farm": Uncle Bernie's Farm is a song about ugly toys and the people who make them. Implied here is the possibility that the people who buy the ugly toys might be as ugly as the toys themselves.

"Son Of Suzie Creamcheese": Son of Suzie Creamcheese is a stirring saga of a young groupie. Her actions are all motivated by a desire to be "in" at all times. Hence the drug abuse (blowing her mind on too much Kool-aid: acid... Stealing her boyfriend's stash: a hidden supply of drugs... and leaving Los Angeles for a protest march in Berkeley).

"Brown Shoes Don't Make It": Brown Shoes Don't Make It is a song about the people who run the government, the people who make

the laws that keep you from living the kind of life you know you should lead. These unfortunate people manufacture inequitable laws and ordinances, perhaps unaware of the fact that the restrictions they place on the young people in a society are a result of their own hidden sexual frustrations. Dirty old men have no business running your country.

"America Drinks And Goes Home": America Drinks and Goes Home is an unsubtle parody of adult conduct in neighbourhood cocktail lounges in America. The humour is aimed at (1) the type of music your parents like to listen to, (2) the manner in which they like to have it performed (the insincerity of the night-club crooner in his closing address to the alcoholics at the bar), (3) the manner in which the audience persists in talking above the level of the music while it is being performed (which belies their disrespect as an art and for anyone involved in the performance of music).

MGM refused to print the words to the songs because they deemed them to be obscene, even though the same words could be sung on record. Zappa...

"There's a legal difference between what's on the record and what's on paper. You can sing it, and that's part of a work of art; but the liner notes to an album are not – you can't defend that in court as a work of art. MGM legal department decided that."

Zappa explained the problems to an American interviewer...

"Look what they censored out of it (the libretto) 'She's only thirteen and she knows how nasty' (from 'Brown Shoes Don't Make It'). You know what they took out? The word 'thirteen,' not 'nasty'.

"Look: 'Magnificent Instrumental, Ejaculation Number 1.' They had to cross it out and change to 'Climax.' (Laughter) You dig? They wanted to change, 'I'd like to make her do a nasty on the White House lawn,' (from 'Brown Shoes') they wanted to change it to 'I'd like to make her do the crossword puzzle on the back of TV Guide'!

"You want to know something else? MGM says, 'Now, we know – you and I both know – that you want to make her do a nasty on the

White House lawn can mean only one thing: you want to make her shit on the White House lawn.' That's what he said. Like dig the way these guys think, man.

"Also, 'She's only 13 and I hear she gets loaded,' [also from 'Brown Shoes'] MGM says, 'We might run into trouble', because in some States you're not supposed to drink until you're eighteen."
[Zappa: 1968]

Zappa published the libretto himself and printed details of where to send for copies on the album sleeve. ("Send money… make sure it's at least $1.00.")

MAY
LUMPY GRAVY [Album 3] released.

"It was a really weird deal. At the time they asked me to do it, I had never been asked by MGM or anybody else to do any serious music, any possible variation from the ordinary rock and roll format. Capitol came along and asked me to write something for an orchestra. My contract with MGM was as a

producer and not as an artist so it was cool. But then MGM threatened to sue Capitol and Capitol threatened them. Then they both figured they needed each other; MGM had a record deal with the Capitol Record Club. It all settled down to a regular American business deal: Buy it from Capitol and put it out on MGM. By now I was really pissed with MGM anyway."
[Zappa: 1968]

In 1968 Zappa listed "Pigs & Ponies" on *Lumpy Gravy* as one of his favourite tracks…
"Pigs and Ponies" really says what I wanted it to say and the performance is as good as I could have hoped for. It is 100% of what I'd intended. I tend to judge our songs on a percentage basis."
[Zappa: 1968]

Q: On *Lumpy Gravy* there's a disjointed conversation, you know: "I hear you've been having trouble with pigs and ponies"… was that the result of a lot of conversations?
A: More or less. I sat groups of people inside a grand piano with a

blanket over the top so they couldn't see out. I sat various combinations in there and got them to talk about anything they wanted to, and suggested things when they ran out. It took about three days and the bits on the record come from eight or nine hours of taped conversation.
[Zappa: 1968]

(Some of this material also appeared on *Uncle Meat*).

The Mothers of Invention line-up: August 1967 – Dec 1967 European tour; Frank Zappa – guitar, vocals / Ian Underwood – wind instruments, keyboards / Don Preston – keyboards / Ray Collins – vocals / Motorhead Sherwood – saxophone / Roy Estrada – bass, vocals / Bunk Gardner - wind instruments / Jimmy Carl Black – drums, trumpet, vocals / Billy Mundi – drums / Pamela Zarubica – Suzy Creamcheese

JULY
A contemporary report: " *Frank was standing in the street outside the theater. He seemed to be turning in slow circles, signing autographs, talking with fans, hustling people to buy tickets for the*

show, seeing how the tickets were selling. He was wearing tight, flower-patterned pants. It was a dramatic set. It began with the stage in total darkness except for the control lights on the amplifiers. An imperceptible drum roll began, grew louder, and when everyone was fully focused on the stage, a dim light came on at the back of the stage, growing brighter, silhouetting Frank who was standing at the rear of the sloping stage next to a large gong, like the J. Arthur Rank trademark.

There were a lot of girls on stage, some playing tambourine, others being mauled by the group. The Mothers threw a lot of vegetables about - particularly while playing "Call Any Vegetable", and the girls had brooms and would sweep the stage clean again. The set included many favourites like "Brown Shoes Don't Make It." The group was not particularly tight but they knew a lot of hand signals, some of which were virtually invisible. The group would be playing an extended rockout, seemingly totally improvised, when suddenly they would all change tempo. It was very impressive."
[Miles: 1967]

AUGUST – SEPTEMBER

Recording sessions for *We're Only In It For The Money*, Mayfair Studios, NYC

5 SEPTEMBER

Summer season at the Garrick Theater ended.

SEPTEMBER

New York City.
Detroit, Mi.
Cincinnati, Oh.
Miami, Fl.

23 SEPTEMBER

Royal Albert Hall, London, UK.

SEPTEMBER

Amsterdam, Holland.
Gothenburg, Sweden.
Lund: Sweden.

30 SEPTEMBER

Konserthuset, Stockholm, Sweden.

1 OCTOBER

Falkoner Theatre, Copenhagen, Denmark.

OCTOBER

The Speakeasy, London, UK.
Royal Albert Hall (with members of the London Symphony Orchestra).
The Tivoli, Copenhagen, Denmark.

New York: working simultaneously on *We're Only In It For The Money* and *Lumpy Gravy* at Apostolic Studios, NYC.

– 1968 –

When Frank and Gail returned to Los Angeles from New York, Frank decided that he wanted to move into the Log Cabin. This was a prototype hippie commune, lived in by Miss Christine and Miss Sandra (who later formed the GTO's), Carl Franzoni, and others. The Log Cabin was built by Tom Mix, the hero of over 400 low budget Westerns, on a huge acreage on the corner of Laurel Canyon and Lookout Mountain Avenue, high in the Santa Monica Mountains above Hollywood. In the grounds was a stream, a small lake, caves and a huge variety of semi-tropical vegetation. There was supposed to be a secret passageway leading from the Log Cabin to Harry Houdini's mansion across the street. Carl Franzoni lived in the personal bowling alley that Tom Mix had built in the back of the house, under which he had buried his beloved horse. It was a real log cabin, as befitted a cowboy movie star, and the huge living room had walls made from actual logs, with a giant log-burning stone fireplace at the end.

LUMPY GRAVY
US Verve V8741 (mono)
Released May 1967
US Verve V6 8741 (stereo)
Released May 1967
US CD Rykodisc RCD 40024
(w / We're Only In It For The Money)
Released 1986

UK Verve SVLP 9223
Released October 1968
UK CD Zappa CDZAP 13
(w/ We're Only In It For The Money)
Released December 1988

Side 1:
Lumpy Gravy - Part I

Side 2:
Lumpy Gravy - Part II

Solo album released as 'Francis Vincent Zappa Conducts Lumpy Gravy, a curiously inconsistent piece which started out to be a BALLET but probably didn't make it,' with the players described as the 'ABNUCEALS EMUUKHA ELECTRIC SYMPHONY ORCHESTRA & CHORUS with maybe even some of The Mothers of Invention'

Line-up:
Paul Smith, Mike Lang, Lincoln Mayorga, Pete Jolly - keyboards / Johnny Guerin, Frankie Capp, Shelly Manne - Drums / Emil Richards, Gene Estes, Alan Estes, Victor Feldman - percussion / Ted Nash, Jules Jacob, John Rotella, Bunk Gardner, Don Christlieb, Gene Cipriano - woodwinds / Arthur Maebe, Vincent De Rosa, Richard Parisi - french horns / Jimmy Zito - trumpet / Kenneth Shroyer - trombone / Jim Haynes, Tommy Tedesco, Tony Rizzi, Al Viola, Dennis Budimer - guitars / Bob West, John Balkin, Jimmy Bond, Lyle Ritts, Chuck Berghofer - bass / Alexander Koltun, Tibor Zelig, Ralph Schaefter, Bernard Kundell, William Kurasch, James Getzoff, Philip Goldberg, Leonard Selic, Arnold Belnick, Leonard Malarsky, Harold Ayres, Jerome J. Reisler, Harry Hyams, Joseph di Fiore, Jerome A. Kessler, Raymond J. Kelly, Joseph Saxon, Jesse Ehrlich, Harold J. Bemko - strings / Ronnie Williams, Dick Barber, Roy Estrada, Jimmy Carl Black, Jim Sherwood, Gail Zappa, Larry Fanoga, Cal Schenkel, Louie the Turkey, and Billy, Monica, Gilly and Becky from Apostolic Studio, plus various others - the chorus

Producer: Frank Zappa
Recorded at Capitol studios, Los Angeles in December 1966, and at Apostolic Studio, New York City during February 1967
Engineers: Joe, Rex, Pete, Jim, Bob, Gary, Dick Kunc engineered at Apostolic (named after its prototype Scully 12-track - 12 apostles)

The orchestral parts were conducted by Sid Sharp at Capitol Studios.

1968

Frank and The Mothers
sightseeing in London

The landlady was crazy and it did not take long for Frank to get Carl Franzoni and all the girls evicted. Frank and Gail moved in with their new daughter, Moon Unit. Shortly afterwards, Miss Christine moved back in as full-time nanny for Moon and all of Christine's girlfriends began hanging out at the cabin. It was there that Frank named them The GTO's though the title "Miss" before their names came from Tiny Tim. The Log Cabin was always filled with members of The Mothers, with one or two usually staying over. Herb Cohen conducted much bizarre business there and a constant stream of secretaries, roadies and assorted music people flooded in and out.

The Mothers of Invention line-up: December 1967 - Spring 1969; Frank Zappa – guitar, vocals / Ian Underwood – wind instruments, keyboards / Don Preston – keyboards / Motorhead Sherwood – saxophone / Roy Estrada – bass, vocals / Bunk Gardner – wind instruments / Jimmy Carl Black – drums, trumpet, vocals / Art Tripp – percussion. [Ray Collins added for recording *Ruben and Uncle Meat.*]

1 FEBRUARY
Royal Albert Hall, London, UK.

FEBRUARY
Birmingham, UK.
Denver, Co.

4 MARCH
Fullerton, Ca.

MARCH
Thee Image, Miami, Fl.
Hartford, Ct.
Fillmore Auditorium, San Francisco, Ca.
Berkeley Community Center, Berkeley, Ca.

MARCH – APRIL
Sunset Studios, Los Angeles, overdubbing Uncle Meat.

20 APRIL
Fillmore East, NYC.

APRIL
The Arena, Philadelphia, Pa.

9 MAY
Fillmore East, NYC. (Mother's Day concert)

JUNE
Shrine Exposition Hall, Los Angeles, Ca.

JUNE
The Guildhall, Portsmouth, Mass.

4 JULY
The Ark, Boston, Mass.

3 AUGUST
New York City.

SEPTEMBER
WE'RE ONLY IN IT FOR THE MONEY
[Album 4] released.

"They sent me a test pressing of We're Only In It for the Money that had a whole bunch of stuff censored out of it. This is one line they cut: 'And I still remember mama with her apron and her pad, feeding all the boys at Ed's café.' Now, this not only didn't make any sense to cut, it fucked up the piece of music by removing four bars before the bridge. And they changed the equalization. They removed the highs, boosted the bottom and the middle to obscure the words.
"So they sent me this test pressing and I'm supposed to sign a paper saying they can release it. I called them up and said, 'You can't put this record out!' And they've already pressed 40,000 of them. Then, six or eight weeks later, I got a call about Lumpy Gravy. They had just pressed 12,000 of them and they had already been shipped, and I hadn't even been sent a release to sign." [Zappa: 1968]

"'Idiot Bastard Son'... I like what it says. I'm not too thrilled by the performance but I like the structure, especially the talking part in the middle and the way that relates to the chord changes." [Zappa: 1968]

Q: What kind of digital repair did you do to master tapes of the older records? *We're Only In It For The Money*, for example, has new digital bass and drum tracks.
A: **"The original two-track masters - they're almost twenty years old now – didn't survive the storage at MGM. They were stored so badly that the oxide had flaked off the tape. You couldn't listen to it any more. So the thing had to be remixed. I had to go back and find all the original elements. You listen**

to 'We're Only In It for the Money' and go, 'My God, there's a million edits in this thing.' And they all had to be redone." [Zappa: 1986]

Zappa's lawsuit with MGM was settled in 1976, when the master tapes were returned to him, so either they were not checked when he received them, or Frank didn't get around to picking them up for another decade.

7 SEPTEMBER
Bremen, Germany.

28 SEPTEMBER
Essen, Germany.

3 OCTOBER
The Tivoli, Copenhagen, Denmark.

9 OCTOBER
Deutsches Museum Kongressaal, München, Germany. "Total Music Theatre".

16 OCTOBER
Berlin, Germany.

20 OCTOBER
Concertgebouw, Amsterdam, Holland.

OCTOBER
The Olympia, Paris, France.
Vienna, Austria.

WE'RE ONLY IN IT FOR THE MONEY

US Verve V 5045 (mono)
US Verve V6 5045 (stereo)
Released September 1968
US CD Rykodisc RCD 40024
(w/Lumpy Gravy)
Released 1986

UK Verve VLP 9199 (mono)
UK Verve SVLP 9199 (stereo)
Released October 1968
UK CD Zappa CDZAP 13
(w/Lumpy Gravy)
Released December 1988

Side 1:
1. Are You Hung Up / 2. Who Needs The Peace Corps / 3. Concentration Moon / 4. Mom & Dad / 5. Bow Tie Daddy / 6. Harry, You're A Beast / 7. What's The Ugliest Part of Your Body? / 8. Absolutely Free / 9. Flower Punk / 10. Hot Poop

Side 2:
1. Nasal Retentive Calliope Music / 2. Let's Make The Water Turn Black / 3. The Idiot Bastard Son / 4. Lonely Little Girl / 5. Take Your Clothes Off When You Dance / 6. What's The Ugliest Part of Your Body? (Reprise) / 7. Mother People / 8. The Chrome Plated Megaphone of Destiny.

Line-up:
Frank Zappa - guitar, piano, lead vocals / Billy Mundi - drums, vocal, talk / Bunk Gardner - woodwinds, mumbling / Roy Estrada - bass, vocals / Don Preston - listed as retired (keyboards?) / Jimmy Carl Black - drums, trumpet, vocals / Ian Underwood - piano, woodwinds / James Motorhead Sherwood - soprano and baritone saxophone / Dick Barber - snorks / Suzy Creamcheese - telephone conversation / Garry Kellgren - whispering / Dick Kunc - interruptions / Eric Clapton - conversation

Producer: Frank Zappa
Recorded at Mayfair Studios, New York during August and September, 1967, then at Apostolic Studio, New York in October, 1967
Engineers: Gary Kellgren at Mayfair / Dick Kunc at Apostolic
Composed, arranged and conducted: Frank Zappa

Sid Sharp conducted the orchestral parts

The Mothers with Suzy
Creamcheese

25 OCTOBER
Royal Albert Hall, London, UK.

NOVEMBER
CRUISING WITH RUBEN AND THE JETS
[Album 5] released.

"We compressed things beyond belief for a lot of that stuff. I mean like the sound of the drums. I mean there's hardly anything left of them they sound like oatmeal boxes, they're squashed and they're squeezed. After we got the bass on there, there's a lot of bass in the mix, it's just that the bass tone has been clipped off and the highs have been reinforced. It gives a little bit more scratchy sound to it."
[Zappa: 1970]

"They're more than recreations, they're careful conglomerates of archetypical clichés. For instance, one song on the 'Ruben & The Jets' album simultaneously has quotes from background chants sung by 'The Moonglows', the opening theme of 'The Rite of Spring', in fact the tune is 'Fountain Of Love', it's on the fadeout but nobody ever heard that as 'The Rite Of Spring' because there's like five different levels of musical accompaniment going on, not counting the band. There's all these different vocal parts and they're all clichés and they're all carefully chosen for nostalgia value and then built into this song with the most imbecile words in the world." [Zappa: 1969]

"I like that kind of music. I'm very fond of close harmony group vocal OO-Wah Rock & Roll. I really like it. But the scientific side of 'Ruben & The Jets' is that it was an experiment in cliché collages because that music was just riddled with stereotyped motifs that made it sound the way it did. Not only did it give it its characteristic sound but it gave it its emotional value. Like there's a real science to playing Rock & Roll triplets, not everybody who can play three notes at once on the piano can play Rock & Roll triplets, and make it sound convincing. There's little weird things in there so there was a lot of exploration done at the time we were putting 'Ruben & The Jets' together.

"We scaled down the instrumentation of the group and I tried to make it sound reasonably modern and also reasonably stereo so we toyed with the idea of doing a really crappy production on it and making it sound old but I didn't think I would enjoy listening to it over and over again at all... I like a little stereo now and then, I can dig that! We discussed different kinds of background chants and the emotional implications of them. Because I think that they have emotional implications the same as morning ragas and evening ragas and things like that. It's a different level, that's where those tracks were at. Also the falsettist, the type of lyric that you would associate with a song that has a low bass voice prominent is different from the type of lyric you would associate with a song that's sung in two-or three-part harmony with a falsetto over it. So we were tinkering around with all these things." [Zappa: 1969]

"Later That Night" is a close parody of "The Letter" by The Medallions. Zappa started his own record labels: Bizarre and Straight. The first release on Bizarre was a concert by Lenny Bruce – the first unexpurgated full concert ever released:

LENNY BRUCE: THE BERKELEY CONCERT (double album) released.

AN EVENING WITH WILD MAN FISCHER (WITH WILD MAN FISCHER) (double album) released.

"That's not his mother on the album sleeve. We staged that. That's a cardboard cut-out of the grandmother of the photographer who took the cover picture. Can't you tell it's a cardboard cut-out?

CRUISING WITH RUBEN AND THE JETS
US Verve V6 5055
Released November 1968
US CD Rykodisc RCD 10063
Released 1985

UK Verve SVLP 9237
Released February 1969
US CD Zappa CDZAP 4
Released October 1987

Side 1:
1. Cheap Thrills / 2. Love Of My Life / 3. How Could I Be Such A Fool / 4. Deseri / 5. I'm Not Satisfied / 6. Jelly Roll Gum Drop / 7. Anything

Side 2:
1. Later That Night / 2. You Didn't Try To Call Me / 3. Fountain Of Love / 4. No. No. No / 5. Any Way The Wind Blows / 6. Stuff Up The Cracks

Line-up:
Frank Zappa - lead guitar / Ray Collins - lead vocals / Roy Estrada - bass, vocals / Jimmy Carl Black - drums / Arthur Tripp - drums / Ian Underwood - keyboards, tenor and alto saxophone / Don Preston - keyboards / Jim Motorhead Sherwood - baritone saxophone, tambourine / Bunk Gardner - tenor and alto saxophone

Producer: Frank Zappa
Recorded at Apostolic Studio, New York City from October 1967 to February 1968
Recorded simultaneously with *Uncle Meat*
Engineer: Dick Kunc

LENNY BRUCE: THE BERKELEY CONCERT
(double album)
US Bizarre 6329
Released 1968
US CD Enigma 1989

UK CD Demon Verbals VERBCD 7
Released 1980

All four sides contain the Lenny Bruce live show

Executive producers: Frank Zappa and Herb Cohen
Engineer (and therefore effective producer): John Judnich

AN EVENING WITH WILD MAN FISCHER (WITH WILD MAN FISCHER)
(double album)
US Bizarre 6332
Released 1968

UK Reprise RSLP 6332
Released 1968

Side 1:
The Basic Fischer:
1. Merry-Go-Round / 2. New Kind Of Songs For Sale / 3. I'm Not Shy Anymore! / 4. Are You From Clovis? / 5. The Madness & Ecstasy

Side 2:
Unaccompanied:
1. Which Way Did The Freaks Go? / 2. I'm Working For The Federal Bureau Of Narcotics / 3. The Leaves Are Falling / 4. 85 Times / 5. Cops & Robbers / 6. Monkeys Versus Donkeys / 7. Start Life Over Again / 8. The Mope / 9. Life Brand New / 10. Who Did It Johnny? / 11. Think Of Me When Your Clothes Are Off / 12. Taggy Lee / 13. Rhonda / 14. I Looked Around You / 15. Jennifer Jones

Side 3:
Some Historical Notes:
1. The Taster / 2. The Story Of The Taster / 3. The Rocket Rock / 4. The Rocket Rock Explanation & Dialogue / 5. Dream Girl / 6. Dream Girl Explanation / 7. Serrano (Sorrento?) Beach / 8. Success Will Not Make Me Happy / 9. Wild Man On The Strip Again

Side 4:
In Conclusion:
1. Why I Am Normal / 2. The Wild Man Fischer Story / 3. Balling Isn't Everything / 4. Ugly Beautiful Girl / 5. Larry & His Guitar / 6. Circle / 7. Larry Under Pressure

Line-up:
Wild Man Fischer, all except 'The Madness & The Ecstasy' which is by Kim Fowley & Rodney Bingenheimer, assisted by the GTO's and with a few words from Miss Johna at the end. Frank Zappa recorded the backing tracks for 'The Taster' and 'The Circle.' Art Tripp provided the percussion backing tracks on Side 1 tracks one through four

Producer: Frank Zappa
Engineer: live tracks by Dick Kunc Recorded on the Strip outside the Whisky A-Go-Go Unaccompanied songs by Jerry Hansen at Studio 2 of Sunset Sound, Hollywood, and Dick Kunc in the basement of The Log Cabin, Frank Zappa's house in Laurel Canyon

"We originally wanted blood, but we thought it would be a little bit too gory. I'd like to get a tape of his mother when she calls the office. Man, she is weird. She's afraid of him. He's tried to kill her three times. He does things like he sneaks into the house and he hides in the closet and sits for hours until she opens the closet, then he jumps out to scare her and then he runs away. He's real zany.

"This guy smells so bad. He comes into the office, you know, and you can smell him and tell he's coming, honest to God. He goes over to Warner Brothers and asks for copies of his album and if they give them to him, he goes out into the street and sells them. They're always saying, 'Please keep your artists away'." [Zappa: 1969]

30–31 NOVEMBER
Berkeley Community Theater, Berkeley, California.

DATE UNKNOWN
Thee Image, Miami, Fl.
Criteria, Miami, Fl.

6–7 DECEMBER
Shrine Exposition Hall, Los Angeles, California. (With The GTOs, Alice Cooper and Wild Man Fischer.)

–1969–

In 1969, Frank and Gail bought a home of their own, a large wood and stucco house off Mulholland Drive in the Santa Monica Mountains overlooking Laurel Canyon, not far from the Log Cabin. They have lived there ever since. A contemporary report described it as follows:

In the driveway, shaded by trees, is a white Jaguar – bought off Captain Beefheart and with all the seats slashed by the LA police searching unsuccessfully for drugs. Next to it, a late model fully automatic Buick Riviera, and the panel truck in which The Mothers' amplifiers and equipment is kept. The house is set back from the road, surrounded by palm trees, cut deep into the side of the mountain so that the front ground floor is the back basement level. The windows are shuttered, and the only indication that it is not a normal Hollywood home is the double-door on the ground floor to enable equipment to be brought in and out of the studio.

Inside it is a typical Hollywood home: the kitchen has all the latest in blenders, extractors, choppers and grinders: a triple door eye-level ice-box, a twin-sink with garbage disposal units, a water cooler with paper cups. Hanging like a frieze around the edge of the ceiling is Frank's large collection of hotel room keys and the walls are covered with weird newspaper cuttings and odd photographs and drawings, most of them sent in to United Mutations, the nearest thing that The Mothers have to a fan-club.

Zappa's house functions like a court, with everything designed to facilitate and serve Frank and his work. Gail is in charge and never appears to sleep. The house is in operation 24 hours a day, with huge quantities of clothes being bundled into the laundry room, and gigantic quantities of food – particularly muffins – being prepared for the children and endless visitors. Shrieks of laughter come from the GTOs planning a concert in the

kitchen in an apparent state of perpetual hysteria. Herb Cohen and an assistant whisper to each other over a sheet of hieroglyphic figures – doesn't he have an office he could work in?

Two year old Moon Unit is eating, perched on a stool. Her new brother, Dweezil, sits in a plastic baby bucket on the work counter, watching a miniature television set about 18 inches from his toes, presided over by "Gabby" Janet Ferguson, who lives in a small cottage in the garden, its walls covered with colour photographs of friends. Kansas, the road manager, is taking a call from a girl in Saginaw, but afterwards reveals he can't remember her at all. Pete, who describes herself as an "innocent country-girl" says she came south from Oregon that summer "to be with her Mothers." She is living in one of the bedrooms.

Gail smiles her benevolent liquid smile and lets it all wash over her. Frank's brother Carl is living in the changing

rooms by the pool. He does all the things that Frank sings about. Right now he is working at a car-wash. And before that he was a short order cook. Gail asked him to demonstrate a dance called The Slop. Carl is very good at it. He and Gail tut-tut over an ad that Frank's father has run in the local paper: "Frank Zappa's father offers car for sale…" Gail thinks it's cheap and demeaning.

In the large living room one wall is dominated by the Ed Beardsley painting which featured on the cover of Alice Cooper's Pretties For You album which Frank released on Straight. On the settee are Tony Secunda, visiting from London, and "H", Jimi Hendrix's London roadie who is staying at Frank's for an unspecified amount of time. When he arrived H gave Frank one of Jimi's smashed guitars which now sits propped against the wall.

And in the basement, crouched over his tape machines, single-sided razor blade in hand, sits Frank. On the door leading to the basement from the main house is a small black card on which is written, in neat white letters, DR ZURKON'S LAB IN HAPPY VALLEY. The basement is huge. The windows looking south over Hollywood from the front of the house are covered by sound-proofed patterned shutters. Two enormous speakers stand five feet high and between them, a Cal Schenkel assemblage of plastic, wood, auto-hoods and other collage elements, covers the hatch through which films are projected from an ante-room.

The baby blue, deep pile carpet is littered with instrument cases, an electric organ, an antique wheelchair and more of Schenkel's collage material. Paintings, concert posters and a framed, broken plaque proclaiming ZAPPA'S GRUBBY CHAMBER in large white letters on a dingy green background cover the walls. The sunlight is completely excluded and some parts of the room, particularly around the huge settee, are very dark, too dark to read in. A long row of cupboards holds Frank's collection of more than 7,000 R&B records and his tapes – seemingly thousands of them, mostly on 10" NAB spools to fit the Scully 280 2-track machine which occupies the centre of his life.

The Scully stands by the wall, connected to a TEAC A1200U for making tape transfers and has its own patchboard for making connections between the record player and amplifiers in the small adjoining record room. In this room are

more tape boxes, several guitars, leads, and more and more tapes. Frank says that no-one will insure the tapes because the house is in a fire zone. Many of them are tapes of concerts.

Frank seizes the top one, "Here's one which has a crazed groupie from Miami!" He picks up the next box, "Like to hear 'Absolutely Free' without the vocal overdubs?" There are conversations and oddments, final mixes and out-takes in apparently random order. A row of tapes are labelled:
"Merely Entertaining"
"Songs & Old Clothes #1"
"Sex In The 60s"
"Rustic Protrusion #2"
"Lovely Lips"
"The Mad Gummer #2"
"Cucamonga Era #2"
"Criteria: Right There Bunk Finale"
"What Does It All Mean?"

The index sheet taped to one box reads:

1. CHUKY BOB
Mono (highly compressed)
high level . . . . 1:35'
2. *LAUGHING BOY MAMBO
high level . . . . 3:15'

3. GARY WHISPERING "Famous people all suck…" low level . . . . 41 secs
4. Collection of Dick's Piano Slates/ BOSS CHROME TRIM/Spider Extracts.1:05'
5. CHEESE TRIM (Uncle Tom Wilson & Herbie)/Boss Snork Finale 96 Tears . . . . 1:22'
6. JIMMY CARL BLACK INDIAN OF THE GROUP "It sure wasn't between her legs" . . . . 14 secs
7. 15ips Xrer PIANO EXERCISE #3 low level . . . . 48 secs
8. 15ips LOVE OF MY LIFE Phoney stereo compressed center . . 58 secs
9. *SNORES . . . . 1:41'
10.*"Dark Water" RUN HOME WATER MUSIC . . . . 26½ secs
11.*CHROME PLATED GUITAR MUSIC . . . . .1:49'
12.*PONYSKIN TOWEL RACK/ "I feed them clouds"low level . . . . . 8 secs
13.*CZACL CUTS with Ums . . . . 48 secs
14.*AYEEEE HA HA HA HAH low level . . . . 35 secs
15.*MARIMBA CREEPINESS . . . . 17 secs
16.*High Speed CARTOON SAX MUSIC . . . . 9½ secs
17.*BLOOD UNIT MASTER replaced w DOG B rewind . . . . 1:28'
18.*RELAXED RAGA SNORK COLLAGE

with MOODY PIANO – Very Boss
Stereo – Slightly deficient in highs
At approx 1:35' goes into uptemp
section . . . . 2:41'
19.*GOD, I SEE GOD. . . . Talk Dirty
In French (Mono) high level . . . . . . 11 secs
20.*ALBERT HALL INTRO WITH
SURF . . . . 39 secs
21.*WHISKY A GOGO ROCKOUT #1
with electronic ending . . . . 1:30'
22.*WHISKY A GOGO ROCKOUT #2
(with whip) – level needs boosting
on front – electronic ending . . . . 4:37'
23.*HIGH SPEED RAGA with Snorks
& Ronnie – high level . . . . 1:33'

Total time . . . . 30:18'

At 5:45am the basement is quiet.
The huge speakers give off a low hiss.
The ceiling is not soundproofed and there
is a distant rumbling as the kittens play
on the floor above. The coffee percolator
gurgles imperceptibly. Frank sits at his
desk, at his elbow black sugarless coffee
and cigarettes, both of which he enjoys
intensely.

He writes music jerkily, pausing
to gaze into blank space, then scribbling
several bars of quavers. Chord clusters
grow and pose difficulties which, after
a while, cause him to reach for his Gibson
Les Paul, propped against his chair.
The sound is loud in the pre-dawn quiet.
Score paper and guitar cases are scattered
across the floor, crossed by headphone
leads and surrounded by little leaves
of discarded paper leader tape like
daisies in a summer field. At 9am he
will go to bed.

In the garden, Georgie, the German
Shepherd, is already stalking the semi-
tropical vegetation in the early morning
light. The surface of the pool is very still.
Muffled guitar lines coming from the
house are absorbed by the lush foliage.

Frank never goes out: "There are
steady streams of people walking through
the door. All I have to do is sit here, man."
And he's right. That evening Captain
Beefheart arrives to eat. Like Frank,
he lives at night, avoiding the sun.
At 6:30am Frank and Don are walking
in the garden.

Zappa: "That was an earthquake...
Did you feel it?"

Beefheart "Yes, but it was so small
that it made the people seem enormous!"
[Miles: 1969]

The Mothers of Invention line-up:
Spring 1969 tour; Frank Zappa – guitar,

Facing page: Ian Underwood
whips it out

vocals / Ian Underwood – wind instruments, keyboards / Don Preston – keyboards / Motorhead Sherwood – saxophone / Roy Estrada – bass, vocals / Bunk Gardner – wind instruments / Jimmy Carl Black – drums, trumpet, vocals / Art Tripp – percussion / Buzz Gardner – horns / Lowell George – guitar, vocals. (Billy Mundi added on drums on some concerts)

13 FEBRUARY
The Factory, The Bronx, NYC.

FEBRUARY
Stratford, Ct.

21 FEBRUARY
Lecture at the New School for Social Research, NYC, followed by concert at Fillmore East, NYC.

23 FEBRUARY
Toronto, Canada.

APRIL
MOTHERMANIA [Album 6]
(Compilation) released.

The sleeve reprints an article from a German newspaper about a riot which occurred after their Berlin concert.
"I don't know the direct translation of that. But I can tell you roughly what it says. It's a minute by minute account of a riot that occurred in Berlin that some students caused. Because of our appearance... It was in the newspaper the next morning."
[Zappa: 1968]

CAPTAIN BEEFHEART & HIS MAGIC BAND: TROUT MASK REPLICA
released.

LORD BUCKLEY: A MOST IMMACULATELY HIP ARISTOCRAT
released.

APRIL
UNCLE MEAT [Album 7]
(double album) released.

"'Uncle Meat' is sort of the missing link between the early albums which were basically song-type things, stuff like 'Monster-Magnet', into what we're doing now which is a lot more like serious music, if you want to use that expression, and very little of it is vocal music, you see.

MOTHERMANIA
Compilation
US Verve V6 5068
Released April 1969

UK Verve SVLP 9239
Released April 1969

Side 1:
1. Brown Shoes Don't Make It /
2. Mother People / 3. Duke Of Prunes / 4. Call Any Vegetable /
5. The Idiot Bastard Son

Side 2:
1. It Can't Happen Here /
2. You're Probably Wondering Why I'm Here / 3. Who Are The Brain Police / 4. Plastic People /
5. Hungry Freaks, Daddy /
6. America Drinks & Goes Home

Line-up:
Frank Zappa / Jimmy Carl Black / Don Preston / Bunk Gardner / Euclid James Sherwood / Ian Underwood / Roy Estrada and Arthur Tripp

Producers: Frank Zappa and Tom Wilson
Engineers: Ami Hadani, Tom Hidley, Gary Kelgren and Dick Kunc

This is the only authorised compilation of the Verve material ever issued. Track selection by Zappa taken from the albums *Freak Out*, *Absolutely Free* and *We're Only In It For The Money*

CAPTAIN BEEFHEART & HIS MAGIC BAND: TROUT MASK REPLICA
US Straight STS 1053
Released 1969
US CD Reprise 2027-2

UK Straight STS 1053
re-issued as Reprise K 64026

Side 1:
1. Frownland / 2. The Dust Blows Forward 'N' The Dust Blows Back / 3. Dachau Blues /
4. Ella Guru / 5. Hair Pie: Bake 1 /6. Moonlight On Vermont

Side 2:
Pachuco Cadaver / 2. Bill's Corpse / 3. Sweet Sweet Bulbs /
4. Neon Meate Dream Of A Octafish / 5. China Pig /
6. My Human Gets Me Blues /
7. Dali's Car

Side 3:
1. Hair Pie: Bake 2 / 2. Pena /
3. Well / 4. When Big Joan Sets

Up / 5. Fallin' Ditch / 6. Sugar 'N' Spikes / 7. Ant Man Bee

Side 4:
1. Orange Claw Hammer /
2. Wild Life / 3. She's Too Much For My Mirror / 4. Hobo Chang Ba / 5. The Blimp / 6. Steal Softly Thru Snow / 7. Old Fart At Play /
8. Veteran's Day Poppy

Line-up:
Captain Beefheart - vocals, bass clarinet, tenor saxophone, soprano saxophone / Zoot Horn Rollo - guitar, flute / Antennae Jimmy Semens - steel guitar / The Mascara Snake - vocals, bass clarinet / Rockette Morton - bass, narration

Producer: Frank Zappa
Engineer: Dick Kunc

UNCLE MEAT
(double album)
US Bizarre MS 2024
Released April 1969
US CD Rykodisc 10064/65
(double CD) Released 1987

UK Transatlantic TRA 197
Released September 1969
UK CD Zappa CDDZAP 3
(double CD)
Released October 1987

Side 1:
1. Uncle Meat: Main Title Theme / 2. The Voice Of Cheese /
3. Nine Types Of Industrial Pollution / 4. Zolar Czakl /
5. Dog Breath, In The Year Of The Plague / 6. The Legend Of The Golden Arches / 7. Louie Louie (At The Royal Albert Hall In London) / 8. The Dog Breath Variations

Side 2:
1. Sleeping In A Jar / 2. Our Bizarre Relationship / 3. The Uncle Meat Variations / 4. Electric Aunt Jemima. 5. Prelude To King Kong (Live At The Whisky A Go Go) /
7. A Pound For A Brown On The Bus / 8. Ian Underwood Whips It Out (Live On Stage In Copenhagen)

Side 3:
1. Mr. Green Genes / 2. We Can Shoot You / 3. If We'd All Been Living In California... / 4. The Air /
5. Project X / 6. Cruising For Burgers

Side 4:
1. King Kong Itself (As Played By The Mothers In A Studio) /
2. King Kong (Its Magnificence As Interpreted By Dom DeWild) /
3. King Kong (As Motorhead Explains It) / 4. King Kong (The Gardner Varieties) / 5. King Kong (As Played By 3 Deranged Good Humor Trucks) / 6. King Kong (Live On A Flat Bed Diesel In The Middle Of A Race Track At A Miami Pop Festival... The Underwood Ramifications)

The double CD version adds three tracks before 'King Kong' as follows

CD Disc 2:
Track 1: Uncle Meat Film Excerpt Part 1 / 2. Tengo Na Minchia Tanta / 3. Uncle Meat Film Excerpt Part 2

The film excerpts are spoken word only and last for just over 41 minutes

Line-up:
Frank Zappa - guitar, vocals, percussions / Ray Collins - vocals / Jimmy Carl Black - drums / Roy Estrada - bass, vocals / Don (Dom De Wild) Preston - keyboards / Billy Mundi - drums / Bunk Gardner - brass and woodwinds / Ian Underwood - keyboards, brass and

woodwinds / Art Tripp - drums, percussion / James Motorhead Sherwood - tenor saxophone, percussion / Ruth Komanoff - marimba, vibes / Nelcy Walker - vocal soprano on 'Dog Breath' and 'The Uncle Meat Variations'

Producer: Frank Zappa
Recorded at Apostolic Studio, New York and Sunset Sound in Los Angeles / Live recordings are listed in titles / The Copenhagen recording was at the Tivoli / Recorded simultaneously with 'We're Only In It For The Money' between October 1967 and February 1968
Engineers: Dick Kunc at Apostolic Studio, New York, and Jerry Hansen at Sunset Sound, Los Angeles

LORD BUCKLEY: A MOST IMMACULATELY HIP ARISTOCRAT
US Straight STS 1054
Released 1969
US CD Enigma Retro
(number unknown)

UK Demon Verbals 8. Release date unknown (mid-eighties?)
UK CD Demon Verbals VERBCD 8
Released 1989

Side 1:
1. The Bad-Rapping Of The Marquis De Sade / 2. The King Of Bad Cats / 3. Governor Slugwell

Side 2:
1. The Raven / 2. The Train /
3. The Hip Einie

Producer: Lyle Griffin
Engineer: Lyle Griffin
Edited: Frank Zappa

1969

MAY
Toronto, Canada.

23 MAY
University of Wisconsin, Appleton, Wi. (home of the Appleton Decency Convention).

Five days "outskirts of London" tour. Including TV and a talk at London School of Economics.

30 MAY
Birmingham, UK.

31 MAY
Newcastle, UK.

1 JUNE
Palace Theatre, Manchester, UK.

3 JUNE
Bristol, UK.

5 JUNE
Portsmouth, UK.

6 JUNE
Royal Albert Hall, London, UK.

7 JUNE
Paris late June-Early July: recording The GTOs album *Permanent Damage* in Los Angeles.

AUTUMN
Touring Germany, including TV. Denmark, Holland, France, including TV.

DATE UNKNOWN
Framington, Mass.

2 AUGUST
Central Park, NYC.

6 AUGUST
Highland Park Outdoor Music Center, Los Angeles, Ca.

AUGUST
Hot Rats recording sessions, Los Angeles.

10–17 AUGUST
Eight day tour of Canada ending: Montreal, Quebec, Canada.

AUGUST – SEPTEMBER
Hot Rats recording sessions at Whitney Studios, Glendale; TT&G Studios, Los Angeles and Sunset Sound, Los Angeles.

"A lot depends on how well 'Uncle Meat' sells as to whether or not we're going to be able to even survive continuing in that direction. Because if you stop singing, the audience stops listening. You have to either talk to them or sing to them but they're not prepared to listen to music at all, they just don't want to sit through it. They have a bad interest span for instrumental music unless it happens to be glandular music, you know those loud blues. They can dig it because they can tap their feet to it. But you whip a bunch of atonal 5 and ⅞ths on 'em and THAT they can't uh... groove with and that they have to think about. Then you're in dangerous territory when you consider that next week you're going to have to pay your rent. [Zappa: 1969]

"Here's an interesting thing about this album: A lot of it was written in the studio. While they were recording one section of a song I'd be in the control room writing the next score and then copy the parts. The album was put together basically by me, Bunk, Ian and Art Tripp. Because we did most of the overdubbing, 'cause they're the ones that read best in the group." [Zappa: 1969]

"I get kind of a laugh out of the fact that other people are going to try and interpret that stuff and come up with some grotesque, I mean really grotesque, interpretations of it. It gives me a certain amount of satisfaction. You can imagine how insane that must get on a song 'Electric Aunt Jemima' which was written about an amplifier. Yes, it's a Standall amplifier, about this big, that I used on a couple of sessions." [Zappa: 1969]

1969

OCTOBER
Mothers officially disbanded.

10 OCTOBER
HOT RATS [Album 8] released.

OCTOBER
Zappa on vacation in Europe attended the Amougis Festival in Belgium where he jammed with the Pink Floyd and Captain Beefheart.

NOVEMBER
Press conference.

JEFF SIMMONS: LUCILLE HAS MESSED MY MIND UP released.

NOVEMBER
GTO'S GIRLS TOGETHER OUTRAGEOUSLY: PERMANENT DAMAGE released.

Pamela des Barres describes one of the recording sessions in her autobiography *I'm With The Band – Confessions Of A Groupie*. Morrow, New York 1987:
"We recited some of our lyrics for Nicky [Hopkins] and Jeff [Beck], and they were rolling on the floor within thirty seconds! When Frank asked if they would like to put some of their virtuosity on our record, Jeff asked, "When do we start?" We were all in the dimly lit little studio, humming along with Mercy as she belted out 'Shock Treatment' optimistically off-key, when the entire Jeff Beck Group sauntered in to add some amazingness to the proceedings. I was very pleased to see that Jeff brought Rod Stewart, whom we all became instantly chummy with, calling him Rodney Rooster because of his choppy stick-up hairdo. Frank put Jeff and Nicky right to work, and they bombarded our meager efforts with brilliant bravura. We

sat watching, enthralled and captured while Rod the Mod hunched forlornly, then paced round and round in circles, then finally left the building. After Jeff's solo on 'The Eureka Springs Garbage Lady' we went out to the suburbs of Glendale calling 'Rodneeeee, Rodneeeee!' until we found him sitting on the steps of a grade school, peevish and petulant, feeling left out. We ooh'd and ahh'd over him and dragged him back to the studio, where he enhanced 'Shock Treatment' with his raspy sandpaper shouting. We all stood around in a circle with headphones on, following Rod Stewart's lead: 'Shock Treatment, oh let me go-oo shock treatment, oh let me go-oo.' I couldn't believe my eyes and ears. Frank was smiling away with his baton, the girls were caterwauling as best they could, Rod had his eyes closed and was sweaty and wailing, Nicky and Jeff were rocking out to the music, and I was in the middle of my own recording session!"

"Why am I getting into the GTO's? That's a very personal question! I don't spend much time working with the GTO's at all. I finished their album and my partner in the record company heard it and he just shit his pants. He said we can't put that out. He says there's no distributor in the world who would ever take that record.

"They are not good musicians but they write interesting material and they have something to say. They're about as good as any other girlie type rock 'n' roll, and they're generally weird." [Zappa: 1969]

NOVEMBER 1969 – FEBRUARY 1970

Shooting *Uncle Meat* movie.

6–7 DECEMBER

Shrine Exposition Hall, Los Angeles.

HOT RATS

US Bizarre RS 6356
Released 10 October 1969
US CD Rykodisc RCD 10066
Released 1987

UK Reprise RSLP 6356
Released February 1970
UK CD Zappa CDZAP 2
Released October 1987

Side 1:
1. Peaches En Regalia / 2. Willie The Pimp / 3. Son Of Mr. Green Genes

Side 2:
1. Little Umbrellas / 2. The Gumbo Variations / 3. It Must be A Camel

The CD release is labelled as 'Remixed from the original multi-track masters with added material from the original sessions. In fact all selections except 'The Gumbo Variations' are shorter than on the original

album. 'The Gumbo Variations' is 3 minutes 53 seconds longer

Line-up:
Frank Zappa - guitar, bass, percussion / Ian Underwood - piano, keyboards, brass and woodwind / Don Van Vliet - vocals on 'Willy The Pimp' / Sugar Cane Harris - violin on 'Willy the Pimp' and 'The Gumbo Variations' / Jean-Luc Ponty - violin on 'It Must be A Camel' / John Guerin - drums on 'Willie the Pimp', 'Little Umbrellas' and 'It Must be A Camel.' / Paul Humphrey - drums on 'Son Of Mr. Green Genes' and 'The Gumbo Variations' / Ron Selico - drums on 'Peaches En Regalia' / Max Bennett - bass on 'Willie the Pimp', 'Son Of Mr. Green Genes', 'Little Umbrellas', 'The Gumbo Variations' and 'It Must be A Camel.' Shuggy Otis - bass on 'Peaches En Regalia'

Producer: Frank Zappa.
Recorded at Whitney Studio in Glendale, T.T.G in Hollywood and Sunset Sound, Los Angeles during August and September 1969
Engineers: Dick Kunc at Whitney Studios, Jack Hunt at T.T.G., Cliff Goldstein at T.T.G. and Brian Ingoldsby at Sunset Sound

Dick Kunc (having left Apostolic in New York to work for Zappa) in charge of engineering

JEFF SIMMONS: LUCILLE HAS MESSED MY MIND UP

Straight STS 1057
Released 1969
(probably October)

Side 1:
1. Appian Way / 2. Zondo Zondo / 3. Madame Du Barry / 4. I'm In The Music Business / 5. Lucille Has Messed My Mind Up

Side 2:
1. Raye / 2. Wonderful Wino / 3. Tigres / 4. Aqueous Humore / 5. Conversations With A Recluse

Producer: Frank Zappa
(using the name La Marr Bruister) Zappa wrote the title track 'Lucille Has Messed My Mind Up' and co-wrote 'Wonderful Wino' with Simmons

Line-up:
Jeff Simmons - vocals, bass, piano, organ, accordion / Frank

Zappa - lead guitar on 'Lucille' and 'Raye' / Ian Underwood - saxophones / Craig Tarwater - guitars / Ron Woods - drums, percussion / John Kehlior - drums on 'Lucille' and 'Raye'

Engineer: Chris Huston at Mystic Studios, Hollywood and Whitney Studios, Glendale

GTO'S GIRLS TOGETHER OUTRAGEOUSLY: PERMANENT DAMAGE

US Straight STS 1059
Released November 1969
US CD Enigma Retro 7 73397-2
Released 1989

UK Straight STS 1059
Released 1970

Side 1:
1. The Eureka Springs Garbage Lady / 2. Miss Pamela and Miss Sparky discuss STUFFED BRAS and some of their early gym class experiences / 3: Who's Jim Sox? / 4. Kansas and the BTO's / 5. The Captain's Fat Theresa Shoes / 6. Wouldn't It Be Sad If There Were No Cones? / 7. Do Me In Once And I'll Be Sad, Do Me In Twice And I'll Know Better (Circular Circulation) / 8. The Moche Monster Review / 9. TV Lives

Side 2:
1. Rodney / 2. I Have A Paintbrush In My hand To Color A Triangle / 3. Miss Christine's First Conversation With The Plaster Casters Of Chicago / 4. The Original GTO's / 5. The Ghost Chained To The Past, Present, And Future (Shock Treatment) / 6. Love On An Eleven Year Old Level / 7. Miss Pamela's First Conversation With The Plaster Casters Of Chicago / 8. I'm In Love With The Oo-Ooo Man

Line-up:
Miss Pamela (Des Barres) / Miss Sandra / Miss Cinderella / Miss Christine / Miss Mercy

Frank Zappa: tambourine on 'I'm In Love With The Oo-Oo Man'

The Jeff Beck Group and Nicky Hopkins on piano on 'The Eureka Springs Garbage Lady' and 'Shock Treatment' (and maybe more tracks) Jimmy Carl Black, Roy Estrada, Ian Underwood and Don Preston on 'Circular Circulation' / 'TV Lives' / 'I Have A Paintbrush In My Hand To Color A Triangle' and maybe more / Rod Stewart vocals on 'Shock Treatment'. Miss Sparky (an original GTO's member) on Side 1, track two. Kansas, Mothers' road manager, on Side 1, track four; Rodney Bingenheimer

Producer: Frank Zappa
Engineer: Dick Kunc

DECEMBER
BURNT WEENY SANDWICH
[Album 9] released.

A contemporary report: *"I was present at TT&G when Ian Underwood dubbed his sax piece on the 16-track for 'Overture to a Holiday in Berlin'. Ian played facing the wall so the sound bounced off, rebounded off the the ceiling and was caught by the microphone set up behind him. 'That's how they got that greasy feeling' – Zappa. The band was playing deliberately slightly out of tune to get that Fifties feeling. Zappa was in the control booth and leading the band was Johnny Otis; Deeply tanned and looking just like his album sleeves with jet black gelled hair. He was clapping his hands high in the bass player's face, who didn't like it. Johnny's hair fell down over his eyes but a simple flick and the entire Fifties hair ensemble was back in place, just like Jerry Lee Lewis. I was impressed to see that Johnny was wearing black silk socks with calf-suspenders, which were of course revealed when he stomped his feet. [Miles: 1970]*

–1970–

JANUARY
KING KONG: JEAN-LUC PONTY PLAYS THE MUSIC OF FRANK ZAPPA
released.

MAY
Spent in the editing room, working on the film *Uncle Meat* between other projects. The previous summer, Zappa had been talking about getting special effects done in Japan, but without major backing all that went by the boards. Zappa did a lot of scrabbling around to get money to finish the film off. One deal, which brought in a small amount of money, required that Zappa shoot some continuity consisting of interviews with all the members of The Mothers, past, present, and future, and also find documentary footage to help to explain the mythology and validity of The Mothers. To this end Haskell Wexler would do a week's shooting interviews for free.

"We had a business meeting with The Mothers, just prior to that week of shooting, and there was a whole bunch of arguments and bullshit and hysteria. Four of the guys decided they wanted to have nothing whatsoever to do with any of the projects. That radically changed my plans for that week's shooting, which I had all blocked out. So two days before we were supposed to go – we had already hired the crew and had the lights and the stock bought and all that shit – to the tune of about maybe $12,000 for the week. Even though Haskell was free, the stuff that goes with him costs you some money. So I said, "Oh, what am I going to do here?"**

At the beginning of May, Zappa arranged a screening of the film as it stood for the money people...
"They were very distressed. They said, 'That's not the movie that you told us you were going to make.' And one of the other guys says, 'Why, that's horrible. It's so dull.' It's not going to be very easy to please those guys."
[Zappa: 1970]

"We had money to finish that picture, and all of a sudden, the people who gave us the money took the money back. I couldn't do anything more with it. I had 40 minutes of it cut at the time the money ran out." [Zappa: 1971]

BURNT WEENY SANDWICH
US Bizarre RS 6370
Released December 1969
US CD Rykodisc RCD 10163
Released 1990

UK Reprise RSLP 6370
Released March 1970
UK CD Zappa CD ZAP 35
Released October 1991

Side 1:
1. WPLJ / 2. Igor's Boogie, Phase One / 3. Overture To A Holiday In Berlin / 4. Theme From Burnt Weenie Sandwich / 5. Igor's Boogie, Phase Two / 6. Holiday In Berlin, Full Blown / 7. Aybe Sea (Piano Solo by Ian Underwood)

Side 2:
Little House I Used To Live In (Piano Solo By Ian Underwood, Violin Solo By Sugar Cane Harris, Piano Solo By Don Preston, Organ Solo By Frank Zappa) / 2: Valarie

Line-up:
Frank Zappa - guitar /
Roy Estrada - bass, vocals /
Jimmy Carl Black - drums, trumpet, vocals / Bunk Gardner - woodwinds / Buzz Gardner - trumpet / Ian Underwood - keyboards, clarinet, piano / Art Tripp - bass / Don Preston - keyboards, mini-moog / Sugar Cane Harris - violin / Jim Motorhead Sherwood - saxophone, vocals / Gabby Furggy - vocals on 'WPLJ'

Producer: Frank Zappa
Studio and live recordings from 1968 and 1969 / 'Overture To A Holiday In Berlin' was recorded at TT&G, Los Angeles as part of the Hot Rats sessions (The day after 'Willy the Pimp') The guitar solo on 'Holiday In Berlin, Full Blown' was recorded at The Arc in Boston, 1968
Engineer: Dick Kunc

KING KONG: JEAN-LUC PONTY PLAYS THE MUSIC OF FRANK ZAPPA
US World Pacific Jazz ST-20172
Released 1970
UK Liberty LBS 83375
Released 1970

Side 1:
1. King Kong / 2. Idiot Bastard Son / 3. Twenty Small Cigars / 4. How Would You Like To Have A Head Like That?
Side 2:
1. Music For Electric Violin And Low Budget Orchestra / 2. America Drinks And Goes Home

Line-up:
Jean-Luc Ponty - baritone violectra (on Side 1), electric violin / George Duke, piano, electric piano / Frank Zappa - guitar on 'How Would You Like To Have A Head Like That?' / Gene Estes - vibes, percussion on 'King Kong' / Buell Neidlinger - bass on 'King Kong' and 'Music For Electric Violin And Low Budget Orchestra' / Arthur Tripp - drums on 'King Kong' and 'Music For Electric Violin And Low Budget Orchestra' / Ian Underwood - tenor saxophone on 'King Kong' / Wilton Felder -Fender bass on 'Idiot Bastard Son', 'Twenty Small Guitars', 'America Drinks And Goes Home' and 'How Would You Like To Have A Head Like That?' / John Guerin - drums on 'Idiot Bastard Son', 'Twenty Small Guitars' , 'America Drinks And Goes Home' and 'How Would You Like To Have A Head Like That?' / Ernie Watts - alto saxophone and tenor saxophone on 'Idiot Bastard Son', 'Twenty Small Guitars' , 'America Drinks And Goes Home' and 'How Would You Like To Have A Head Like That?' / Donald Christlieb - bassoon on 'Music For Electric Violin And Low Budget Orchestra' / Gene Cipriano - oboe, English horn on 'Music For Electric Violin And Low Budget Orchestra' / Vincent DeRosa - French horn, descant on 'Music For Electric Violin And Low Budget Orchestra' / Arthur Maebe - French horn, tuben (sic) on 'Music For Electric Violin And Low Budget Orchestra' / Jonathan Meyer - flute on 'Music For Electric Violin And Low Budget Orchestra' / Harold Bemko - cello on 'Music For Electric Violin And Low Budget Orchestra' / Milton Thomas - viola on 'Music For Electric Violin And Low Budget Orchestra'

Producer: Richard Bock
Composer: Frank Zappa (except 'How Would You Like To Have A Head Like That' by Jean-Luc Ponty)
Arranged: Frank Zappa
'Music For Electric Violin And Low Budget Orchestra' conducted by Ian Underwood
Engineer: Dick Kunc

Uncle Meat eventually emerged on video but was clearly not at all the film that Zappa originally envisaged. 41 minutes from the soundtrack appear on the CD *Uncle Meat* and give a very accurate idea of the film.

Frank Zappa & The Mothers Of Invention line-up: August 1969 – March 1970 Frank Zappa – guitar, vocals / Ian Underwood – alto saxophone / Aynsley Dunbar – drums / Don Sugar Cane Harris – violin / keyboards, vocals / Max Bennett – bass.

28 FEBRUARY
Sports Arena, San Diego, Ca.
(with the *Hot Rats* line-up).

7 MARCH
Olympic Auditorium, Los Angeles, Ca.
(with the *Hot Rats* line-up).

Frank Zappa & The Mothers Of Invention line-up: April-May: Frank Zappa – guitar, vocals / Ray Collins – vocals / George Duke – keyboards / Aynsley Dunbar – drums / Billy Mundi – drums / Jeff Simmons – bass.

DATE UNKNOWN
El Monte Legion Stadium, Los Angeles, Ca.
Chicago, Ill.
Madison, Wi.
Philadelphia, Pa.
Minneapolis, Mi.

APRIL
Miami, Fl.

8–9 MAY
Fillmore East, NYC.

10 MAY: MOTHER'S DAY
Academy of Music, Philadelphia, Pa.
Zappa described the three previous engagements as…
"Strictly to get our chops up to the L.A. concert".

15 MAY
"200 Motels" performed in concert with the L.A. Philharmonic, at Pauley Pavilion, UCLA for the *Contempo 70* festival. Line-up: Frank Zappa – guitar, vocals / Jeff Simmons – bass, vocals / Aynsley Dunbar – drums / Ian Underwood – flute, saxophone / Don Preston – keyboards / Jim Motorhead Sherwood – saxophone / Ray Collins – vocals / Billy Mundi – drums / The Los Angeles Philharmonic Orchestra, conducted by Zubin Mehta.

The concert with Zubin Mehta was brought about by a chance meeting at KPFK-FM. Zappa was with David Raksin and had been complaining to him about how hard it was to get a piece of music played by an orchestra. A radio interview with Zubin Mehta was in progress at KPFK and Raksin invited Zappa to join in. **"I joined them and started yakking it up on the air. After it was over, I talked to Mehta for about ten minutes, during which – he probably won't remember – he commissioned me to write a piece of music for the** 1971 season – just sort of offhand. I said, 'Well, I got this other thing that's been sitting around for a while. Do you want to take a look at it?' He was too busy to look at it, but Fleishman, the manager of the Hollywood Bowl, looked at it, and he liked the score very much and got Zubin to check it out."**

This led to three months of meetings to discuss the financial feasibility of the project. In the end, Zappa was given six rehearsals and the concert was held at UCLA in the Pauley Pavilion,

an 11,000 capacity basketball dome. Two of the six rehearsals were just to balance the sound...

"If that works out and you can actually hear what's supposed to come out, then we'll be lucky." [Zappa: 1970]

Zappa was not convinced that Mehta was totally serious but was pleased that...

"He's going along with the gig."

Zappa played excerpts from *200 Motels*. The entire piece runs two and a half hours. Mehta played movements one, three and four. Zappa explained...

"Movement three is only one page long, but it's a special system that's got a lot of choreography in it – a special deal. The second movement is this big dramatic movement with a chorus and the dancers and vacuum cleaner and all that stuff. That was too expensive to do, so they couldn't put that in.

"I've been writing this for three years. It's based on sketches and material that were actually completed on the road or in motels, for one reason or another, and then

the final orchestration was done in my house over about three months, just prior to Christmas last year.**

21 MAY
Fillmore East, NYC.

Frank Zappa & The Mothers of Invention line-up: June 1970 - February 1971 Frank Zappa – guitar, vocals / Mark Volman – vocals / Howard Kaylan – vocals / Jeff Simmons – bass, vocals / George Duke – keyboards / Aynsley Dunbar – drums / Ian Underwood – flute, saxophone.

18 JUNE
Live on VRRP – Dutch TV.

24 JUNE
Fillmore West, San Francisco, Ca.

28 JUNE
Bath Festival, UK: Zappa and The Mothers had a mansion in Littlehampton placed at their disposal where they could relax from the rigours of the road and spend some time with other festival players, Dr. John, Canned Heat and the remains of The Turtles. Dr. John gave an impromptu grass show in preparation for

their English début. Zappa restricted his response to alternate verbal and physical gestures of appreciation and disgust.

7 AUGUST
Pauley Pavilion, UCLA, Los Angeles, Ca.

AUGUST
WEASELS RIPPED MY FLESH
[Album 10] released.

"What I've been doing is ripping up the twelve albums, which were already edited – I had them ready to go. Chopping them up and I put together a new album called 'Weasels Ripped My Flesh'. So 'Weasels Ripped My Flesh' is an all-live album. Most of the music on it – I'd say 80% of it – is group improvisation, not just accompaniment with solos, but where the group was conducted into a spontaneous piece of music." [Zappa: 1970]

WEASELS RIPPED MY FLESH
US Bizarre RSLP 2028
Released August 1970
US CD Rykodisc RCD 10163
Released 1990

UK Reprise RSLP 2028
Released September 1970. CD
Zappa CDZAP 24
Released 21 May 1990

Side 1:
1. Didja Get Any Onya /
2: Directly From My Heart To You / 3. Prelude To The Afternoon Of A Sexually Aroused Gas Mask / 4. Toads Of The Short Forest / 5. Get A Little

Side 2:
1. Eric Dolphy Memorial Barbecue / 2. Dwarf Nebula Processional March & Dwarf Nebula / 3. My Guitar Wants To Kill Your Mama / 4. Oh No / 5. The Orange County Lumber Truck / 6. Weasels Ripped My Flesh

Line-up:
Frank Zappa – lead guitar, vocal on "My Guitar"/ Ian Underwood – alto saxophone/ Bunk Gardner – tenor saxophone/ Jim Motorhead Sherwood – baritone saxophone, snorks/ Buzz Gardner – trumpet, flugelhorn / Roy Estrada – bass, vocal on "Prelude To The Afternoon" Jimmy Carl Black – drums/ Art Tripp – drums / Don Preston – keyboards/ Ray Collins – vocals on "Oh No" / Sugar Cane Harris – electric violin, vocals on "Directly From My Heart" Lowell George – rhythm guitar, vocal on "Didja Get Any Onya"

Producer: Frank Zappa
Recorded at various locations:
Side 1, track 1: Philadelphia Arena / 2. T.T.G. Studios, Hollywood / 3. Festival Hall, London / 4. First half, Whitney Studios, Glendale – second half Thee Image, Miami / 5. The Factory, Bronx, New York
Side 2: 1. A & R Studios, New York / 2. Apostolic Studio, New York / 3. Criteria Studios, Miami with final overdubs at T.T.G. Studios, Hollywood and Whitney Studios, Glendale / 4. Apostolic Studio, New York / 5. Festival Hall, London / 6. Birmingham, UK
Recorded between 1967 and 1969
Engineer: Dick Kunc in most cases

21 AUGUST
Santa Monica, Ca.

23–25 AUGUST
Pepperland, San Rafael, Ca.

10 SEPTEMBER
Hollywood Bowl, Los Angeles, Ca.

23 OCTOBER
CHUNGA'S REVENGE [Album 11]
released.

5–8 NOVEMBER
Fillmore West, San Francisco, Ca.

13–14 NOVEMBER
Fillmore East, NYC.

"The whole 40-minute sequence
that we perform of *200 Motels* was
learned in about 50 hours, like 10
days, five hours a day, in a rehearsal
hall. Scheduled from say 4 pm 'til
9 pm, just go down there and hit it.
There's a liquor store next door, get
a bottle of brandy... Joni Mitchell
sat in with us last night during the
second show and we improvised a
thing that was really good. And we
ended it with her singing 'Duke of
Earl'. Really far out, she came on
stage: 'Now OK and we're going to
improvise this thing...' and we did
a few chords for her and she started
reciting this poem which began:
'Penelope wants to fuck the sea...'
And the audience did a double-take
'Yuuunk!'... a little hush falls over
the Fillmore... JONI MITCHELL ?"
[Zappa: 1970]

NOVEMBER
Tyrone Guthrie Theater.
Minneapolis, Ma.

Frank with manager
Herbie Cohen

20 NOVEMBER
Veterans' Memorial Stadium,
Columbus, Oh.

26 NOVEMBER
Liverpool, UK.

27 NOVEMBER
Manchester, UK.

29 NOVEMBER
The Coliseum, London, UK.

1 DECEMBER
Stockholm, Sweden.

2 DECEMBER
K.B.Hallen, Copenhagen, Denmark.

4 DECEMBER
Hamburg, Germany.

5 DECEMBER
Düsseldorf, Germany.

6 DECEMBER
Concertgebouw, Amsterdam, Holland.

12 DECEMBER
Vienna, Austria.

13 DECEMBER
Munich, Germany.

15 DECEMBER
Gaumont Palace, Paris, France.

16 DECEMBER
Brussels, Belgium.

17 DECEMBER
Lille, France.

DECEMBER
Uddel, Belgium.

–1971–

JANUARY
At a press conference at the ICA, in
Nash House, London, Zappa announced
that he will make a film called *200 Motels*.

"For our stars we hoped to have
Donovan as the Good Conscience and
Ginger Baker as the Bad, but it just
didn't come off... We have been
working on it for about four years."
[Zappa]

Zappa's final remarks were directed
at the press...
"There's a bit in the film where
a reporter comes on stage, sits down,
and asks a lot of banal questions. So
I get up and put a rubber dummy in
my place and the reporter carries on
interviewing it. Then, after a pause,
I throw it into a mass of dancers who
kick the stuffing out of it and the
reporter, still asking questions,
begins to play with a rubber hand."
Zappa said that he would be
concentrating on the movie and the only
time off would be a ten-day tour in May
and a pop festival in Köln in August.

8 FEBRUARY
Royal Albert Hall. 4000 fans arrived to
find that a concert of Zappa and the
Royal Philharmonic Orchestra playing
the music from *200 Motels* had been
cancelled by the Hall on the grounds that
the lyrics were objectionable. A protracted
law suit followed.
Q: Why are you banned from the
Royal Albert Hall?
A: Because the woman who runs
it is insane. She's an old lady, very
prudish and very sick. She gave us

CHUNGA'S REVENGE
US Bizarre MS 2030
Released 23 October 1970
US CD Rykodisc RCD 10124
Released 1990

UK Reprise RSLP 2030
Released November 1970
UK CD Zappa CDZAP 23 Released
UK 21 May 1990

Side 1:
1. Transylvania Boogie /
2. Road Ladies / 3. Twenty Small
Cigars / 4. The Nancy & Mary
Music

Side 2:
1. Tell Me You Love Me /
2. Would You Go All The
Way? / 3. Chunga's Revenge /
4. The Clap / 5. Rudy Wants To
Buy Yez A Drink / 6. Sharleena

Line-up:
Frank Zappa – guitar, vocals,
drums, percussion / Ian
Underwood – keyboards,
saxophones, guitar / Max
Bennett – bass / Aynsley
Dunbar – drums / Jeff Simmons –
bass, vocals / George Duke –
organ, trombone, electric piano /
Howard Kaylan – vocals /
Mark Volman – vocals / John
Guerin – drums / Sugar Cane
Harris – organ

Producer: Frank Zappa
Recorded at The Record Plant,
Hollywood / Trident Studios,
London / T.T.G. Hollywood /
Whitney Studios, Glendale,
in 1970 / "The Nancy & Mary
Music" recorded live at the Tyrone
Guthrie Theater, Minneapolis, Minn
Engineers: Dick Kunc,
Stan Agol, Roy Baker /
Bruce Margolis engineered
"The Nancy & Mary Music"

Mark Volman, Aynsley Dunbar,
Jeff Simmons, Ian Underwood,
Howard Kaylan, Frank and
George Duke

a list of 12 words we couldn't say on stage. One of them was brassière, so you know where she's at. There's about a dozen other bands that are banned from the Albert."
[Zappa: 1973]

FEBRUARY
Filming and recording *200 Motels* at Pinewood Film Studios, UK.

APRIL – MAY
Overdubs for 200 Motels recorded at Whitney Studios, Glendale, Ca.

United Artists agreed to back 200 Motels with a budget of $630,000 without many of the usual hassles.

"Considering the ease with which the deal was made it was unbelievable – we sent them a tape and a 10-page treatment, and a few days later we had a meeting. We walked in and the guy says 'You've got a deal', just like that. I would like to have more money for the budget, but considering the amount that it is, we'll be able to do it. It's going to be tight."

Miles: "Is that why you're shooting in England?"

"Yes. Well, that's one of the reasons. I figured it would be fun to do it over there. The main enticement was the cost of the orchestra. We got the Royal Philharmonic for a thousand pounds a session."

Miles: "Which is cheap?.. "
"For a hundred men! You ain't kidding... We'll be shooting at Pinewood, we have two stages there... Tony Palmer is going to be the video-director. We're doing a video thing which is transferred to 35 mil – that's for the orchestra section... We're negotiating for Theodore Bikel to be the heavy in the film... he's really good. Certain things have been added to the script. For instance, the original concept for the orchestral environment was going to be a mountain made out of urethane foam. We got a cost estimate on making that – it was just too much. You can make the foam cheap but you can't reinforce it strong enough to hold 100 people cheap – the scaffolding and the man hours is what runs up the cost. So we canned that and now the orchestra lives in a concentration camp. It's Camp Untermünchen and

it's a music camp sponsored by the United States government – we're going to build a stylised one inside the sound stage.

"The concentration camp is at the end of the main street of Centreville... there's a main stage in the camp, a Busby-Berkeley type stage which laps into the concentration camp, and there's a barbed wire fence which is continued across our stage by a set of iron bars. There is a sliding door and we can go in and out of the camp at will because we can buy-off the guards. Then on Main Street, there is a newt-ranch for Motorhead and his girlfriend, and a bank, and the Rantz Mahamet's Colonic Parlour, and the meat market and a motel: an endless motel which just goes streaming down to infinity with fraudulent perspective. And at the end of the street is this airport with huge, out of proportion 747's lurking... just painted on the wall in black. And then there's a psychedelic night-club called the Electric Circus Factory and there's a bar called RED NECK EATS and there's a neon sign in the window that blinks on and off that says: 'Eat Beer!'...

"The narration is stylised. At one point, when I'm doing some narration and some action, I'm sitting in a motel room with an open window and I'm writing and I'm talking about how I'm doing this thing called Fleeting Gazelle and then the camera pans over my shoulder and you can see through the window the action that I'm describing: which is this girl coming out of the Colonic Parlour wearing the overcoat with the weanies on the shoulder and all that stuff...
"Cal (Schenkel) has designed this great environment, most of it stylised stuff, like the front wall of a house would be scrim on a framework, painted so that if you frontlight it you can see what's painted on it and if you back-light it, it transparentises and you can see the characters behind in sort of a dreamland type thing. And just a vague outline of what was on the front. There's a lot of things done that way... the special effects we'll be using consist mostly of wire-work: flying people in and out of situations...

"United Artists gets the sound-track album and they said that no matter how much music there is in

the film, they'll put it all out, even if it's four records. They said that at the first meeting. The deal itself – the distribution splits, etc., is an excellent deal, at least 10% better than the average deal, which is a lot in the movie business. I couldn't believe it! It only took about two weeks.

"A half an hour of the film's going to be animated: The Red Throbber, that whole sequence. The Red Throbber is the thing about this guy who's a Customs' Inspector and has a cardboard dog named Babette that's been trained by the government to sniff out hash and marijuana at the airport. He just recently managed to shack up with his high school friend, Charlene, that he's been secretly beating off for over ten years, and they've been going steady for three weeks, and he gets home from work one night with a lot of beer and he's ready to get it on, and Charlene has gone! So he goes into this frenzy, gets drunk, whips out his ouija board and asks it what's going on – the ouija board spells out: R.E.D. T.H.R.O.B.B.E.R. And he passes out in a coma and in this dream he imagines that this girl is at the Château Marmont, Bungalow B (Hollywood's hip hotel) being thrashed and eroticised by the Led Zeppelin. Then there is this elaborate dream sequence in which you see the guy that's doing it to her standing over the bed, (this is really not the Led Zeppelin you know – it's a figure of speech). The guy, all he's got on are these python boots and a black mask and this battery belt over his shoulder and this huge vibrator with wires hanging out. And he's holding it like a Krupp armament, standing over this chick on the bed. The thing goes off like a pneumatic drill on the street. And that's the kind of stuff that's going to be animated. Cal is doing all the designs all the characters, all the backgrounds, and then the stuff is executed by this company.

"The only overdubbing that will take place is on the track to The Red Throbber which we will pre-record and then the animators will work to the track. But that will also be done in England.

Frank with Atlantic Records head Ahmet Ertegun

We have made a deal for a mobile 16-track that'll come in with two NEV boards – two 24-input boards, for five hundred pounds a day and four engineers: Neat! One of the engineers is the guy that recorded our Albert Hall shift."

In one scene, where Zappa is being interviewed by a girl reporter from a big rock magazine, she asks: "I just want to verify a rumour. Is it true that you did this show at the Festival Hall?" Zappa continued… "Then it cuts to the rehearsal at the Festival Hall which is pixilated footage that was shot out at this pub on Seven Sisters Road when we were rehearsing. It was great. We had 15 members of the BBC Symphony Orchestra and The Mothers in the back room of this pub – it was the only place we could find to rehearse. We wheeled in a baby grand piano. Really great.

"Then the orchestra starts up again and she stops them again and says: 'Is it also true that you were in Vienna and you made this movie of your wife and an unidentifed foot?' And then there is this sequence of my writing some of the music for the film dissolving into shots of my wife with my foot on her tit, like this… strangling her tit, and she starts laughing. And that cuts in 'n' out of a couple of scratches, my nose over the page,

a bunch of people walking round the room. Then this percussion music comes back for a while and then she stops them again and says: 'And you insisted on mounting your silly little production against the best judgement of Herbie Cohenl! You had the audacity to perform it twice at the very Royal Festival Hall itself on one night whereupon it swiftly received a Chris Welch Melody Maker review pronouncing it totally rancid and devoid of minimum entertainment value and social blah blah…'

"And then we go into the Festival Hall footage where Jimmy Carl Black comes out drunken on stage and he starts saying: 'I'm quitting The Mothers…' and shit like that.

"In 200 Motels I want to make sure that the concept tracks from beginning to end. It's easy to say 'It's a fantasy, you can stick any fuckin' thing you want in there'. But I want somebody to be able to follow the course of the fantasy so that when they do get out there, they can look back and see what they meant and go: What? What am I doing here, without just going 'Yaannttz!' and them saying 'I don't understand it.' I want to get 'em out there and make 'em know that they went someplace and then get 'em back again. And that ain't easy to do." [Zappa: November 1970]

DATE UNKNOWN
Pomona, Ca.
Fillmore West, San Francisco, Ca.

Frank Zappa & The Mothers line-up:
May – December 1971 US, Canada and
European tour Frank Zappa – guitar &
vocals / Ian Underwood – keyboards, wind
instruments / Don Preston – mini-moog /
Jim Pons – bass / Howard Kaylan – vocals /
Mark Volman – vocals / Aynsley Dunbar –
drums / Bob Harris – keyboards on part
US tour only.

MAY
Claremont College, Claremont, Ca.

21 MAY
Chicago, Ill.

22 MAY
Wesleyan University, De.

23 MAY
Ohio Theater, Columbus, Oh.

25 MAY
Detroit, Mi.

Live on WABX, Detroit, Mi: line-up
Frank Zappa – guitar, vocals / Mark
Volman – vocals / Howard Kaylan – vocals /
Aynsley Dunbar – drums / Dick Barber –
vocals / Dave Dixon – ?

5 – 6 JUNE
Fillmore East, NYC. (*Fillmore East,
June 1971* recorded at June 6 concert
with John Lennon and Yoko Ono).

JUNE
Boston, Ma.

7 JULY
Pauley Pavilion, UCLA, Los Angeles, Ca.

JULY
El Monte Legion Stadium, Los Angeles, Ca.

AUGUST
FILLMORE EAST JUNE 1971
[Album 12] released.

AUGUST
Portland, Or.

7 AUGUST
Pauley Pavilion, UCLA, Los Angeles, Ca.
(*Just Another Band From L.A.* recorded).

SEPTEMBER
Noel Redding fell down the steps at

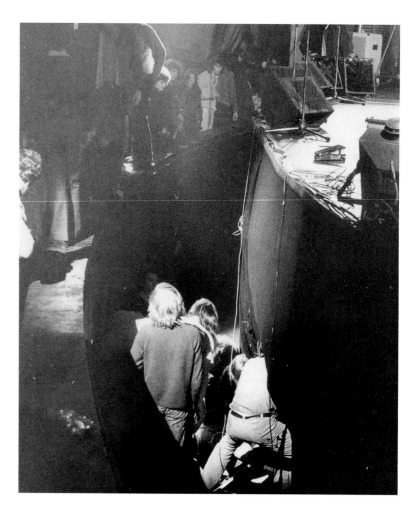

Zappa's home in L.A. and, according
to Noel, "broke me arm and bent
me back a bit." Lawyers and insurance
companies brought the suit so
Redding would have his medical
expenses paid. He and Frank remained
good friends and the suit "has nothing
to do with us."

OCTOBER
200 MOTELS [Album 13]
(double album) released.

200 Motels film released...
**"Within the scope of the budget
that we were given, I'd say I got
maybe 40 to 50 per cent of what
I wanted to get out of it. You just
have to kiss the rest of it good-bye
because there's not enough time
or money to do it perfect.
[Zappa: 1972]**

6 OCTOBER
Music Hall, Boston, Ma.

NOVEMBER
Odense, Denmark.

19 NOVEMBER
Konserthuset, Stockholm.

20 NOVEMBER
Aarhus, Denmark.

21 NOVEMBER
KB-Hallen, Copenhagen, Denmark.

23 NOVEMBER
Rheinhalle, Düsseldorf, Germany.

24 NOVEMBER
Deutschlandhalle, Berlin, Germany.

26 NOVEMBER
Hamburg, Germany.

27 NOVEMBER
The Ahoy, Rotterdam, Holland.

28 NOVEMBER
Jahrhunderthalle, Frankfurt, Germany.

29 NOVEMBER
Munich, Germany.

30 NOVEMBER
Vienna, Austria.

4 DECEMBER
The Casino, Montreux, Switzerland. In
the middle of Don Preston's synthesizer
solo on "King Kong" the building caught

fire. Zappa calmed the crowd of 3,000 which was well over capacity. The owners had chained shut the exit doors because there were people still trying to get in so one of the roadies smashed a large plate glass window to enable the audience to escape. The auditorium filled with smoke and shortly after the band had escaped through the backstage tunnel, the heating system exploded blowing several people through the window. No-one was killed. The building was gutted and Zappa lost all of his equipment with ten tour dates to go.

The band voted to continue the tour, cancelled one week's worth of gigs to break in new equipment ready for the two sold-out nights - two shows a night - at the 3000 seater Rainbow in London.

10 DECEMBER

The Rainbow Theatre, London. The band played the first show, and returned to play an encore. Since they were in England, Frank chose to play The Beatles' "I Want To Hold Your Hand". A member of the audience ran up the side steps of the stage and pushed Zappa off the stage, ten feet into the orchestra pit, knocking him unconscious and breaking his leg. Members of the audience immediately seized the man, Trevor Charles Howell, as he tried to get away. Zappa's roadies then taught him a few manners.

Chaotic scenes ensued outside the Rainbow where the audience for the second concert were joined on the street by the audience from the first. Wild rumours that Frank had been killed flashed through the massive crowd, and for upwards of an hour no-one knew what was happening. Eventually the crowd dispersed, most of them none the wiser about the evening's dramatic events.

Police arrested Howell, a 24-year-old manual worker, and charged him with assault with malicious intent to commit bodily harm. Bail was set at £100.

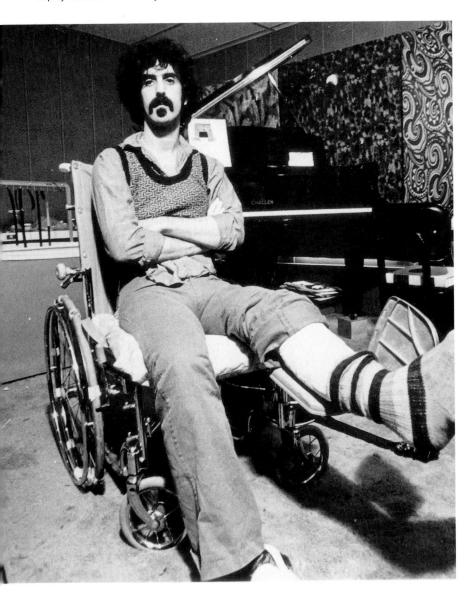

FILLMORE EAST, JUNE 1971
US Bizarre MS 2042
Released August 1971
US CD Rykodisc RCD 10167
Released 1990

UK Reprise K 44150
Released August 1971
CD Zappa CD ZAP 29
Released 21 May 1990

Side 1:
1. Little House I Used To Live In / 2. The Mud Shark / 3. What Kind Of Girl Do You Think We Are? / 4. Bwana Dik / 5. Latex Solar Beef / 6. Willie The Pimp, Part One

Side 2:
1. Do You Like My New Car? / 2. Happy Together / 3. Lonesome Electric Turkey / 4. Peaches En Regalia / 5. Tears Began To Fall

Line-up:
Frank Zappa - guitar, dialogue / Mark Volman - lead vocals, dialogue / Howard Kaylan - lead vocals, dialogue / Ian Underwood - wind instruments, keyboards, vocals / Aynsley Dunbar - drums / Jim Pons - bass, vocals, dialogue / Bob Harris - 2nd keyboard, vocals / Don Preston - mini-moog

Produced: Frank Zappa
Recorded at Fillmore East, 2nd Avenue, New York City, 5 - 6 June 1971, mixed and mastered at Whitney Studios, Glendale
Engineer: Barry Keene

200 MOTELS
(double album)
US United Artists UAS 9956
Released October 1971

UK United Artists UDF 50003
Released November 1971

Side 1:
1. Semi-Fraudulent: Direct From Hollywood Overture / 2. Mystery Roach / 3. Dance Of The Rock & Roll Interviewers / 4. This Town Is A Sealed Tuna Sandwich (Prologue) / 5. Tuna Fish Promenade / 6. Dance Of The Just Plain Folks / 7. This Town Is A Sealed Tuna Sandwich (Reprise) / 8. The Sealed Tuna Bolero / 9. Lonesome Cowboy Burt

Side 2:
1. Touring Can Make You Crazy / 2. Would You Like A Snack? / 3. Redneck Eats / 4. Centerville / 5. She Painted Up Her Face / 6. Janet's Big Dance Number / 7. Half A Dozen Provocative Squats / 8. Mysterioso / 9. Shove It Right In / 10. Lucy's Seduction Of A Bored Violinist & Postlude

ide 3:
1. I'm Stealing The Towels / 2. Dental Hygiene Dilemma / 3. Does This Kind Of Life Look Interesting To You? / 4. Daddy, Daddy, Daddy / 5. Penis Dimension / 6. What Will This Evening Bring Me This Morning

Side 4:
1. A Nun Suit Painted On Some Old Boxes / 2. Magic Fingers / 3. Motorhead's Midnight Ranch / 4. Dew On The Newts We Got / 5. The Lad Searches The Night For His Newts / 6. The Girl Wants To Fix Him Some Broth / 7. The Girl's Dream / 8. Little Green Scratchy Sweaters & Corduroy Ponce / 9. Strictly Genteel (The Finale)

Line-up:
The Mothers: Frank Zappa - guitar, bass / Mark Volman - vocals, special material / Howard Kaylan - vocals, special material / Ian Underwood - keyboards, wind instruments / Aynsley Dunbar - drums / George Duke - keyboards, trombone / Martin Lickert - bass / Jimmy Carl Black - vocal on 'Lonesome Cowboy Burt' / Ruth Underwood - orchestra drum set / Jim Pons - voice of the 'Bad Conscience' / The Royal Philharmonic Orchestra, conducted by Elgar Howarth / The Top Score Singers, conducted by David Van Asch / The Classical Guitar Ensemble, supervised by John Williams

Narrator: Theodore Bikel
Producer: Frank Zappa
Recorded at Pinewood Film Studios, London, on The Rolling Stones Mobile in February 1971, with overdubs recorded at Whitney Studios, Glendale, Ca during April - May, 1971
Engineers: Bob Auger in Stones Mobile and Barry Keene at Whitney Studios

Frank with his leg in plaster following his fall from the Rainbow stage

Frank with his leg in plaster following his fall from the Rainbow stage
Left to right: Tom Fowler,

According to a member of the audience, Howell kept mumbling something about his woman being in love with Zappa.

20 DECEMBER
Trevor Howell, appeared in court charged with "maliciously inflicting grievous bodily harm" on Frank Zappa. Howell pleaded guilty and said "I did it because my girl friend said she loved Frank." He was sentenced to a year in jail…

"The man was deranged. The show was over and the band was leaving the stage when this guy jumped onstage and ran up behind me. He pushed me into the orchestra pit, 15 feet down to the concrete. I had a hole put in the back of my skull, twisted my neck, broke my wrist and leg. I was in a wheel chair for nine months and off the road for over a year." [Zappa: 1973]

–1972–

Zappa spent a month in hospital in a wheelchair with a cast on his leg. He spent the next few months in a wheelchair and on crutches before the cast was replaced with a leg brace. By September of 1972 he was able to walk around without using crutches all the time but his leg was still in a brace. He spent the first half of the year

**JUST ANOTHER BAND
FROM L.A.**
US Bizarre MS 2075
Released May 1972
US CD Rykodisc RCD 10161
Released 1990

UK Reprise K 44179
Released June 1972
UK CD Zappa CD ZAP 25
Released 21 May 1990

Side 1:
1. Billy The Mountain

Side 2:
1. Call Any Vegetable / 2. Eddie,
Are You Kidding? / 3. Magdalena /
4. Dog Breath

Line-up:
Frank Zappa - guitar, vocals /
Mark Volman - lead vocals /
Howard Kaylan - lead vocals /
Ian Underwood - wind
instruments, keyboards, vocals /
Aynsley Dunbar - drums /
Don Preston - keyboard, mini-
moog / Jim Pons - bass, vocals
Producer: Frank Zappa
Engineer: Barry Keene
Recorded live at Pauley Pavilion,
UCLA, Los Angeles, Ca
on 7 August 1971

**SOMETIME IN
NEW YORK CITY**
(double album)
US Apple SVBB 3392
Released 12 June 1972
US CD CEMA C21V-46782

UK Apple PCSP 716
Released 15 September 1972
UK CD EMI CDS-746782-8

(Side 1 & 2 comprised a studio
album by John Lennon and Yoko
Ono, Side 3 was a live John
Lennon and Yoko Ono concert
from the London Lyceum)

Side 4:
Track 1. Well (Baby Please
Don't Go) / 2. Jamrag /
3. Scumbag / 4 Aü

Line-up:
Frank Zappa - lead guitar,
dialogue / John Lennon - guitar,
vocals / Yoko Ono - vocals / Mark
Volman - vocals, dialogue /
Howard Kaylan - vocals,
dialogue / Ian Underwood - wind
instruments, keyboard, vocals /
Aynsley Dunbar - drums / Jim
Pons - bass, vocals, dialogue /
Bob Harris - 2nd keyboard,
vocals; Don Preston - mini-moog /
Klaus Voorman - overdubbed
bass
Produced: John Lennon,
Yoko Ono and Phil Spector
Recorded 6 June 1971, live at
the Fillmore East, New York City
Engineer: Roy Sicala
Mixed at the Record Plant,
New York City

WAKA/JAWAKA
US Bizarre MS 2094
Released 5 July 1972
US CD Rykodisc 10094
Released 1988

UK Reprise K 44203
Released August 1972
UK CD Zappa CDZAP 10
Released June 1989

Side 1:
1. Big Swifty

Side 2:
1. Your Mouth / 2. It Just
Might Be A One-Shot Deal /
3. Waka/Jawaka

Line-up:
Frank Zappa - guitar, percussion /
Tony Duran - slide guitar, vocal
on "Big Swifty", "Your Mouth",
"It Just Might Be A One-Shot
Deal" / George Duke - piano on
"Big Swifty" and "Your Mouth";
Sal Marquez - trumpets, chimes,
vocal, flugelhorn; Erroneous (Alex
Dmochowski) - bass / Aynsley
Dunbar - drums / Chris Peterson -
vocal on "Your Mouth" / Joel
Peskin - tenor saxophone on
"Your Mouth" / Mike Altschul -
brass and woodwind on "Your
Mouth" and "Waka/Jawaka" /
Jeff Simmons - Hawaiian guitar,
vocal on "It Might Just Be A
One-Shot Deal" / Sneaky Pete
Kleinow - pedal steel guitar on
"It Might Just Be A One-Shot
Deal" / Janet Ferguson - vocal on
"It Might Just Be A One-Shot
Deal" / Don Preston - piano, mini-
moog on "Waka/Jawaka" /
Bill Byers - trombone, baritone
horn on "Waka/Jawaka" / Ken
Shroyer - trombone, baritone
horn on "Waka/Jawaka"

Producer: Frank Zappa
Recorded at Paramount Studios,
Los Angeles, in the spring of
1972
Engineer: Kerry McNabb

at his home in Los Angeles recuperating,
during which time he worked on a new
movie project, produced a nine-piece
doo-wop group called Ruben and The
Jets, and made the album Waka / Jawaka
in Paramount Studios while he was still in
the wheelchair.

MAY
JUST ANOTHER BAND FROM L.A.
[Album 14] released.

12 JUNE
JOHN LENNON AND YOKO ONO:
SOMETIME IN NEW YORK CITY
(double album) released.

5 JULY
WAKA/JAWAKA [Album 15] released.

**"One of the projects I've been
working on for the past few months
has been assisting in putting**

1972-73

Frank and Gail inspect the Oval pitch before the Grand Wazoo concert

with tambourines and saying zany stuff – we're not supplying that this season." [Zappa: 1972]

Frank Zappa / Mothers & the Grand Wazoo Orchestra line-up: September 1972 Frank Zappa – guitar, vocals / Malcolm McNabb – trumpet / Sal Marquez – horns / Tom Malone – trumpet, brass / Bruce Fowler – trumpet / Glenn Ferris – trumpet / Kenny Shroyer – trumpet, horns / Jay Migliori – flute, saxophone / Mike Altschul – flute, saxophone / Ray Reed – saxophone, clarinet / Charles Owens – saxophone / Joanne McNabb – bassoon / Earl Dumler – oboe, double bass / Jerry Kessler – electric cello / Ian Underwood – woodwinds, piano / Dave Parlato – bass / Tony Duran – guitar / Jim Gordon – drums / Tom Raney – percussion / Ruth Underwood – percussion.

10 SEPTEMBER
Hollywood Bowl, Los Angeles, Ca. "The Grand Wazoo"

15 SEPTEMBER
Deutschlandhalle, Berlin, Germany.

16 SEPTEMBER
Oval Cricket Ground, London, UK.

17 SEPTEMBER
Hourast Halls, Den Haag, Holland.

SEPTEMBER
Two days in Electric Ladyland Studios, NYC. Recording sessions for *Apostrophe (')*.

23 SEPTEMBER
Felt Forum, NYC. "The Grand Wazoo Comic Book Extravaganza"

24 SEPTEMBER
Music Hall, Boston, Mass.

25 SEPTEMBER
Los Angeles, Ca.

The Petit Wazoo Orchestra October – December line-up: Frank Zappa – guitar, vocals / Gary Barone – trumpet / Earl Dumler – oboe, double bass / Malcolm McNabb – tuba, horns / Tom Malone – trumpet, brass / Bruce Fowler – trombone / Glenn Ferris – trombone, horns / Dave Parlato – bass / Tony Duran – slide guitar / Jim Gordon – drums.

28 OCTOBER
Syracuse, NY.

together a real *Ruben and The Jets*. If there's another album like that, then they'll make it, not me." [Zappa: August 1972] (The record was released in 1973).

During the summer Zappa put together and rehearsed a 20-piece rock ensemble called The Grand Wazoo Orchestra, consisting mostly of people who played on the Waka / Jawaka album… **"It's a group you've never seen before – 20 pieces including six reeds, six brass, two concert percussionists, one drum set, one electric bass, two guitars, keyboard and synthesizers, and an electric cello. It's really nice. The only names** people will recognise from past associations will be Ian Underwood on keyboard and Ruth Underwood playing percussion one. Most of the people who are on the "Waka / Jawaka" album are in this group. We'll probably be billed as The Mothers. What we really have here is an electric symphony orchestra… Aside from the recognisable pieces which are rock-oriented, there are two or three semi-symphonic-type pieces, [in the act] which are of a humorous nature simply because of the subject matter. But we're not going to have people jumping around on stage or falling down

29 OCTOBER
Harper College, Binghamton, NY.

31 OCTOBER
Capitol Theater, Passaic, NJ.
"Hallowe'en Show".

7 NOVEMBER
Commack, NY.

NOVEMBER
Bloomington, Id.

10 NOVEMBER
Irvine Auditorium, Philadelphia, Pa.

11 OCTOBER
Constitution Hall, Washington, DC.

DECEMBER
THE GRAND WAZOO [Album 16]
released.

2 DECEMBER
Cowtown Palace, Kansas City, Mo.

12 DECEMBER
Paramount Theater, Portland, Or.

31 DECEMBER
Constitution Hall, Washington, DC.

– 1973 –

The Mothers of Invention January –
December World tour line-up: Frank
Zappa – guitar, vocals / Jean-Luc Ponty –
violin / George Duke – keyboards, violin /
Ian Underwood – saxophones, woodwinds
/ Ruth Underwood – percussion / Bruce
Fowler – trumpet / Tom Fowler – bass /
Ralph Humphrey – drums. [Sal Marquez –
trumpet US and Far East only]

23 FEBRUARY
Fayetteville, Nc.

24 FEBRUARY
Duke University, Durham, Nc.

27 FEBRUARY
Athens, Ga.

1 MARCH
Daytona Beach, Fl.

2 MARCH
Curtis Hickson Hall, Tampa, Fl.

5 MARCH
Miami, Fl.

7 MARCH
Veterans' Memorial Hall, Columbus, Ga.

11 MARCH
Texas Hall Auditorium, Arlington, Tx.
"The Petite Wazoo".

APRIL
Circle Star Theater, Phoenix, Az.

27 APRIL
Princeton University, Princeton, NJ.

1 MAY
Kent State University, Kent, Oh.

2 MAY
Coliseum, Indianapolis, Ind.

4 MAY
Maple Leaf Gardens, Toronto, Canada.

6 MAY
Syria Mosque, Pittsburgh, Pa.

9 MAY
Capitol Theater, Passaic, NJ.

11 MAY
Milwaukee, Wi.

13 MAY
University of Ohio, Cincinnati, Oh.

16 MAY
Auditorium Theater, Chicago, Ill.

17 MAY
Hofstra College, Hempstead, NY.

18 MAY
Nassau Coliseum, Uniondale, NY.

JUNE
OVER NITE SENSATION
[Album 17] released.

THE GRAND WAZOO
US Bizarre MS 2093
Released December 1972
US CD Rykodisk RCD 10026
Released 1986

UK Reprise K 44209
Released January 1973
Import CD Rykodisk RCD 10026
released 1986 followed by
UK CD Zappa CDZAP 31
(digitally remixed at UMRK 1990)
Released 1990

Side 1:
1. For Calvin (And His Next Two
Hitch-hikers) / 2. The Grand
Wazoo

Side 2:
1. Cletus Awreetus-Awrightus /
2. Eat That Question / 3. Blessed
Relief

Line-up:
Frank Zappa - lead guitar,
percussion / George Duke -
keyboards Side 2 only /
Tony Duran - bottle-neck guitar
on 'Grand Wazoo', 'For Calvin' and
rhythm on 'Eat That Question' /
'Blessed Relief' / Sal Marquez -
trumpet / Don Preston - mini-
moog on Side 1 / Mike Altschul -
woodwind / Erroneous (Alex
Dmochowski) - bass / Aynsley
Dunbar - drums / Janet Neville-
Ferguson - vocals on Side 1 / Earl
Dumler - woodwind on Side 1 /
Tony 'Bat Man' Ortega - woodwind
on Side 1 / Joanne Caldwell
McNabb - woodwind on Side 1 /
Johnny Rotella - woodwind on
Side 1 / Fred Jackson - woodwind
on Side 1 / Malcolm McNabb -
trumpet on Side 1 / Bill Byers -
trombone on Side 1 / Ken
Shroyer - trombone on Side 1 and
'Cletus...' / Ernie Tack - brass
on Side 1 / Bob Zimmitti -
percussion on Side 1 / Alan Estes
- percussion on Side 1 / Ernie
Watts - saxophone on 'Cletus...' /
'Chunky' - vocals on 'Cletus...' /
Lee Clement - gong on 'Eat That
Question' / Joel Peskin -
woodwind on 'Eat That Question'
and 'Blessed Relief'

Producer: Frank Zappa
Recorded at Paramount Studios,
Hollywood, 1972
Engineer: Kerry McNabb

OVER NITE SENSATION
US DiscReet MS 2149
Released June 1973
US CD (w/APOSTROPHE)
Rykodisc RCD 40025
Released 1987

UK DiscReet K 41000
Released August 1973
UK CD (w/APOSTROPHE)
Zappa CD ZAP 18
(digitally remixed at UMRK 1989)
Released 1990

Side 1:
1. Camarillo Brillo / 2. I'm The
Slime / 3. Dirty Love / 4. Fifty-Fifty

Side 2:
1. Zomby Woof / 2. Dinah-Moe
Humm / 3. Montana

Line-up:
Frank Zappa - guitar, vocals /
Sal Marquez - trumpet, vocals /
Tom Fowler - bass / Bruce Fowler-
trombone / Ralph Humphrey -
drums / Ruth Underwood -
marimba, vibes, percussion /
Ian Underwood - flute, clarinet,
alto saxophone, tenor
saxophone / George Duke -
keyboards, synthesizer / Jean-Luc
Ponty - violins / Ricky Lancelotti -
vocal on 'Zomby Woof' and 'Fifty-
Fifty' / Kin Vassy - vocal on 'I'm
The Slime', 'Montana' and 'Dinah-
Moe Humm'

Producer: Frank Zappa
Recorded at Bolic Sound,
Inglewood / Whitney Studios,
Glendale / Paramount Studios,
Los Angeles, in 1973
Engineers: Barry Keene,
Terry Dunavan, Fred Borkgren,
Steve Desper
Re-mix by Kerry McNabb at
Paramount

"My experiences have changed, they're getting less specific in certain ways, more specific in others. It used to be that I would write specific things about obvious social phenomena that a large number of people could identify with because they had seen it in action. But that's less specific in terms of my own personal experience. You know, I could observe something happen that may or may not have happened to me personally and I could still write about it. These days such weird things have happened to me as a person that I'd rather put some of those down and do it that way. That's why I have songs like "Penguin in Bondage," and "Montana." I write about the things that are part of my personal experience."

"'Montana', which is, in part, about a man who dreams of raising dental floss on a ranch in Montana, started out this way: I got up one day, looked at a box of dental floss and said, hmmm. I assumed that nobody had done the same thing and

I felt it was my duty as an observer of floss to express my relationship to the package. So I went downstairs and I sat at the typewriter and I wrote a song about it. I've never been to Montana, but I understand there's only 450,000 people in the whole State. It has a lot of things going for it, plenty of space for the production of dental floss... and the idea of travelling along the empty wasteland with a very short horse and a very large tweezer, grabbing the dental floss sprout as it pooches up from the bush... grabbing it with your tweezers and towing it all the way back to the bunkhouse... would be something good to imagine.

"Sometimes I show the lyrics to my wife, or after a while I'll get her to read them to me so I can see what the sounds are like, because part of the texts are put together phonetically as well as what the information is supposed to be. I change lyrics all the time. A lot of them get changed by accident. Somebody will read them wrong and it'll sound so funny I'll leave it wrong." [Zappa: 1974]

RUBEN AND THE JETS: FOR REAL
released.

21 JUNE
Brisbane, Australia.

24 – 26 JUNE
Horden Pavilion, Sydney, Australia.

28 – 29 JUNE
Festival Hall, Melbourne, Australia.

4 JULY
Adelaide, Australia.

6 JULY
Melbourne, Australia.

7 – 8 JULY
Horden Pavilion, Sydney, Australia.

18 AUGUST
KB Hallen, Copenhagen, Denmark.

19 AUGUST
Gothenburg, Sweden.

21 AUGUST
Skansen, Stockholm, Sweden.

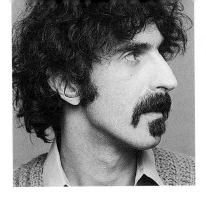

23 AUGUST
Helsinki, Finland.

26 AUGUST
Oslo, Norway.

29 AUGUST
Palasport, Rome, Italy.

30 AUGUST
Stadio Communale, Bologna, Italy.

31 AUGUST
Milan, Italy.

1 SEPTEMBER
Verona, Italy.

2 SEPTEMBER
Mehrzweckhalle Wetzikon, Zurich,
Switzerland.

3 SEPTEMBER
Deutsches Museum, Munich, Germany.

4 SEPTEMBER
Stadthalle, Freiburg, Germany.

5 SEPTEMBER
Stadthalle, Offenbach, Germany.

6 SEPTEMBER
Hamburg, Germany.

8 SEPTEMBER
Voorst Nationaal, Brussels, Belgium.

9 SEPTEMBER
Amsterdam, Holland.

10 SEPTEMBER
Paris, France.

11 SEPTEMBER
Liverpool Stadium, Liverpool, UK.

13 SEPTEMBER
Birmingham, UK.

14 SEPTEMBER
Empire Pool, Wembley, London, UK.

31 OCTOBER
Auditorium Theater, Chicago, Ill.

4 NOVEMBER
Brooklyn College, NYC.

6 NOVEMBER
Hofstra College, Hempstead, NY.

9 NOVEMBER
Syracuse, NY.

11 NOVEMBER
William Patterson College, Wayne, NY.

17 NOVEMBER
Rochester, NY.

18 NOVEMBER
Waterloo, Toronto, Ontario, Canada.

19 NOVEMBER
Ontario, Canada.

21 NOVEMBER
Buffalo, NY.

22 NOVEMBER
Avery Fisher Hall, Lincoln Center, NYC.

23 – 24 NOVEMBER
Massey Hall, Toronto, Canada.

26 NOVEMBER
Edmonton, Alberta, Canada.

30 NOVEMBER
Lowell, Mass.

1 DECEMBER
State University of NY at Stoneybrook.

2 DECEMBER
North Dartmouth, Dartmouth, Mass.

DECEMBER
Seattle, Wa.
Fresno, Ca.
Oakland, Ca.

7 – 12 DECEMBER
The Roxy, Hollywood, Los Angeles, Ca.
   Line-up for recording of *Roxy &
Elsewhere* on 10 - 12 December: Frank
Zappa – guitar, vocals / George Duke –
keyboards, violin / Ruth Underwood –
percussion / Jeff Simmons – rhythm guitar,
vocals / Bruce Fowler – trumpet / Tom
Fowler – bass / Walt Fowler – trumpet /
Napoleon Murphy Brock – tenor
saxophone, flute, lead vocals / Ralph
Humphrey – drums.

**RUBEN AND THE JETS:
FOR REAL**
Mercury SRM 1-659
Released 1973

Side 1:
1. If I Could Only Be Your Love
Again / 2. Dedicated To The One
I Love / 3. Show Me The Way
To Your Heart / 4. Sparkie /
5. Wedding Bells

Side 2:
1. Almost Grown / 2. Charlena /
3. Mah Man Flash / 4. Santa
Kari / 5. Spider Woman /
6. All Night Long

Line-up:
Ruben Guevara - vocals,
tambourine / Tony Duran - lead
and slide guitar, vocals / Robert
'Frog' Camarena - rhythm guitar,
vocals / Johnny Martinez - bass,
organ, vocals / Robert 'Buffalo'
Roberts - tenor saxophone /
Bill Wild - bass, vocals / Bob
Zamora - drums / Jim Motorhead
Sherwood - baritone saxophone,
tambourine

Producer: Frank Zappa
Zappa wrote and arranged
'If I Could Only Be Your Love
Again' and co-arranged 'Santa
Kari' and 'Mah Man Flash' with
Ruben Guevara

Engineers: Kerry McNabb at
Paramount Studios, Hollywood /
Buck Herring and Wally Duguid at
Sun West Studios, Hollywood

(The cover of Just Another
Band From LA is reproduced on
a hamburger on the inner sleeve)

January – February: "200 Years Old", "Cucamonga" and the introduction to "Muffin Man" on *Bongo Fury* recorded at The Record Plant, Los Angeles…

"I have a solo album called 'Apostrophe' coming out in January. I play everything but drums on it." [Zappa]

Q: "Any special songs on it?"
"There's one inspired by the Mennen foot spray commercial where the god keels over after the guy takes his shoes off. Do you know how hard it is to write a song about something like that?" [Zappa: November 1973]

22 APRIL
APOSTROPHE (') [Album 18] released.

Apostrophe (') entered the CASH BOX top twenty at number 18.
"I don't know why this one is so popular, Over-nite Sensation looked like it would have gone big if we hadn't been caught with the vinyl shortage. I think the impact of that one made Warners put the extra effort they put into Apostrophe."
[Miles: August 1974]

The album was promoted using television advertising spots. Zappa and Cal Schenkel designed a thirty-second spot featuring a frenzied deejay hollering over an animated video skit. We tried to place them in conjunction with monster movies because with our material that's our audience." [Miles: August 1974]

LATE APRIL
Zappa back on road to celebrate "10 Years of The Mothers"

8 MAY
State College, Edinboro, Penn.
[Material on *Roxy & Elsewhere* recorded].

12 MAY
Duke University, Durham, NC.

15 MAY
Ahmet Rodan Zappa born, named after Ahmet Ertegun and the Japanese monster that ate Boeing 707s.

MAY – JULY
Studio overdubs on *Roxy & Elsewhere*.

Frank Zappa & The Mothers; line-up

September 1974 – March 1975 US and European tour: Frank Zappa – guitar, vocals / Ruth Underwood – percussion / Napoleon Murphy Brock – saxophone, vocals / Chester Thompson – drums / Tom Fowler – bass / George Duke – keyboards.

15 – 16 FEBRUARY
Berkeley Community Center, Berkeley, Ca.

17 FEBRUARY
Robertson's Gymnasium, Santa Barbara, Ca.

5 MARCH
Dallas, Tx.

9 MARCH
Travel & Transport Building, Oklahoma City, Ok.

15 – 16 MARCH
Paramount Theater, Seattle, Wa.

24 APRIL
Coliseum, Indianapolis, Ind.

29 APRIL
Trenton, NJ.

1 MAY
Broome County Arena, Binghamton, NY.

4 MAY
Washington, DC.

8 MAY
Edinboro State College, Edinboro, Pa.

10 MAY
Flint, Mi.

11 MAY
Auditorium Theater, Chicago, Ill.
"Mother's Day"

12 MAY
Notre Dame University, South Bend, Idaho.

MAY
St. Louis, Mo.
Indianapolis, Minn.
Milwaukee, Wi.

Facing page: The Mothers in 1974

6 JULY
Robinson Auditorium, Little Rock, Ark.

7 JULY
Tampa, Fl.

12 JULY
Fronton Jai Alai, Miami, Fl.

13 JULY
St. Petersburg, Fl.

17 JULY
Phoenix, Az.

19–21 JULY
Circle Star Theater, San Carlos, Ca.

6–7 AUGUST
Television Special, Culver City Studios, open to TV audience.

8 AUGUST
Shrine Auditorium, Los Angeles, Ca.

11 AUGUST
San Diego, Ca.

6 SEPTEMBER
Rome, Italy.

7 SEPTEMBER
Palazzo Della Sport, Udine, Italy.

8 SEPTEMBER
Palasport, Bologna, Italy.

9 SEPTEMBER
Vigorelli, Milan, Italy.

10 SEPTEMBER
ROXY & ELSEWHERE [Album 19]
(double album) released.
Palermo, Sicily.

11 SEPTEMBER
Wighalle, Vienna, Austria.

12 SEPTEMBER
Jahrhunderthalle, Frankfurt, Germany.

13 SEPTEMBER
Munich, Germany.

14 SEPTEMBER
Deutschlandhalle, Berlin, Germany.

16 SEPTEMBER
CCH, Hamburg, Germany.

APOSTROPHE (')
US DiscReet DS 2175
Released 22 April 1974
US CD (w/Overnite Sensation)
Rykodisc RCD 40025
Released 1987

UK DiscReet K 59201
Released April 1974
UK CD (w/Overnite Sensation)
Zappa CD ZAP 18
(digitally remixed at UMRK 1989)
Released 1990

Side 1:
1. Don't Eat The Yellow Snow /
2. Nanook Rubs It / 3. St.
Alfonzo's Pancake Breakfast /
4. Father O'Blivion / 5. Cosmik
Debris

Side 2:
1. Excentrifugal Forz /
2. Apostrophe' / 3. Uncle
Remus / 4. Stink Foot

Line-up:
Frank Zappa - lead vocals,
all guitars, bass / Jim Gordon -
drums / Johnny Guerin - drums /
Aynsley Dunbar - drums /
Ralph Humphrey - drums /
Jack Bruce - bass / Erroneous
(Alex Dmochowski) - bass / Tom
Fowler - bass / George Duke -
keyboards, back-up vocals /
Sugar Cane Harris - violin /
Jean-Luc Ponty - violin /
Ruth Underwood - percussion /
Ian Underwood - saxophone /
Napoleon Murphy Brock -
saxophone, back-up vocals /
Sal Marquez - trumpet / Bruce
Fowler - trombone / Ray Collins -
back-up vocals / Kerry McNabb -
back-up vocals / Susie Glover -
back-up vocals / Debbie - back-up
vocals / Lynn - back-up vocals /
Ruben Ladron De Guevara -
back-up vocals / Robert 'Frog'
Camarena - back-up vocals

Producer: Frank Zappa
Recorded at Electric Lady,
New York City, Bolic, Inglewood,
Paramount, Hollywood,
1973-1974
Engineers: Steve Desper,
Terry Dunavan, Barry Keene,
Bob Hughes, Kerry McNabb
Re-mixed by Kerry McNabb

Side 1:
1. Preamble / 2. Penguin In
Bondage / 3. Pygmy Twylyte /
4. Dummy Up

Side 2:
1. Preamble / 2. Village Of
The Sun / 3. Echidna's Arf
(Of You) / 4. Don't You Ever
Wash That Thing?

Side 3:
1. Preamble / 2. Cheepnis /
3. Son Of Orange County /
4. More Trouble Every Day

Side 4:
1. Preamble / 2. Be-Bop Tango
(Of The Old Jazzmen's Church)

Line-up:
Frank Zappa - lead guitar,
vocals / George Duke - keyboards,
synthesizer, vocals / Tom Fowler -
bass / Ruth Underwood -
percussion / Jeff Simmons -
rhythm guitar, vocals / Don
Preston - synthesizer / Bruce
Fowler - trombone / Walt Fowler -
trumpet / Napoleon Murphy
Brock - tenor saxophone, flute,
lead vocals / Ralph Humphrey -
drums / Chester Thompson -
drums (additional back-up vocals
on 'Cheepnis' by Debbi, Lynn,
George, Ruben Ladron de
Guevara and Robert 'Frog'
Camarena)

Producer: Frank Zappa
Recorded live at the Roxy
Hollywood

10, 11 and 12, December 1973
Other portions recorded at the
second show of the Mothers' Day
concert at Auditorium Theater in
Chicago, 1974 and at Edinboro
State College, Edinboro, Penn,
8 May 1974
The Roxy material was
overdubbed at Bolic Studios,
Inglewood, and Paramount
Studios, Hollywood
The Chicago and Edinboro
material was not overdubbed

Engineers: Kerry McNabb
at the Roxy, using the
Wally Heider Remote
Bill Hennigh at Chicago
and Edinboro
Kerry McNabb re-mixed the
entire album The girl adjusting
Zappa's clothing on the sleeve
is Susan Bressman

ROXY & ELSEWHERE
(double album)
US DiscReet DS 2202
Released 10 September 1974

UK DiscReet K 69201
Released September 1974
UK CD Zappa CD ZAP 39
Released January 1992

17 SEPTEMBER
Helsinki, Finland.
[material used on *One Size Fits All*.]

18 SEPTEMBER
Oslo, Norway.

19 SEPTEMBER
Stockholm, Sweden.

20 SEPTEMBER
KB-Hallen, Copenhagen, Denmark.

22 SEPTEMBER
Helsinki, Finland. [most of the concert used on *You Can't Do That On Stage Anymore Vol. 2*].

25 SEPTEMBER
Gothenburg, Sweden.

27 SEPTEMBER
Paris, France.

28 SEPTEMBER
Rotterdam, Netherlands.

29 SEPTEMBER
Ancienne Belgique, Brussels, Belgium.

1 OCTOBER
Festhalle Mustermesse, Basel, Switzerland.

2 OCTOBER
Lyons, France.

3 OCTOBER
Marseilles, France.

4 OCTOBER
Barcelona, Spain.

29 OCTOBER
Orpheum, Boston, MA.

30–31 OCTOBER
Felt Forum, New York City.

31 OCTOBER
Zappa threw a Hallowe'en Party for himself at the Blue Hawaii Room of the Roosevelt Hotel, New York, in celebration of the 10th anniversary of The Mothers of Invention. Labelle sang 'Happy Birthday'. Guests included Carly Simon, James Taylor, Bianca Jagger, Dory Previn.

NOVEMBER
Freedom Hall, Louisville, GA.

6 NOVEMBER
Pittsburgh, Pa.

8 NOVEMBER
Capitol Theater, Passaic, NJ.

9 NOVEMBER
Orpheum, Boston, Mass.

17 NOVEMBER
Spectrum, Philadelphia, Pa.

18 NOVEMBER
Capitol Theater, Passaic, NJ.

30 NOVEMBER
North Central College, Naperville.

1 DECEMBER
Richfield Coliseum, Cleveland, Oh.

DECEMBER
Recording "A Token Of My Extreme" TV Special at KCET-TV, Los Angeles.

Recording material used on Sleep Dirt at Caribou Studios, Colorado.

31 DECEMBER
Long Beach Arena, Ca.

–1975–

FEBRUARY
Tivoli Gardens, Copenhagen, Denmark.

14 APRIL
Bizarre Productions began their suit against the Royal Albert Hall in London before Mr. Justice Mocatta in Number Seven Court of the Law Courts in the Strand. At issue was the cancellation of The Mothers Of Invention / London Philharmonic presentation of "200 Motels" originally scheduled for

8 February 1971, at the Royal Albert Hall.
At the last minute, the Albert Hall
cancelled Zappa's booking and refused to
allow the concert to take place, their
reason being that they considered parts of
the script to be obscene and objectionable. On the night of the concert, TV news
showed apparently angry protests by fans
outside the Albert Hall.

Zappa and Herb Cohen, his business
manager, sued the management of the
Albert Hall for damages for both the
financial loss caused by the cancellation
and the resulting loss of important
publicity. The case took four years to
come to court.

16 APRIL

Zappa was on the witness stand for the
second day. Under examination he spoke
very quietly and on a number of occasions,

the judge requested that he speak up. The counsel for the defence had a large dictionary of American slang and a stereo system was set up in court. The judge was given a copy of *200 Motels* to play. He reacted with alarm, as if he had never even seen a long playing record before, "What's this?" he demanded.

He listened to *200 Motels* with his head sunk in his hands and complained that he couldn't hear the words. He refused to have the track "Penis Dimension" played in court. He read the lyrics and found them objectionable.

Judge Mocatta was puzzled by the word "groupie". "Is a groupie a girl who is a member of a group?" he asked.

Zappa shook his head…

"No. She is a girl who likes members of a rock-and-roll band."

Judge Mocatta: "When I started this case. I knew very little about pop and beat music. I knew it was to do with rhythm, banging and an infectious atmosphere. I didn't know it was anything to do with sex or drugs." Zappa carefully explained that the majority of pop music has some kind of sexual connotations.

One of the points of the Bizarre case was that if the Albert Hall management had objected to the lyrics, Zappa would have been both willing and able to adapt and change the words at short notice, had he been consulted. In order to demonstrate, Zappa's counsel handed him a script of "200 Motels" and asked him to 'render the lyrics suitable for a socially-retarded audience".

"The places she goes/Are filled with guys from Pudsey/Waiting for a chance/To buy her Sudsy," wrote Zappa. He read the lines to the court in a slow deadpan voice. The judge was confused by the reference to Pudsey. "Pudsey?" he enquired.

"Pudsey. Yorkshire, m'lud," offered Zappa's counsel helpfully. "It's produced some fine cricketers, I believe."

There was no way that Zappa could win - and he didn't.

"Breach of contract, that's what the whole lawsuit was really about, not whether '200 Motels' was obscene or not. This point was very clear in the judge's final statement It was a breach of contract trial and not an obscenity trial with us versus the Albert Hall which is the Queen by proxy.

"The judge was right when he said there had been a breach of contract, because we had a contract to play there, and he was also right when he said that '200 Motels' wasn't obscene. But when it came down to whether the Albert Hall would pay damages, the judge said, **'Well now, wait a minute. The Royal Albert Hall is a royal institution and we can't go around giving these Americans money'.**

"I would probably have felt a lot worse about it if I had gone through with the appeal and spent a lot more money. but I thought, $50,000 is enough. Besides, I'll give her (the Queen) a backstage pass just to show there's no ill-feeling." [Zappa: 1977]

Frank Zappa & The Mothers
April – May US "Bongo Fury" Tour line-up: Frank Zappa – guitar, vocals / Bruce Fowler – trumpet / Napoleon Murphy Brock – saxophone, vocals / Terry Bozio – drums / Tom Fowler – bass / Denny Walley – guitar, vocals / George Duke – keyboards / Captain Beefheart – harmonica, vocals / Chester Thompson – drums on first few gigs of the tour.

11 APRIL
Bridges Auditorium, Claremont College, Pomona, Ca.

18 APRIL
New Haven, Ct.

19 APRIL
Capitol Theater, Passaic, NJ.

20 APRIL
Kurztown, Pa.

22 APRIL
Syracuse, NY.

24 APRIL
Albany, NY.

25 APRIL
Nassau Coliseum, Uniondale, NY.

26 APRIL
Providence, RI.

27 APRIL
Music Hall, Boston, Mass.

29 APRIL
Trenton, NJ.

30 APRIL
Johnstown, Pa.

2 MAY
Hampton Rhodes, Va.

3 MAY
Civic Center, Baltimore, Md.

4 MAY
Charleston, NC.

6 MAY
Normal, Ill.

7 MAY
Frankfort, Ky.

9 MAY
Athens, Ga.

10 MAY
Indianapolis, Ind.

11 MAY
Chicago, Ill.

13 MAY
Kiel Auditorium, St. Louis, Mo.

14 MAY
Evansville, Oh.

16 MAY
Cincinnati, Oh.

17 MAY
Kalamazoo, Mi.

18 MAY
18 May: Detroit, Mi.

20 – 21 MAY
Austin Tx, Armadillo World HQ
[*Bongo Fury* recorded].

MAY
Dallas, Tx.
Zappa works on *Bongo Fury*.

25 JUNE
ONE SIZE FITS ALL [Album 20] released.

The release of *One Size Fits All* was held up by contractual matters. "I figure that I spent a long time on this album. I was in the studio for four months, 10 to 14 hours a day, and by God I want people to hear the thing. I went to Warners in the States and played it to the president of the company and two or three other executives and I watched them listen to it, so I know they heard at least one of my records... It has some story type songs, but it's pretty much rock and roll oriented. You could actually dance to this record.
"It's a very good title when you consider that the front cover shows

a picture of a sofa and the back cover is references to the Universe in general. I think that it's applicable." [Zappa: 1975]

17 – 18 SEPTEMBER
Royce Hall, UCLA, Los Angeles, CA.
[*Orchestral Favorites* recorded with a 37-piece orchestra].

2 OCTOBER
BONGO FURY [Album 21]
(w/Captain Beefheart) released.

Zappa on inappropriate soundtracks...
**"Oh the ultimate worst is in a Mexican science fiction movie called The Brainiac. It's one of the worst movies ever made and when the monster appears, not only is the monster cheap, he's got a rubber mask that you can see over the collar of the guy's jacket and rubber gloves that don't quite match up with the sleeves of his sport coat. When the monster appears there's this trumpet lick that isn't scary. It's not even out of tune, it's just exactly the wrong thing to put there, it doesn't scare you, that's the greatest example I can think of.
"Did you ever hear the song 'Debra Kadabra' (on 'Bongo Fury')? That's what that song is about and when you hear in the background DA-DA-DA-DA- DAHH, that's making fun of that stupid trumpet line that's in that movie but nobody's seen it over here so you can't appreciate the humour of the song.**

ONE SIZE FITS ALL
released
US DiscReet DS 2216
Released 25 June 1975
US CD Rykodisc RCD 10095
Released 1988

UK DiscReet K 59207
Released June 1975
UK CD Zappa CDZAP11
Released January 1989

Side 1:
1. Inca Roads / 2. Can't Afford No Shoes / 3. Sofa No. 1 / 4. Po-Jama People

Side 2:
1. Florentine Pogen / 2. Evelyn, A Modified Dog / 3. San Ber'dino / 4. Andy / 5. Sofa No. 2

Line-up:
Frank Zappa - all guitars, lead vocals, backing vocals / George Duke - keyboards, synthesizers, lead vocals, backing vocals / Napoleon Murphy Brock - flute, tenor saxophone, lead vocals, backing vocals / Chester Thompson - drums / Tom Fowler - bass / Ruth Underwood - vibes, marimba, percussion / James 'Bird Legs' Youman - bass on 'Can't Afford No Shoes' / Johnny Guitar Watson - vocals on the choruses of 'San Ber'dino' and 'Andy' / Bloodshot Rollin' Red (Captain Beefheart) - harmonica

Producer: Frank Zappa
Recorded at The Record Plant, Los Angeles / Caribou Studios / Paramount Studios / Finnlevy Studios, Helsinki / the Wally Weider Remote Truck
'Inca Roads' and 'Florentine Pogen' recorded live at KCET-TV, Los Angeles, during the

production of 'A Token Of My Extreme' TV special December 1974 / Guitar solo on 'Inca Roads' taken from a concert in Helsinki, 17 September 1974
Engineers: Kerry McNabb, Gary O and Jukka
Re-mix by Kerry McNabb

**BONGO FURY
(w/CAPTAIN BEEFHEART)**
US DiscReet DS 2234
Released 2 October 1975
US CD Rykodisc RCD 10097

UK CD Zappa CD ZAP 15
Released May 1989
(No UK album because Virgin Records had Beefheart under UK contract and claimed it as theirs)

Side 1:
1. Debra Kadabra / 2. Carolina Hard-Core Ecstasy / 3. Sam With The Showing Scalp Flat Top / 4. Poofter's Froth Wyoming Plans Ahead / 5. 200 Years Old

Side 2:
1. Cucamonga / 2. Advance Romance / 3. Man With The Woman Head / 4. Muffin Man

Line-up:
Frank Zappa - lead guitar, vocals / Captain Beefheart - harmonica, vocals / George Duke - keyboards, vocals / Napoleon Murphy Brock - saxophone, vocals / Bruce Fowler - trombone / Tom Fowler - bass / Denny Walley - slide guitar, vocals / Terry Bozzio - drums / Chester Thompson - drums on '200 Years Old' and 'Cucamonga'

Producer: Frank Zappa
Recorded live at Armadillo World Headquarters, Austin, Texas on 20 and 21 May 1975 using the Record Plant, Los Angeles, Remote '200 Years Old', 'Cucamonga' and the introduction to 'Muffin Man' were recorded at The Record Plant, Los Angeles, January and February 1974
Overdubs and mixing done at The Record Plant
Engineers: Kerry McNabb, Mike Braunstein, Kelly Kotera, Mike Stone, Davey Moire and Frank Hubach

Facing page: Captain Beefheart and Frank

1975-76

"When he's saying 'Make me grow Brainiac fingers' that's what he's referring to, because Vliet and I have both seen that movie and it's so fucking stupid. Mexican monster movies are great, The Aztec Mummy's Ghost that's a good one too." [Zappa: 1983]

Frank Zappa & The Mothers of Invention September 1975 - March 1976 line-up : Frank Zappa - guitar, vocals, Napoleon Murphy Brock - saxophone, vocals, André Lewis - keyboards, Terry Bozzio - drums, Roy Estrada - bass, vocals.

27 SEPTEMBER
Robertsons Gymnasium, Santa Barbara, Ca.

1 OCTOBER
Vancouver, Canada.

4 OCTOBER
Paramount Theater, Seattle, Wa.

12 OCTOBER
Memorial Auditorium, Dallas, Tx.

23 OCTOBER
Music Hall, Boston, Mass.

25 OCTOBER
Capitol Theater, Passaic, NJ.

26 OCTOBER
Hofstra College, Hempstead, NY.

29 OCTOBER
Waterbury Palace Theater, Waterbury, Ct.

31 OCTOBER
Felt Forum, NYC, Hallowe'en Concert. [line-up as above plus Norma Bell – saxophone, vocals]

2 NOVEMBER
University of Maryland, Baltimore, Md.

3 NOVEMBER
The Spectrum, Philadelphia, Pa.

30 NOVEMBER
Auditorium Theater, Chicago, Ill.

7 DECEMBER
McMaster University, Hamilton, Ontario, Canada.

DECEMBER
Trip to Yugoslavia with concerts in Ljubljana and Zagreb.

26 DECEMBER
Paramont Theater, Oakland, Ca.

27 DECEMBER
Winterland, San Francisco, Ca.

31 DECEMBER
The Forum, Inglewood, Los Angeles, Ca.

–1976–

18 JANUARY
Sydney, Australia.

JANUARY
Perth, Australia.

22 – 23 JANUARY
Festival Hall, Melbourne, Australia.

24 – 25 JANUARY
Apollo Stadium, Adelaide, Australia.

27 JANUARY
Brisbane, Australia.

3 FEBRUARY
Kosei Nenkin Kaikan, Osaka, Japan. [material used on Zoot Allures]

4 FEBRUARY
Kyodai Seibu Kodo, Kyoto, Japan.

13 FEBRUARY
Kurhalle, Vienna.

14 FEBRUARY
Deutsches Museum, Munich, Germany.

15 FEBRUARY
Friedrich Ebert Halle, Ludwigshafen, Germany.

17 FEBRUARY
Sporthalle, Köln, Germany.

18 FEBRUARY
Niedersachsenhalle, Hanover, Germany.

19 FEBRUARY
Grugahalle, Essen, Germany.

20 FEBRUARY
CCH, Hamburg, Germany.

21 FEBRUARY
Vejlby Risskov Hallen, Aarhus, Denmark.

23 FEBRUARY
Njardhallen, Oslo, Norway.

24 – 25 FEBRUARY
Stockholm, Sweden.

26 FEBRUARY
Helsinki, Finland.

29 FEBRUARY
Falkoner Theatret, Copenhagen, Denmark.

2 MARCH
Lund, Holland.

3 MARCH
Tivoli Gardens, Copenhagen, Denmark.

4 MARCH
Berlin, Germany.

6 MARCH
Jaap Edenhal, Amsterdam, Holland.

7 MARCH
Vorst Nationaal, Brussels, Belgium.

8 MARCH
Palais des Sports, Paris.

10 MARCH
Saarbrucken, Germany.

11 MARCH
Oberheinhalle, Offenburg, Germany.

12 MARCH
Kongresshaus, Zurich, Switzerland.

13 MARCH
Palasport, Lugano, Italy.

17 MARCH
Bilboa, Spain.

MAY
Zappa ended his ten-year association with his manager Herb Cohen, claiming that Herb and his lawyer brother were stealing money.

MAY – JUNE
Zappa recording *Zoot Allures* at the Record Plant, Los Angeles.

AUGUST
GRAND FUNK RAILROAD: GOOD SINGIN' GOOD PLAYIN' released.

Q: What are you doing with Grand Funk?
"I'm not doing anything with them. All I did was in a documentary way make a record which tells you

exactly what they really sound like. For the first time on record, you can hear Grand Funk Railroad... and they're fantastic, fan-tastic with an F three times taller than you!"
[Zappa]

Don Brewer, drummer with Grand Funk: "His whole viewpoint on what rock 'n'roll is all about is basically the same as ours. You go in and do exactly what you do live, without overproduction. Keep it as simple as possible and really bring the balls out of this thing. He was totally different from what we expected."

"The best rock 'n' roll of the year."
[Zappa: 1976]

Frank Zappa October 1976 – March 1977 line-up: Frank Zappa – guitar, vocals / Ray White – guitar, vocals / Eddie Jobson – violin, keyboards / Patrick O'Hearn – bass / Terry Bozzio – drums / Bianca – keyboards, vocals on some dates.

16 – 19 OCTOBER
University of Florida, Miami. Fl.

23 – 27 OCTOBER
Music Hall, Boston, Mass.

29 OCTOBER
ZOOT ALLURES [Album 22] released.
"'Ms. Pinky' is a song about a lonely person device. We have this fan in Finland called Eric and every time we come to Finland, he's there with his shopping bag. I think he works in a Volvo factory. One time he showed up with presents; candy and his favourite Finnish pornographic magazine. A publication called *Kalle*. Had the worst pictures you've ever seen.

"There's a problem with litho-graphy when you don't get your colour balance right. Things either go too red or too blue. Well, split pink is one thing, but split pink that looks infected is another. And when the people are homely... There was this one article called: "And Now, from Leningrad", and this girl looked like she had just come out of a concentration camp, doing this split on a bleak little bed in a bleak little room. It looked like a medical picture.

"And then they had ads for lonely person devices. There was an ad for Pinky. It was a head with its mouth wide open and its eyes shut and a short haircut. And I thought: Hmmmm, anyone who's gonna buy a plastic head just to give himself a gum job is Right Out There.

"By the time we got to Amsterdam I sent Smothers out to buy one, to use onstage. Sure enough, for $69.95 he came back with Ms. Pinky. It was even worse than I had imagined. Not only is it a head, it's the size of a child's head. The throat is sponge rubber and it's got a vibrator in it with a battery pack and a two-speed motor. Sticking out of its neck is a nozzle with a squeezebulb that makes the throat contract."

"'Black Napkins' is a song I've had for a year or more but it was finally named last Thanksgiving when we were having this horrible Thanksgiving dinner in Milwaukee. Sliced turkey roll with the fucking preservatives just gleaming off of it, and this beat-up cranberry material. The final stroke to this ridiculous dinner was the black napkins, sitting next to the dishes. That really said the most about the dinner."
[Zappa: 1976]

"'Disco Boy' came about because we were in Denmark and we went to a place there called the The Disc Club, and it was really poot. It was so make-believe sophisticated that it was embarrassing. The place was decorated like a playboy-type living room would sorta be like – lowboy chairs and snackettes on the table, and everybody drinks and dances to these robot beat records, which I happen to like you know. I'm very fond of monotony, I think it's an integral part of contemporary civilisation and once you adapt to it you're better in phase with reality. I think that it's probably one of the funnier commentaries on the disco syndrome." [Zappa: 1977]

One of the problems caused by Frank's lawsuit with Herbie Cohen was that he was unable to get the 30ips master tapes of *Zoot Allures* from the Record Plant. Zappa had this to say…
"Listen to this: I am the chairman of the board of DiscReet and the president of the company – also those guys are supposed to be my friends – but they wouldn't release the master tapes to me unless Warner Bros indemnified the studio from any legal action that Herbie might take against them."

Warner Bros agreed – provided Frank indemnified them:
"Can you believe it? An individual artist having to indemnify one of the

biggest record companies in the world so that they can bring his record out?"

Frank mastered the album from his own 15ips safety copy of the album. He always takes 15ips safeties home after each recording session.
"When I go home after 20 hours in the studio, what am I gonna listen to? Bob Dylan records?"

Another casualty of the lawsuit with Herbie Cohen was Captain Beefheart, whose album *Bat Chain Puller* got caught up in the arguments. Frank said…
"One of the reasons I argued with Herbie was because he used my royalty cheques to pay for the production costs of Beefheart's album when I was away on tour… It's his best album since *Trout Mask Replica*, it's really good."

The album was produced by Beefheart himself using Kerry McNabb who was the engineer on Zappa's *One Size Fits All*. Frank had the master tapes in his basement studio but much as he would have loved to see the album released, he was unable to send them to Beefheart's label, Virgin Records in London, because he was sure that both he and Virgin would be sued by Cohen if Virgin released the album.
"I can't do anything until this Herbie thing is cleared up. Herbie is holding out for a settlement."

Cohen wanted the advance money paid to him from Virgin on delivery of the album whereas Zappa thought the money should go to him, since he (inadvertently) paid for its production. It was a classic record business wrangle which resulted in the artist getting screwed. *Bat Chain Puller* was never released, though parts of it came out in a different form later on *Shiny Beast*.

Another legal matter: Frank's $2M lawsuit against MGM Records which he began in August 1975 was finally settled…
"We made a settlement in which we get the masters back plus $100,000. But MGM gets a 3% production over-ride on all future use of them."

The money, however, was all tied up in Frank's lawsuit with Cohen.

29 OCTOBER
Spectrum, Philadelphia, Pa.

30 – 31 OCTOBER
Felt Forum, NYC [material on *Zappa In New York* recorded during three of the shows]

4 NOVEMBER
Capitol Center, Key Largo, Fl.

6 NOVEMBER
RPI Fieldhouse, NYC.

7 NOVEMBER
Civic Center, Springfield, Mass.

ZOOT ALLURES
US Warner Bros, BS 2970
Released 29 October 1976
US CD Rykosic RCD 10160
Released 1990

UK Warner Bros K 56298
Released December 1976
UK CD Zappa CDZAP 22
Released UK 21 May 1990

Side 1:
1. Wind Up Workin' In A Gas Station / 2. Black Napkins / 3. The Torture Never Stops / 4. Ms. Pinky

Side 2:
1. Find Her Finer / 2. Friendly Little Finger / 3. Wonderful Wino / 4. Zoot Allures / 5. Disco Boy

Line-up:
Frank Zappa - guitar, lead vocal, synthesizer, keyboards, bass / Terry Bozzio - drums, backing vocal / Davey Moire - lead vocal, backing vocal on 'Wind Up Workin' In A Gas Station' and 'Disco Boy' / André Lewis - organ, vocal on 'Black Napkins', 'Find Her Finer' and 'Disco Boy' / Roy Estrada - bass, vocal on 'Black Napkins', 'Ms Pinky', 'Find Her Finer' and 'Disco Boy' / Napoleon Murphy Brock - saxophone, vocal on 'Black Napkins' / Ruth Underwood - marimba, synthesizer on 'Ms Pinky', 'Zoot Allures' and 'Friendly Little Finger' / Captain Beefheart - harmonica on 'Find Her Finer' / Dave Parlato - bass on 'Zoot Allures' / Lu Ann Neil - harmonica on 'Zoot Allures' / Sparky Parker - backing vocal on 'Disco Boy' / Ruben Ladron De Guevara - backing vocal on 'Find Her Finer'

Producer: Frank Zappa
Recorded at The Record Plant, Los Angeles
'Black Napkins' recorded live in Osaka, Japan, 3 February 1976
Engineers: Michael Braunstein, Davey Moire
Re-mixed by Frank Zappa

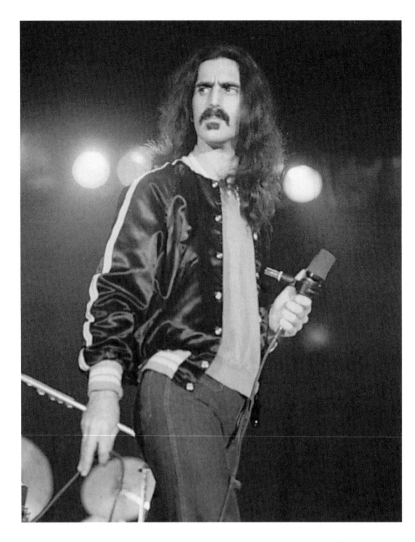

16 NOVEMBER
Maple Leaf Gardens, Toronto, Canada.

19 NOVEMBER
Cobo Hall, Detroit, Mi. The Zappa band drew the biggest crowd since The Rolling Stones played Cobo Hall 18 months before. Flo and Eddie appeared as the opening act then later guested with the band. Also in the closing jam were Ralph Armstrong of The Mahavishnu Orchestra and drummer Don Brewer of Grand Funk Railroad. Frank has a high regard for Brewer's playing and since Grand Funk had just broken up…
"I immediately offered Brewer a job since he wasn't doing anything."

Brewer went away to think about it and eventually declined.

Flo and Eddie had been touring to promote their new album, *Moving Targets*, but their guitarist Phil Reed fell from a hotel window and was killed. Flo and Eddie asked if they could tag on to Frank's tour and he agreed. Bruce and Walt Fowler, ex-Zappa sidemen were in Flo & Eddie's group

and at the Roxy in Los Angeles, Ian Underwood joined their line-up.

20 NOVEMBER
Public Hall, Cleveland, Oh.

6 DECEMBER
Frank Zappa introduced Black Sabbath to their NY audience but did not play with them.

11 DECEMBER
The Frank Zappa band played a 15-minute set on the *Saturday Night Live* TV show in New York. John Belush played the Be-Bop Samurai Warrior during "The Purple Lagoon."

26–29 DECEMBER
Palladium, NYC, for a theatrical show with dancers and an expanded line-up: Mike Brecker – saxophone, flute / Randy Brecker – trumpet / Ronnie Cuber – reed instruments / Tom Malone – brass / Lou Marini – saxophone, flute / David Samuels – percussion / Ruth Underwood – percussion. [material on *Zappa In New York* recorded.]

ROBERT CHARLEBOIS: SWING CHARLEBOIS SWING released.

13 JANUARY
Falkoner Theatret, Copenhagen, Denmark.

15 JANUARY
Konserthuset, Stockholm, Sweden.

21 JANUARY
Skandinavium, Gothenburg, Sweden.

22 JANUARY
Olso, Norway.

23 JANUARY
Helsinki, Finland.

24 JANUARY
CCH, Hamburg, Germany.

25 JANUARY
Hemmerleinhalle, Nürnburg, Germany.

26 JANUARY
Olympiahalle, Munich, Germany.

27 JANUARY
Philipshalle, Düsseldorf, Germany.

28 JANUARY
Voorst Nationaal Hal, Brussels, Belgium.

30 JANUARY
Rheinmainhalle, Wiesbaden, Germany.

31 JANUARY
Sporthalle, Boblingen, Germany.

2–3 FEBRUARY
Pavilion de Paris, Paris, France.

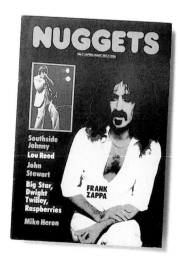

5 FEBRUARY
Jaap Edenhall, Amsterdam, Holland.

6 FEBRUARY
Sporthalle, Köln, Germany.

7 FEBRUARY
Deutschlandhalle, Berlin, Germany.

9 – 10 FEBRUARY
Hammersmith Odeon,
London, UK.

12 FEBRUARY
Stafford, UK.

13 FEBRUARY
The Apollo, Glasgow, Scotland.

14 FEBRUARY
Edinburgh, Scotland.

16 – 17 FEBRUARY
Hammersmith Odeon,
London, UK.

25 FEBRUARY
Amsterdam, Holland.

Frank Zappa October 1977 - April
1978 line-up: Frank Zappa – guitar,
vocals / Patrick O'Hearn – bass / Adrian
Belew – guitar / Tommy Mars – keyboards /
Terry Bozzio – drums / Peter Wolf –
keyboards / Ed Mann – percussion /
Roy Estrada – vocals on some US dates.

9 SEPTEMBER
University of California at San Diego,
San Diego, Ca.

18 SEPTEMBER
Fox Theater, Atlanta, Ga.

23 SEPTEMBER
Champaign, Ill.

30 SEPTEMBER
Cobo Hall, Detroit, Mi.

2 OCTOBER
St. Louis, Mo.

16 OCTOBER
Miami, Fl.

17 OCTOBER
Civic Center, Hartford, Ct.

18 OCTOBER
Mid Hudson Civic Center,
Poughkeepsie, NY.

20 OCTOBER
Music Hall, Boston, Mass.

22 OCTOBER
The Forum, Montreal, Quebec, Canada.

24 OCTOBER
The Spectrum, Philadelphia, Pa.

27 – 31 OCTOBER
Palladium, NYC ending with Hallowe'en
Show.

31 OCTOBER
Was to have been the release date for
Läther, a 4 record box set which was to
be the first release of Zappa Records
(Zappa SRZ 4 -1500) but contractual
difficulties with Warner Bros stopped the
release. Zappa played the entire thing on
American radio, effectively encouraging
listeners to tape record it.

13 NOVEMBER
Denver, Co.

18 NOVEMBER
Sacramento, Ca.

19 NOVEMBER
Maples Pavilion, Stanford University,
Palo Alto, Ca.

20 NOVEMBER
Pauley Pavilion, University of California,
Los Angeles, Ca.

31 DECEMBER
Pauley Pavilion, University of California,
Los Angeles, Ca.

ROBERT CHARLEBOIS:
SWING CHARLEBOIS
SWING
RCA KDL 6436

Frank Zappa plays guitar on the
track 'Petroleum'

-1978-

FLINT: FLINT released.

24 – 28 JANUARY
Hammersmith Odeon, London, UK.

29 JANUARY
Festhalle, Frankfurt, Germany.

30 JANUARY
CCH, Hamburg, Germany.

1 FEBRUARY
Philipshalle, Düsseldorf, Germany.

2 FEBRUARY
Circus Krone, Munich, Germany.

3 FEBRUARY
Stadthalle, Vienna, Austria.

4 FEBRUARY
Wighalle, Zurich, Switzerland.

5 FEBRUARY
Festhalle, Bern, Switzerland.

6 – 9 FEBRUARY
Nouvel Hippodrome, Paris, France.

10 FEBRUARY
Palais des Sports, Lyons, France.

11 FEBRUARY
Parc des Expositions, Colmar, France.

13 FEBRUARY
The Ahoy, Rotterdam, Holland.

14 FEBRUARY
Sporthalle, Köln, Germany.

15 FEBRUARY
Deutschlandhalle, Berlin, Germany.

17 FEBRUARY
Falkoner Theatret, Copenhagen, Denmark.

18 FEBRUARY
Skandinavium, Göteborg, Sweden.

19 FEBRUARY
Konserthuset, Stockholm, Sweden

23 FEBRUARY
Munsterlandhalle, Munster, Germany.

24 FEBRUARY
Heidelberg, Germany
[w/ O'Hearn & Belew, without Willis]

25 FEBRUARY
Hemmerleinhalle, Neunkirchen.

26 FEBRUARY
Voorst Nationaal Hal, Brussels, Belgium.

27 – 28 FEBRUARY
Hammersmith Odeon, London, UK.

3 MARCH
ZAPPA IN NEW YORK [Album 23]
(double album) released.

Some reviewers criticised the album as a rip-off because it was so short for a double album…

"There was one track that got removed, 'Punky's Whips'. They [Warner Bros.] took it out. First of all they had no right to tamper with the tapes. Secondly they didn't pay me for any of the stuff that I delivered to them. I mean, they're just so far in breach of the contract and they're just so grossly unfair. For instance, that track 'Punky's Whips' is 12 minutes and 37 seconds long. It's most of a side. They took it out because they didn't have the permission from Punky Meadows to use it. Then they have the audacity to go ahead and release the album with 12 minutes missing. There was something in one of the papers over here complaining about how short the album was. It wasn't my fault. I didn't have any control over it. I think Herb Cohen was the one who took it out."
[Zappa: 1978]

1 JULY
Circus Krone, Munich, Germany.

26 AUGUST
Friedrichsau Festplatz, Ulm, Germany (open air festival).

3 SEPTEMBER
Saarbrücken Open Air Festival, Ludwigsparkstadion, Germany.
[w/ Ike Willis and without Patrick O'Hearn and Belew]

4 SEPTEMBER
Stadthalle, Bremen, Germany.

5 SEPTEMBER
Folkets Park, Malmo, Sweden.

7 SEPTEMBER
Waldbuhne, Berlin, Germany.

8 SEPTEMBER
Circus Krone, Munich, Germany.

9 SEPTEMBER
Knebworth House Open Air Festival, Herts, UK.

15 SEPTEMBER
STUDIO TAN [Album 24] released.

14 – 15 SEPTEMBER
Convention Hall, Miami, Fl.

17 SEPTEMBER
Fox Theater, Atlanta, Ga.

21 SEPTEMBER
Mid Hudson Civic Center, Poughkeepsie, NY.

28 SEPTEMBER
Uptown Theater, Detroit, Mi.

29 SEPTEMBER
Uptown Theater, Chicago, Ill.

OCTOBER
Harvard Square, Cambridge, Mass.

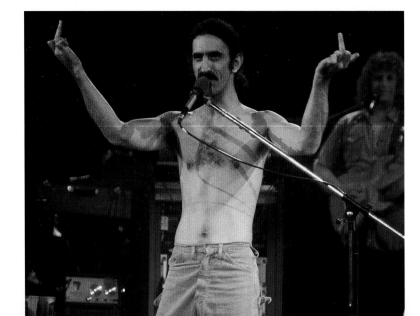

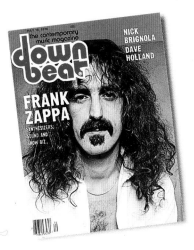

4 OCTOBER
The Forum, Montreal, Quebec, Canada.

9 OCTOBER
Providence, RI.

13 OCTOBER
Capitol Theater, Passaic, NJ.

14 OCTOBER
Cole Fieldhouse, College Park, Baltimore, Md.

15 OCTOBER
State University of NY at Stoneybrook, Stoneybrook, NY.

23 OCTOBER
Philadelphia, Pa.

25 OCTOBER
Northside Coliseum, Danbury, Ct.

25 OCTOBER
Boston, Mass.

27 – 31 OCTOBER
Palladium, NYC (ending with Hallowe'en Show).

9 NOVEMBER
Detroit, Mi.

11 NOVEMBER
Denver, Co.

DECEMBER
Zappa was hit on the shoulder by a flying beer bottle during a concert in Maine. He stopped the show, had the houselights turned on and announced…

"Now I'm not going to start playing again 'til that asshole is taken away."

James Collins, 23, was identified as the culprit and police charged him with

FLINT: FLINT
CBS 83297

Frank Zappa plays guitar on 'Better You Than Me' and 'You'll Never Be The Same.'

ZAPPA IN NEW YORK
(double album)
US DiscReet 2D 2290
Released 3 March 1978

UK DiscReet K 69204
Released April 1978
UK CD Zappa CDDZAP 37
Released 1991

Side 1:
1. Titties & Beer /
2. I Promise Not To Come In Your Mouth / 3. Punky's Whips

Side 2:
1. Sofa / 2. Manx Needs Woman / 3. The Black Page Drum Solo / Black Page No. 1 / 4. Big Leg Emma / 5. Black Page No. 2

Side 3:
1. Honey, Don't You Want A Man Like Me? / 2. The Illinois Enema Bandit

Side 4:
The Purple Lagoon
The CD release adds four new tracks and revises the tracking order:

Side 3:
1. Honey, Don't You Want A Man Like Me? / 2. The Illinois Enema Bandit

Side 4:
The Purple Lagoon

Because Warner Brothers feared legal action from Punky Meadows, who is the subject of 'Punky's Whips', this track was removed after only a few copies got out and the album was re-released with a different tracking order as follows:

Side 1:
1. Titties & Beer / 2. I Promise Not To Come In Your Mouth / 3. Big Leg Emma

Side 2:
1. Sofa / 2. Manx Needs Woman / 3. The Black Page Drum Solo / Black Page No. 1 / 4. Black Page No. 2

Side 3:
1. Honey, Don't You Want A Man Like Me? / 2. The Illinois Enema Bandit

Side 4:
The Purple Lagoon

Disc 1:
1. Titties & Beer / 2. Cruisin' For Burgers / 3. I Promise Not To Come In Your Mouth / 4. Punky's Whips / 5. Honey, Don't You Want A Man Like Me? / 6. The Illinois Enema Bandit

Disc 2:
1. I'm The Slime / 2. Pound For A Brown / 3. Manx Needs Woman / 4. The Black Page Drum Solo / Black Page No. 1 / 5. Big Leg Emma / 6. Sofa / 7. Black Page No. 2 / 8. The Torture Never Stops / 9. The Purple Lagoon / Approximate

Line-up:
Frank Zappa - lead guitar, vocals / Ray White - rhythm guitar, vocals / Eddie Jobson - keyboards, violin, vocals / Patrick O'Hearn - bass, vocals / Terry Bozzio - drums, vocals / Ruth Underwood - percussion, synthesizer / Don Pardo - narrator / David Samuels - timpani, vibes / Randy Brecker - trumpet / Mike Brecker - tenor saxophone, flute / Lou Marini - alto saxophone, flute / Ronnie Cuber - baritone saxophone, clarinet / Tom Malone - trombone, trumpet, piccolo / John Bergamo - percussion overdubs / Ed Mann -

percussion overdubs / Louanne Neil - osmotic harp overdub

Producer: Frank Zappa

Recorded live in New York City: three shows at the Felt Forum during Hallowe'en, 1976 and four shows at the Palladium, during the week between Christmas and the New Year, 1976, using the Fedco Remote recording truck. Studio overdubs and mixing at the Record Plant, Los Angeles
Engineers: Bob Liftin in the Remote, NYC / Rick Smith, Davey Moire at the Record Plant

STUDIO TAN
US DiscReet DSK 2291
Released 15 September 1978
US CD Barking Pumpkin
D2 74237
Released 1991

UK DiscReet K 59210
Released October 1978
UK CD Zappa CDZAP 44

Side 1:
1. Greggery Peccary

Side 2.
1. Let Me Take You To The Beach / 2. Revised Music For Guitar & Low Budget Orchestra / 3. REDUNZL (spelling corrected on CD release to RNDZL / The CD also reverses the order of tracks Side 2, 1 and 2)

Line-up:
Frank Zappa - guitar, vocals, percussion / George Duke - keyboards, vocals (not on 'Lemme Take You...') / Bruce Fowler - trombone on The Adventures... and 'Revised Music...' / Tom Fowler - bass on The Adventures... and 'Revised Music...' / Chester Thompson - drums (not on 'Lemme Take You...') / Davey Moire - vocals on 'Lemme Take You To The Beach' / Eddie Jobson - keyboards, yodelling on 'Lemme Take You To The Beach' / Max Bennett - bass on 'Lemme Take You To The Beach' / Paul Humphrey - drums on 'Lemme Take You To The Beach' / Don Brewer - bongos on 'Lemme Take You To The Beach' / James 'Bird Legs' Youman - bass on 'RNDZL' / Ruth Underwood - percussion, synthesizer on 'RNDZL'

Producer: Frank Zappa
Recorded between 1974 and 1976
CD re-mastered by
Bob Stone at UMRK, 1991

1978-79

"reckless conduct." Collins pleaded not guilty and a hearing was scheduled for December 28th.

1978 US Fall tour line-up: Frank Zappa – guitar, vocals / Ed Mann –– percussion; Peter Wolf – keyboards / Denny Walley – guitar, vocals / Tommy Mars – keyboards, vocals / Arthur Barrow – bass, vocals / Vinnie Colaiuta – drums / Patrick O'Hearn – bass on some concerts.

15 OCTOBER
Stoneybrook, NY.

27 – 31 NOVEMBER
Palladium, New York City.

2 DECEMBER
Zappa reads the "Talking Asshole" section from William Burroughs' *Naked Lunch* at The Nova Convention, Entermedia Theater, NYC. The Nova Convention was a celebration of the work of William Burroughs. Burroughs and Zappa visited and had dinner together during which time Zappa suggested making a Broadway musical from Naked Lunch but the idea never came to anything.

–1979–

19 JANUARY
SLEEP DIRT [Album 25]
[originally titled HOT RATS 3] released.

Frank arrived in London mid-January to examine the possibility of recording orchestral work in Britain, to sign a distribution deal with CBS Records and to record an album with L. Shankar. He was unable to find a studio in the States which had flexible time available:
"I could have done Shankar's album

in Los Angeles but there wasn't a studio to do it. This is the only place in the world where I could find a studio that is workable so I could get lock-out time for the whole period. Everybody else is booked up."
Zappa recorded in Advision and at AIR. **"Advision is primitive, AIR is about like New York studio quality."**
He mixed the album at the Town House.

L. SHANKAR: TOUCH ME THERE released.

1979 European tour line-up: Frank Zappa - guitar, vocals; Tommy Mars – keyboard, vocals / Ike Willis – guitar, vocals / Arthur Barrow – bass / Vinnie Colaiuta – drums / Ed Mann – percussion / Peter Wolf – keyboards / Denny Walley – guitar / Warren Cucurullo – guitar.
"The tour opens in the UK and then goes as far south as Spain, as far north as Norway and as far east as Munich and all the slots in between. The tours keep getting longer and longer and longer. And I need them more and more and more. I was talking to my manager on the phone, 'We want to do this big television show in Paris and would I mind doing it on my day off between Brussels and Paris?' 'Yes I would mind.' 'But it's going out to 3 million people on a Sunday.' 'Yes, I would rather have a day off.' If you don't start having your days off when you come over on these things, your health just starts falling apart. I'm not one for cold weather, weird food, depressing social conditions, busy schedules and not enough sleep. A few months of that and you don't even want to know about playing a guitar or anything else. It's dreadful."
[Zappa: 1979]

10 – 11 FEBRUARY
Birmingham, UK.

12 FEBRUARY
Manchester, UK.

13 FEBRUARY
City Hall, Newcastle, UK.

14 FEBRUARY
The Apollo, Glasgow, UK.

16 FEBRUARY
Brighton, Sussex, UK.

SLEEP DIRT
ORIGINALLY TITLED
HOT RATS 3
US DiscReet DSK 2292
Released 19 January 1979
US CD Barking
Pumpkin D2 74238
Released 1991

UK DiscReet K 59211
Released October 1979
CD Zappa CDZAP 43

Side 1:
1. Filthy Habits / 2. Flam Bay /
3. Spider Of Destiny /
4. Regyptian Strut

Side 2:
1. Time Is Money / 2. Sleep Dirt /
3. The Ocean Is The Ultimate
Solution

Line-up:
Frank Zappa: guitar, keyboards, synthesizer / Dave Parlato - bass on 'Filthy Habits' / Terry Bozzio - drums on 'Filthy Habits' and 'The Ocean...' / George Duke - keyboards on 'Flambay', 'Spider of Destiny' and 'Regyptian Strut' / Patrick O'Hearn - bass on 'Flambay', 'Spider of Destiny' and 'The Ocean...' / Ruth Underwood - percussion on 'Flambay', 'Spider of Destiny', 'Regyptian Strut' and 'Time Is Money' / Chad Wakerman - drum overdubs on 'Flambay', 'Spider of Destiny' and 'Time Is Money' / Thana Harris - vocals on 'Flambay' and 'Time Is Money' / James 'Bird Legs' Youman - bass on 'Regyptian Strut' and 'Sleep Dirt' / Chester Thompson - drum on 'Regyptian Strut' / Bruce Fowler - brass on 'Regyptian Strut'

Producer: Frank Zappa
Recorded between 1974 and 1976
Digitally remixed by Bob Stone at UMRK in 1990 for CD release

L. SHANKAR: TOUCH ME THERE
Mercury 9198289
Released Spring 1979

Side 1:
Dead Girls Of London /
2. Windy Morning / 3. Knee Deep In Heaters; Little Stinker

Side 2:
Darlene / 2. Touch Me There /
3. No More Mr. Nice Girl /
4. Love Gone Away

Line-up:
L. Shankar - acoustic and electric violin, string orchestra, vocal on 'Knee Deep In Heaters' / Phil Palmer - mandolin, acoustic and electric guitars / Dave Marquee - bass / Simon Philips - drums / James Lascelles - Fender Rhodes, organ, acoustic piano, synthesizer / Jack Emblow - accordion on 'No More Mr. Nice Girl' / Frank Zappa (as Stucco Homes) vocal on 'Dead Girls Of London': Vicky Blumenthal - chorus on 'Dead Girls Of London', 'Knee Deep In Heaters' and 'No More Mr. Nice Girl' / Jenny Lautrec - vocal on 'Touch Me There' The vocal on 'Dead Girls Of London' was originally recorded by Van Morrison but had to be replaced by Zappa at mixing stage for contractual reasons / The 'Dead Girls' was inspired by the girls Zappa met in Tramps after recording sessions - the only place he could find to eat in London after 2am
Zappa co-wrote "Touch Me There", "No More Mr. Nice Girl", "Dead Girls Of London" and "Knee Deep In Heaters" with L. Shankar (The initial stands for Lakshmirnarayna)

17 – 19 FEBRUARY
Hammersmith Odeon, London, UK.

21 FEBRUARY
Voorst Nationaal Hal, Brussels, Belgium.

23 – 24 FEBRUARY
Nouvel Hippodrome, Paris, France.

25 FEBRUARY
Chambrai, France.

26 FEBRUARY
Wiesbaden, Germany.

27 FEBRUARY
The Ahoy, Rotterdam, Holland.

28 FEBRUARY
CCH, Hamburg, Germany.

1 MARCH
Falkoner Theatret, Copenhagen, Denmark.

2 MARCH
Ekeberghalle, Oslo, Norway.

3 MARCH
Isstation, Stockholm, Sweden.

SHEIK YERBOUTI [Album 26]
(double album) released.

The Anti Defamation league of B'nai B'rith filed a formal protest with the FCC to ban the track "Jewish Princess" on the grounds that the lyrics contained "vulgar, sexual and anti-Semitic references which leave very little to the imagination." Zappa responded by saying…

"I'm an artist and I have a right to express my opinion. I'm not anti-Semitic. The Jewish princesses I've played this song for think it's funny… Producing satire is kind of hopeless because of the literacy rate of the American public."

He threatened the ADL with a countersuit.

"Open hostility is the only way to go. I'm taking off my gloves. My lawyer has called them up and

demanded an apology. I haven't stalked controversy - controversy has stalked me." [Zappa: 1979]

Zappa on "Tryin' To Grow A Chin"…
"The song was constructed using every kind of cliché that folk-rock brought to the world – all those stupid bass lines. And it's sung by the drummer who has a squeaky little teenage voice. He sings on about four other songs: everybody sings." [Zappa: 1976]

5 MARCH
Falkoner Theatret, Copenhagen, Denmark.

6 MARCH
Skandinavium, Gothenberg, Sweden.

8 MARCH
Strasbourg, France.

9 MARCH
Dijon, France.

11 MARCH
Palais des Sports, Lyons, France.

12 MARCH
Palais des Sports, Montpellier, France.

13 MARCH
Palau Blau Grana, Barcelona, Spain.

14 MARCH
Pabellon De Deportes, Madrid, Spain.

16 MARCH
Pau, Spain.

17 MARCH
Bordeaux, France.

18 MARCH
Palais des Sports, Nantes, France.

19 MARCH
Parc de Loisirs de Pennfeld, Brest, France.

21 MARCH
Rhein-Neckarhalle, Eppelheim, Germany.

22 MARCH
Passau, Germany.

23 MARCH
Graz, Austria.

25 MARCH
Westfalenhalle, Dortmund, Germany.

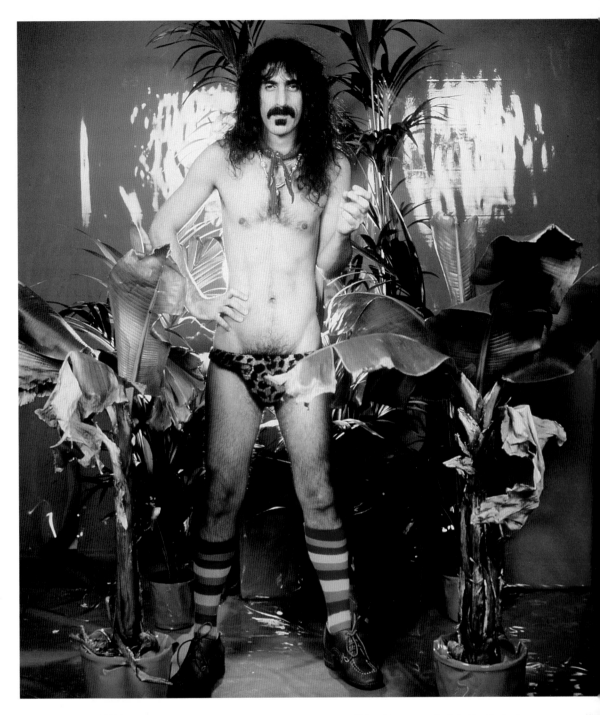

SHEIK YERBOUTI
(double album)
US Zappa Records SRZ-2-1501
3 March 1979
US CD Rykodisc RCD 40162

UK CBS 88339
Released February 1979
UK CD EMI CDP 7-90076-2
(digitally remixed at UMRK by Bob Stone and re-issued as CDZAP 28 on 28 May 1990)

Side 1:
1. I Have Been In You /
2. Flakes / 3. Broken Hearts Are For Assholes / 4. I'm So Cute

Side 2:
1. Jones Crusher / 2. What Ever Happened To All The Fun In The World / 3. Rat Tomago / 4. We've Got To Get Into Something Real / 5. Bobby Brown / 6. Rubber Shirt / 7. The Sheik Yerbouti Tango

Side 3:
1. Baby Snakes / 2. Tryin' To Grow A Chin / 3. City Of Tiny Lites / 4. Dancin' Fool / 5. Jewish Princess

Side 4:
1. Wild Love / 2. Yo' Mama

Line-up:
Frank Zappa - lead guitar, vocals / Adrian Belew - rhythm guitar, vocals / Tommy Mars - keyboards, vocals / Peter Wolf - keyboards / Patrick O'Hearn - bass, vocals / Terry Bozzio - drums, vocals / Ed Mann - percussion, vocals / Dave Ocker -

clarinets on 'Wild Love' / Napoleon Murphy Brock - background vocals / André Lewis - background vocals / Randy Thornton - background vocals / Davey Moire - background vocals

Producer: Frank Zappa
Recorded live with overdubs: The whole of Side 1 / Side 2 tracks 1 and 5 / Side 3 tracks 1-4 and the whole of Side 4 were recorded at The Odeon, Hammersmith, London, 1978

Side 2 tracks 1 and 2 and Side 3 track 5 were recorded at The Palladium, New York City

Side 2 tracks 3 and 7 were recorded at the Deutschland Halle, Berlin, 15 February 1978 The guitar solo from 'Yo Mama' is from the 25 February 1978 concert at the Hemmerleinhalle in Neunkirchen, Germany

The Basing Street Truck and the Manor Truck were used for remote recording in Europe, The RCA Truck and The Ol' Four Track for US recordings / Overdubbing and mixing done at The Village Recorders

Engineers on basic tracks: Peter Henderson, Davey Moire, Claus Wiedemann, Kerry McNab
Overdub engineer Joe Chicarelli
Remixed by Joe Chicarelli and Frank Zappa

1979

26 MARCH
Eilenriedhalle, Hanover, Germany.

27 MARCH
Rhein-Mainhalle, Wiesbaden, Germany.

29 MARCH
Sporthalle, Köln, Germany.

31 MARCH
Rudi-Sedlmayer Halle, Munich, Germany.

1 APRIL
Hallenstadion, Zurich, Switzerland.
The tour then continued to Japan with concerts in Tokyo and Osaka.

11 APRIL
Zappa began recording Joe's Garage.

4 MAY
ORCHESTRAL FAVORITES
[Album 27] released.

AUGUST
Zappa laid off the band and cancelled his late-summer tour. A friend reported to Rolling Stone: "Frank is extremely tired. He rehearses sixteen hours a day, non-stop. His wife is having a baby in August, and the studio he's been building in his home will be finished September Ist. He feels it's irrational to go on tour now."

Zappa finally had his hair cut…
"It's not fashionable, it's short. I used to wear these little rubber- band things in my hair and when I'd lose them, all my hair would just fall into my face. Finally, I just said, 'Fuck it.' and had Gail cut it."
[Zappa: 1979]

17 SEPTEMBER
JOE'S GARAGE ACT I [Album 28]
released.

"I know the world isn't ready for me, so I'll just stay in my basement. But the world may be ready for 'Joe's Garage'. It started out to be just a bunch of songs. But together, they looked like they had continuity. So I went home one night midway through recording, wrote the story and changed it into an opera. It's probably the first opera that you can really tap your feet to and get a couple of good laughs along the way." [Zappa: 1979]

"When we went into the studio to cut 'Joe's Garage' as a single and 'Catholic Girls' as the B side, we stayed in there and cut about sixteen tracks. Then I figured out a story that would hold 'em together. It's all exercise. It's like doing crossword puzzles. In looking at it I saw that not only did it make a continuous story, but it made a good continuous story."
[Zappa: 1979]

ORCHESTRAL FAVORITES
US DiscReet DSK 2294
Released 4 May 1979

UK: DiscReet K 59212
Released June 1979
CD Zappa CDZAP45
Released 21 November 1991

Side 1:
1. Strictly Genteel / 2. Pedro's Dowry / 3. Naval Aviation In Art

Side 2:
1. Duke Of Prunes / 2. Bogus Pomp

Line-up:
Rhythm section:
Frank Zappa - guitar / Dave Parlato - bass / Terry Bozzio - drums / Emil Richards - percussion / The Abnuceals Emuukha Electric Symphony Orchestra was conducted by Michael Zearott and had 37 players

Producer: Frank Zappa
Recorded at Royce Hall, University of California, Los Angeles, 17th and 18th September, 1975
Original engineer unknown, digitally remastered for CD release at UMRK by Bob Stone, 1991

JOE'S GARAGE ACT I
US Zappa Records SRZ-1-1603
Released 17 September 1979
US CD Rykodisc RCD 10060
Released 1987

UK CBS 86101
Released September 1979
UK CD EMI CDP 7-90089-2
Released 1987

Side 1:
1. The Central Scrutinizer / 2. Joe's Garage / 3. Catholic Girls / 4. Crew Slut

Side 2:
1. Wet T-Shirt Nite / 2. Toad-O Line / 3. Why Does It Hurt When I Pee? / 4. Lucille Has Messed My Mind Up

Line-up:
Frank Zappa - lead guitar, vocals / Warren Cucurullo - rhythm guitar, vocals / Denny Walley - slide guitar, vocals / Ike Willis - lead vocals / Peter Wolf - keyboards / Tommy Mars - keyboards / Arthur Barrow - bass, vocals / Ed Mann - percussion / Vinnie Colaiuta - drums / Jeff [?] - tenor saxophone / Marginal Chagrin [?] - baritone saxophone / Stumuk [?] - bass saxophone / Dale Bozzio - vocals / Al Malkin - vocals / Craig Steward - harmonica

Producer: Frank Zappa
Recorded at Village Recorders, studio B and Ken-Dun studio D
Engineers: Joe Chicarelli
Re-mix engineers: Mick Glossop and Steve Nye

Frank and Gail

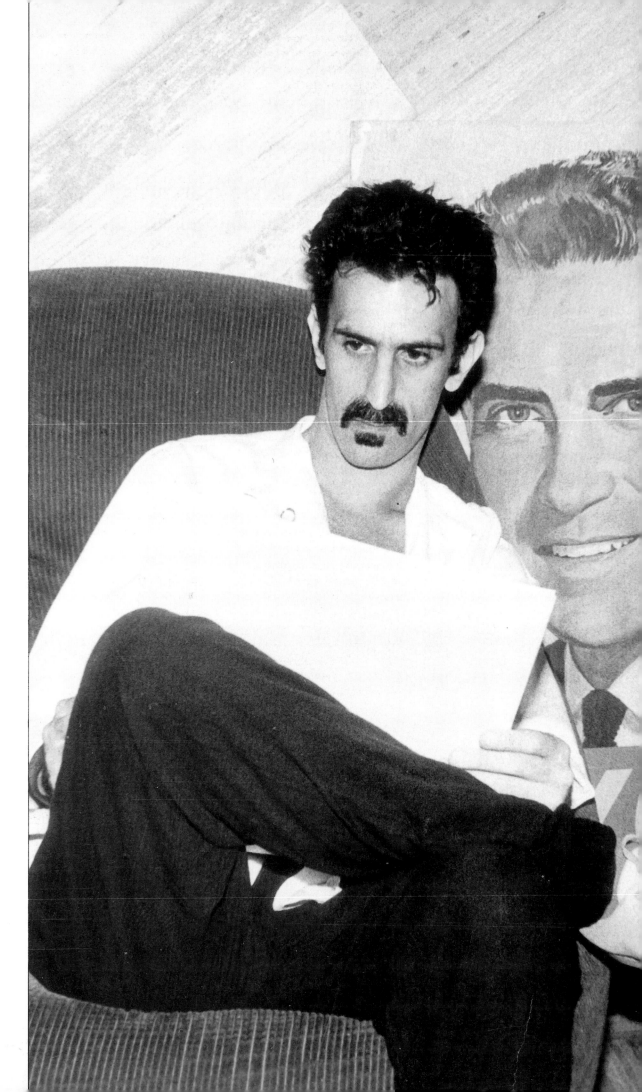

-1979-

"'Joe's Garage' was supposed to be a single three-record set but I changed it into 2 releases because the cost of a 3-record package might be hard on people the way the world is today." [Zappa: 1989]

[liner notes]
Desperate nerds in high offices all over the world have been known to enact the most disgusting pieces of legislation in order to win votes (or, in places where they don't get to vote, to control unwanted forms of mass behavior.)

Environmental laws were not passed to protect our air and water… they were passed to get votes. Seasonal anti-smut campaigns are not conducted to rid our communities of moral rot… they are conducted to give an aura of saintliness to the office seekers who demand them. If a few key phrases are thrown into any speech (as the expert advisers explain to these various heads of state) votes will roll in, bucks will roll in, and, most importantly, power will be maintained by the groovy guy (or gal) who gets the most media coverage for his sleaze. Naturally his friends, in various businesses, will do okay too.

All governments perpetuate themselves through the daily commission of acts which a rational person might find to be stupid or dangerous (or both). Naturally, our government is no exception… for instance, if the President (any one of them) went on TV and sat there with the flag in the background (or maybe a rustic scene on a little backdrop, plus the flag) and stared sincerely into the camera and told everybody that all energy problems and all inflationary problems had been traced to and could be solved by the abolition of MUSIC, chances are that most people would believe him and think that the illegalization of this obnoxious form of noise pollution would be a small price to pay for the chance to buy gas like in the good ol' days. No way? Never happen? Records are made out of oil. All those big rock shows go from town to town in fuel-gobbling 45-foot trucks… and when they get there, they use up enormous amounts of electrical energy with their lights, their amplifiers, their PA systems… their smoke machines. And all those synthesizers… look at all the plastic they got in 'em… and the guitar picks… you name it…

JOE'S GARAGE is a stupid story about how the government is going to try to do away with music (a prime cause of
unwanted mass behavior). It's sort of like a really cheap kind of high school play… the way it might have been done 20 years ago, with all the sets made out of cardboard boxes and poster paint. It's also like those lectures that local narks used to give (where they show you a display of all the different ways you can get wasted, with the pills leading to the weed, leading to the needle etc., etc.).

If the plot of the story seems just a little bit preposterous, and if the idea of The Central Scrutinizer enforcing laws that haven't been passed yet makes you giggle, just be glad you don't live in one of the cheerful little countries where, at this very moment, music is either severely restricted… or, as it is in Iran, totally illegal.

The Cast: Central Scrutinizer, Larry, Father Riley, L. Ron Hoover & Buddy Jones – Frank Zappa / Joe – Ike Willis / Mary – Dale Bozzio / Mrs. Borg – Denny Walley / Officer Butzis – Al Malkin / Sy Borg – Warren Cucurullo & Ed Mann / Bald Headed John – Terry Bozzio

The Utility Muffin Research Kitchen Chorus: Al Malkin, Warren Cucurullo, Dale Bozzio, Geordie Hormel, Barbara Issak & most of the people who work at Village Recorders.

[all the above information missing from UK CD release notes]
Taken from CBS 86101 sleeve [Act 1]

19 NOVEMBER
JOE'S GARAGE ACTS II & III
[Album 29] (double album) released.

During the autumn of 1979 Zappa began recording in his own state of the art studio, the Utility Muffin Research Kitchen [UMRK] which he built in the garden of his house in Los Angeles. From now on, most of Zappa's recordings would be made at UMRK and all road recordings re-mixed there.

JOE'S GARAGE
ACTS II & III
(double album)
US Zappa Records SRZ-2-1502
Released 19 November 1979
US CD Rykodisc RCD 10061
Released 1987

UK CBS 88475
Released December 1979
UK CD EMI CDS 790087-2
Released 1987

Side 1:
[Act II]
1. A Token Of My Extreme /
2. Stick It Out / 3. Sy Borg

Side 2:
1. Dong Work For Yuda /
2. Keep It Greasey / 3. Outside Now

Side 3:
[Act III]
1. He Used To Cut The Grass /
2. Packard Goose

Side 4:
1. Watermelon In Easter Hay /
2. A Little Green Rosetta

Line-up:
Frank Zappa - lead guitar, vocals / Warren Cucurullo - rhythm guitar, vocals / Denny Walley - slide guitar, vocals / Ike Willis - lead vocals / Peter Wolf - keyboards / Arthur Barrow - bass, vocals / Ed Mann - percussion, vocals / Vinnie Colaiuta - drums / Patrick O'Hearn - bass on 'Outside Now'

Producer: Frank Zappa
Recorded at Village Recorders, studio B and Ken-Dun studio D
Engineers: Joe Chicarelli
Re-mix engineers: Mick Glossop and Steve Nye

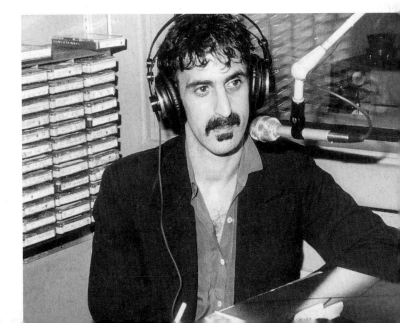

-1980-

Frank Zappa Feb-Aug US, Canada and European tour line-up: Frank Zappa – guitar, vocals / Ike Willis – guitar, vocals / Ray White – guitar, vocals / Arthur Barrow – bass / Tommy Mars – keyboards / David Logeman – drums.

25 MARCH
Seattle Center Arena, Seattle, Wa.

26 MARCH
Coliseum, Vancouver, Canada.

27 MARCH
MacArthur Court, Eugene, Or.

30 MARCH
Sacramento, Ca.

1 APRIL
Berkeley Community Center, Berkeley, Ca.

3 APRIL
Maples Pavilion, San Jose, Ca.

4 APRIL
Sports Arena, San Diego, Ca.

5 APRIL
Swing Auditorium, San Bernardino, Ca.

6 APRIL
Sports Arena, Los Angeles, Ca.

8 APRIL
Scottsdale Center, Phoenix, Az.

12 APRIL
Omaha, Ne.

17 APRIL
Tampa, Fl.

18 APRIL
Sunrise Theater, Fort Lauderdale, Fl.

20 APRIL
Fox Theater, Atlanta, Ga.

22 APRIL
Norfolk, Va.

24 APRIL
Manley Fieldhouse, Syracuse, NY.

25 APRIL
Rutgers Athletic Center, New Brunswick, NJ.

26 APRIL
R.P.I Fieldhouse, Troy, NY.

27 APRIL
Lehigh University, Bethlehem, Pa.

29 APRIL
Tower Theater, Philadelphia, Pa.
[material used on *Tinseltown Rebellion*].

2 MAY
Civic Center, Providence, RI.

3 MAY
Music Hall, Boston, Mass.

4 MAY
Cumberland County Civic Center, Portland, Me.

9 MAY
Nassau Coliseum, Uniondale, NY.

10 MAY
Tower Theater, Philadelphia, Pa.

11 MAY
Civic Center, Baltimore, Md.

23 MAY
Voorst Nationaal, Brussels, Belgium.

24 MAY
The Ahoy, Rotterdam, Holland.

26 MAY
Deutschlandhalle, Berlin, Germany.

27 MAY
Stadthalle, Bremen, Germany.

28 MAY
Ostseehalle, Kiel, Germany.

30 MAY
Forum, Copenhagen, Denmark.

31 MAY
Oslo, Norway.

1 JUNE
Eriksdalshallen, Stockholm, Sweden.

2 JUNE
Scandinavium, Gothenburg, Sweden.

3 JUNE
Oslo, Norway.

4 JUNE
CCH, Hamburg, Germany.

5 JUNE
Eilenriedhalle, Hanover, Germany.

7 JUNE
Sporthalle, Köln, Germany.

8 JUNE
Westfalenhalle, Dortmund, Germany.

9 JUNE
Philipshalle, Düsseldorf, Germany.

10 – 11 JUNE
Palais des Sports, Paris, France.

13 JUNE
Clermont-Ferrand, France.

15 JUNE
Rouen, France.

17 – 18 JUNE
Wembley Arena, London, UK.

19 JUNE
Palais de la Beaujoire, Nantes, France.

20 JUNE
Théâtre Antique, Orange, France.

21 JUNE
Palais des Sports, Geneva, Switzerland.

22 JUNE
Hallenstadion, Zurich, Switzerland.

23 JUNE
Oberrheinhalle, Offenburg, Germany.

25 JUNE
Eisstadion, Mannheim, Germany.

26 JUNE
Hemmerleinhalle, Neuenkirchen,
Germany.

27 JUNE
Stadthalle, Vienna, Austria.

28 JUNE
Messehalle, Sindelfingen,
Germany.

30 JUNE
Théâtre Antique, Vienne, France.

1 JULY
Sous Chapiteau, Toulouse,
France.

2 JULY
Festhalle, Frankfurt, Germany.

3 JULY
Olympiahalle, Munich, Germany.
[Broadcast in USA on 28 June 1981
on King Biscuit Flower Hour.]

6 JULY
Sporthalle, Köln, Germany.

JULY – AUGUST
Recording sessions for *You Are What
You Is* held at UMRK Studios, Los Angeles.

Frank Zappa July – Dec, Fall US and
Canada tour line-up: Frank Zappa –
guitar, vocals / Ike Willis – guitar, vocals /
Ray White – guitar, vocals / Arthur
Barrow – bass / Tommy Mars – keyboards /
Vinnie Colaiuta – drums, vocals / Bob
Harris – keyboards, vocals / Steve Vai –
guitar, vocals.

1 OCTOBER
Seattle, Wa.

3 OCTOBER
Vancouver, Canada.

4 OCTOBER
Eugene, Or.

5 OCTOBER
Portland, Or.

6 OCTOBER
Reno, Na.

7 OCTOBER
Las Vegas, Na.

9 OCTOBER
Tucson, Az.

12 OCTOBER
Johnson Gymnasium, Albuquerque, NM.

13 OCTOBER
Celebrity Theater, Phoenix, Az.

16 OCTOBER
Austin, Tx.

17 OCTOBER
Convention Center, Dallas, Tx.
[material used on *Tinseltown Rebellion*].

18 OCTOBER
Brady Theater, Tulsa, Ok.

WEMBLEY ARENA
Harvey Goldsmith for Umbrella Productions
presents
ZAPPA
WEDNESDAY, 18 JUNE, 1980
at 8 p.m.
SOUTH GRAND TIER
£6.00 ★
JUNE
18
ENTER AT
SOUTH DOOR
ENTRANCE
75
ROW
A
SEAT
99
TO BE RETAINED See conditions on back

21 OCTOBER
Coliseum, Houston, Tx.

22 OCTOBER
Memphis, Tenn.

24 OCTOBER
Civic Center, Hartford, Ct.

25 OCTOBER
Buffalo, NY.

26 OCTOBER
University of NY at Stoneybrook,
Stoneybrook, NY.

27 OCTOBER
Charlotte, Va.

28 OCTOBER
Palace Theater, Albany, NY.

29 OCTOBER
Philadelphia, Pa.
[may not have occurred].

30 OCTOBER – 1 NOVEMBER
Palladium, NYC.

6 NOVEMBER
The Forum, Montreal, Canada.

8 NOVEMBER
Ocean State Performing Art Center,
Providence, RI.

10 NOVEMBER
The Coliseum, Cleveland, Ohio.

11 NOVEMBER
Maple Leaf Gardens, Toronto, Canada.

12 NOVEMBER
The Forum, Montreal, Quebec, Canada.

13 NOVEMBER
Pittsburgh, Pa.

15 NOVEMBER
Carbondale College, Carbondale, Ill.

17 NOVEMBER
Minneapolis, Minn.

18 NOVEMBER
St. Paul, Minn.

22 NOVEMBER
Louisville, Ky.

26 NOVEMBER
Masonic Auditorium, Detroit, Mi.

Frank with Jeff Johnson and his
hand carved Marilyn Monroe guitar

28 – 29 NOVEMBER
Uptown Theater, Chicago, Ill.

30 NOVEMBER
Des Moines, Iowa.

2 DECEMBER
Ft. Collins, Co.

5 DECEMBER
Community Theater, Berkeley, CA.
[material used on *Tinseltown Rebellion*]

11 DECEMBER
Civic Auditorium, Santa Monica, Ca.
[material used on *Tinseltown Rebellion*]

There were a few more December concerts not recorded.

–1981–

17 APRIL
Palladium, NYC: "A Tribute To Edgard Varèse."

Joel Thome, conductor of the Orchestra for Our Time, approached Zappa about participating in a Varèse tribute to be held at the Whitney Museum. Zappa loved the idea because he thought it might draw…
"the kids so they could hear Varèse's music, and come to love it."

He had the venue changed to the more spacious Palladium, (once an opera-house).
"The kids that come may be a little rambunctious. But I've always had a good rapport with them and talked to them like they were my neighbours." [Zappa: 1981]

Zappa wore correct evening dress for the occasion but said that he saw his role as introducer as "comic relief." 91 year old Louise Varèse the composer's widow described Zappa as "a lovely person" and said, "He's very serious about Varèse's music, you know."

11 MAY
SHUT UP 'N PLAY YER GUITAR
[Album 31] released.

**SHUT UP 'N PLAY YER GUITAR
SOME MORE**
[Album 32] released.

**RETURN OF THE SON OF
SHUT UP 'N PLAY YER GUITAR**
[Album 33] released.

SHUT UP 'N PLAY YER GUITAR
US Barking Pumpkin BPR 1111
Released 11 May 1981
(Mail-order only)

Side 1:
1. five-five-FIVE / 2. Hog Heaven /
3. Shut Up 'n Play Yer Guitar /
4. While You Were Out

Side 2:
1. Treacherous Cretins /
2. Heavy Duty Judy /
3. Soup 'n' Old Clothes

Line-up:
Frank Zappa - lead guitar /
Vinnie Colaiuta - drums /
Warren Cucurullo - rhythm guitar on Side 1 tracks 1, 3 and 4, Side 2 track 1 / Denny Walley - rhythm guitar on Side 1 tracks 1 and 3, Side 2 track 1 / Ike Willis - rhythm guitar on Side 1 tracks 1-3 and all of Side 2 / Tommy Mars - keyboards on Side 1 tracks 1-3 and all of Side 2 / Peter Wolf - keyboards Side 1 tracks 1 and 3, and all of Side 2 / Arthur Barrow - bass Side 1 tracks 1-3 and all of Side 2 / Ed Mann - percussion on Side 1 tracks 1 and 3, Side 2 track 1 / Ray White - rhythm guitar on Side 1 track 2, Side 2 tracks 2 and 3 / Bob Harris - keyboards on Side 1 track 2, Side 2 tracks 2 and 3 / Steve Vai - rhythm guitar on Side 2 tracks 2 and 3

Producer: Frank Zappa
Recorded at various locations: Side 1 track 1 and Side 2 track 1 from Odeon, Hammersmith, 17 February 1979 / Side 1 track 3 from Odeon, Hammersmith, 18 February 1979 / Side 1 track 2 from Brady Theater, Tulsa, 18 October 1980 / Side 2 track 2 from the Berkeley Community Theater concert 4 December 1980 / Side 2 track 3 from

Santa Monica Civic Auditorium of 11 December 1980 / Side 1 track 4 recorded at Zappa's UMRK studio, date unknown

Engineer on the Hammersmith Odeon recordings - Mick Glossop using The Rolling Stones Mobile / George Douglas recorded Tulsa and the Santa Monica concerts using the UMRK Remote / Berkeley was recorded by Tommy Fly on the UMRK remote who also cut the studio track / The album was re-mixed by Bob Stone at UMRK

SHUT UP 'N PLAY YER GUITAR SOME MORE
US Barking Pumpkin BPR 1112
Released 11 May 1981
(Mail-order only)

Side 1:
1. Variations On The Carlos Santana Secret Chord Progression / 2. Gee, I Like Your Pants / 3. Canarsie / 4. Ship Ahoy

Side 2:
1. The Deathless Horsie /
2. Shut Up 'n Play Yer Guitar Some More /
3. Pink Napkins

Line-up:
Frank Zappa - lead guitar / Vinnie Colaiuta - drums on Side 1 tracks 1-3 and Side 2 tracks 1 and 2 / Warren Cucurullo - rhythm guitar on Side 1 track 2, Side 2 tracks 1 and 2 / Denny Walley - rhythm guitar on Side 1 track 2, Side 2 tracks 1 and 2 / Ike Willis - rhythm guitar on Side 1 tracks 1 and 2, Side 2 tracks 1 and 2 / Tommy Mars - keyboards on Side 1 tracks 1 and 2, Side 2 tracks 1 and 2 / Peter Wolf - keyboards Side 1 track 2, Side 2 tracks 1 and 2 / Arthur Barrow - bass Side 1 tracks 1 and 2, Side 2 tracks 1 and 2 / Ed Mann - percussion on Side 1 track 2,

Side 2 tracks 1 and 2 / Ray White - rhythm guitar on Side 1 track 1, Side 2 track 3 / Bob Harris - keyboards on Side 1 track 1 / Steve Vai - rhythm guitar on Side 1 track 1 / Patrick O'Hearn - bass on Side 1 track 3 and Side 2 track 3 / André Lewis - keyboards Side 1, track 4 / Roy Estrada - bass side on one track 4 / Terry Bozzio - drums on side on track 4, Side 2 track 3 / Eddie Jobson - keyboards on Side 2 track 3

Producer: Frank Zappa
Recorded at various locations: Side 1 track 1 recorded at the Dallas Civic Center on 17 October 1980 / Side 1 track 4 recorded either in Tokyo or Osaka / Side 1 track 2 recorded at the Odeon, Hammersmith on February 18, 1979 / Side 1 track 3 and Side 2 track 1 recorded at the Odeon Hammersmith on February 19, 1979 / Side 2 track 2 recorded at the Odeon Hammersmith 17 February 1979, Side 2 track 3 recorded at the Odeon Hammersmith, 17 February 1977
Engineers: The 1979 Odeon tracks recorded by Mick Glossop on The Rolling Stones Mobile, the 1977 Odeon gig recorded by Alan P on the Manor Mobile, Dallas recorded by George Douglas on the UMRK remote Album re-mixed by Bob Stone at UMRK

RETURN OF THE SON OF SHUT UP 'N PLAY YER GUITAR
US Barking Pumpkin BPR 1113
Released 11 May 1981
(Mail-order only)
Side 1:
1. Beat It With Your Fist /
2. Return of the Son of Shut Up 'n Play Yer Guitar / 3. Pinocchio's Furniture / 4. Why Johnny Can't Read

Side 2:
1. Stucco Homes / 2. Canard du Jour

Line-up:
Frank Zappa - lead guitar / Vinnie Colaiuta - drums all tracks except 'Canard du Jour' / Warren Cucurullo - rhythm guitar on Side 1 tracks 2, and 4, Side 2 track 1 / Denny Walley - rhythm guitar on Side 1 tracks 2 and 4 / Ike Willis - rhythm guitar on Side 1 / Tommy Mars - keyboards on Side 1 / Peter Wolf - keyboards Side 1 tracks 2 and 4 / Arthur Barrow - bass Side 1 / Ed Mann - percussion on Side 1 tracks 2 and 4 / Ray White - rhythm guitar on Side 1 tracks 1 and 3 / Bob Harris - keyboards on Side 1 tracks 1 and 3 / Steve Vai - rhythm guitar on Side 1 track 3 / Jean-Luc Ponty - baritone violin on Side 2 track 2

Producer: Frank Zappa
Recorded at various locations: Side 1 track 1 at The Palladium, New York City, 30 October 1980 / Side 1 track 2 recorded at the Odeon, Hammersmith on 19 February 1979 / Side 1 track 3 recorded at the Berkeley Community Theater, 5 December 1980 / Side 1 track 4 recorded at the Odeon, Hammersmith, 17 February 1979 / Side 2 track 1 recorded at UMRK and track 2 recorded at Paramount Studios, dates unknown
Engineers: Mick Glossop recorded the Odeon concerts on The Rolling Stones Mobile / George Douglas recorded the NYC gig using the UMRK remote / Tommy Fly recorded the Berkeley concert on the UMRK remote / Steve Nye recorded 'Stucco Homes' at UMRK Central / Kerry McNabb recorded 'Canard du Jour'

11 MAY

SHUT UP 'N PLAY YER GUITAR

[Albums 30-1-2] (3 album boxed set)

"I am glad I did them. I mean, I have been waiting to do it for a long time. And a lot of people thought I was crazy for spending the time to do it. But, right now that group of albums is selling better than 'You Are What You Is' and 'Tinsel Town Rebellion'. We went into a profit position after two weeks on the market. I'm selling more through mail order than in record stores. I am just talking about the cost of making the album, versus what it has brought in in profit after two weeks. I was in profit on the guitar albums and right now 'You Are What You Is' is only being played on the radio in New York and Connecticut. It's not being played any place else and it's not selling worth a shit. And it's a great album. And right now the guitar albums are continuing to sell."

"I like 'Stucco Homes' and 'While You Were Out'. I've always kind of liked those ones. And I like... I think it's the first 'Shut Up and Play Your Guitar' record. I like 'Heavy Duty Judy', I like 'Soup and Old Clothes'. Those are my favourites. The voice segues came because I tried the album... I edited it together with no vocal texture in it and I thought it was flat. I think it needed just a vocal distraction to set you up for the next thing, because one solo after another after another with no interruption is – to me it wasn't dynamic enough." [Zappa: 1982]

17 MAY

TINSEL TOWN REBELLION

[Album 33] (double album) released.

"This is good stuff... it might not be PUNK... it might not be NEW WAVE... it might not be whatever trend you are worshipping at the moment, but it is good stuff nonethless, so, check it out." [Zappa: May 1981]

JUNE

Sessions with the Berkeley Symphony Orchestra.

SEPTEMBER

YOU ARE WHAT YOU IS [Album 34] (double album) released.

27 SEPTEMBER

Robertsons Gymnasium, Santa Barbara, Ca.

28 SEPTEMBER

Memorial Auditorium, Sacramento, Ca.

29 SEPTEMBER

Civic Center, Santa Cruz, Ca.

1 OCTOBER

Portland, Or.

2 OCTOBER

Civic Arena, Seattle, Wa.

3 OCTOBER
Vancouver, BC, Canada.

4 OCTOBER
Eugene, Or.

6 OCTOBER
Reno, Na.

7 OCTOBER
Aladdin Theater, Las Vegas, Na.

9 OCTOBER
Tucson, Az.

10 OCTOBER
Mesa Amphitheater,
Phoenix, Az.

11 OCTOBER
Albuquerque, NM.

13 OCTOBER
Oklahoma City, Ok

14 OCTOBER
Tulsa, Ok.

16 OCTOBER
Dallas, Tx.

17 OCTOBER
Convention Center, Houston, Tx.

18 OCTOBER
University of Texas, Austin, Tx.

20 OCTOBER
Saenger Performing Arts Theater,
New Orleans, La.

22 OCTOBER
Bayfront Arena, St. Petersburg, Fl.

23 OCTOBER
Miami, Fl.

24 OCTOBER
O'Connell Auditorium, Gainsville, Fl.

25 OCTOBER
Fox Theater, Atlanta, Ga.

27 OCTOBER
Charlotte, NC.

**29 OCTOBER –
1 NOVEMBER**
Palladium, NYC. Hallowe'en concert.

3 NOVEMBER
Tower Theater, Philadelphia, Pa.

4 NOVEMBER
Providence, RI.

6 NOVEMBER
Civic Center, Hartford, Ct.

7 NOVEMBER
Case Center, Boston, Mass.

8 NOVEMBER
Montreal, Quebec.

9 NOVEMBER
Maple Leaf Gardens, Toronto,
Canada.

11 NOVEMBER
Shea's Theater, Buffalo, NY.

13 NOVEMBER
Manley Fieldhouse,
Syracuse, NY.

14 NOVEMBER
Albany, NY.

**SHUT UP 'N PLAY
YER GUITAR**
(3 album boxed set)
US Barking Pumpkin 38289
Released 11 May 1981

UK CBS 66368
Released 1981
UK CD Zappa CDDZAP 19
Released UK January 1990

TINSEL TOWN REBELLION
(double album)
US Barking Pumpkin
PW2/37336
Released 17 May 1981
US CD Rykodisc RCD 10166
(Release date unknown)

UK CBS 88516
Released May 1981
UK CD Zappa CDZAP 26
Released June 1990

Side 1:
1. Fine Girl / 2. Easy Meat /
3. For The Young Sophisticate

Side 2:
1. Love Of My Life / 2. I Ain't Got
No Heart / 3. Panty Rap / 4. Tell
Me You Love Me / 5. Now You
See It, Now You Don't

Side 3:
1. Dance Contest / 2. The Blue
Light / 3. Tinsel Town Rebellion /
4. Pick Me, I'm Clean

Side 4:
1. Bamboozled By Love /
2. Brown Shoes Don't Make It /
3. Peaches III

Line-up:
Frank Zappa - lead guitar, vocals /
Ike Willis - rhythm guitar, vocals /
Ray White - rhythm guitar / Steve
Vai - rhythm guitar and vocals /
Warren Cucurullo - rhythm guitar,
vocals / Denny Walley - slide
guitar, vocals / Tommy Mars -
keyboards, vocals / Peter Wolf -
keyboards / Bob Harris -
keyboards, trumpet, high vocals /
Ed Mann - percussion /
Arthur Barrow - bass, vocals /
Patrick O'Hearn - bass on 'Dance
Contest' / Vinnie Colaiuta -
drums / David Logemann - drums
on 'Fine Girl' and the first half
'Easy Meat' / Greg Cowan as an
'eccentric well-to-do Oregonian
party giver'

Producer: Frank Zappa
Recorded live at various locations
using The Rolling Stones Mobile
in London and the UMRK Portable
Studio in the USA / Side 1 track 2
was recorded at the Tower
Theater, Philadelphia, 29 April
1980 with guitar solo taken from
a 11 December 1980 concert
at the Santa Monica Civic
Auditorium / Side 1 track 3, and
all of Side 4 recorded in February
1979 at the Odeon Hammersmith,
London / Side 2 tracks 1-4
recorded at the Berkeley
Community Theater, 5 December
1980, (track four has sections
from the Dallas Convention
Center concert on 17 October
1980 added in) Side 2 track 5 is
from Carbondale College,
Carbondale, Illinois, 15 November

1980 and Side 3 track 1 is from
the 27 October 1978 show at the
Palladium, New York City / The
opening track was recorded at
UMRK Central, summer 1980
Engineers: Mark Pinske,
George Douglas, Joe Chiccarelli /
Alan Sides, Tommy Fly
Re-mix engineer at UMRK Central,
Bob Stone

YOU ARE WHAT YOU IS
(double album)
US Barking Pumpkin
PW 2/37537
Released September 1981
US CD Rykodisc RCD 40165

UK CBS 88560
Released October 1981
UK CD EMI CDP 7-90075-2
Re-issued as Zappa CDZAP 27
Released 21 May 1990

Side 1:
1. Teen-age Wind / 2. Harder
Than Your Husband / 3. Doreen /
4. Goblin Girl / 5. Theme From
The Third Movement Of Sinister
Footwear

Side 2:
1. Society Pages / 2. I'm A
Beautiful Guy / 3. Beauty Knows
No Pain / 4. Charlie's Enormous
Mouth / 5. Any Downers? /
6. Conehead

Side 3:
1. You Are What You Is /
2. Mudd Club / 3. The Meek
Shall Inherit Nothing / 4. Dumb
All Over

Side 4:
1. Heavenly Bank Account /
2. Suicide Chump / 3. Jumbo Go
Away / 4. If Only She Woulda /
5. Drafted Again

Line-up:
Frank Zappa - lead guitar and
vocals / Ike Willis - rhythm guitar
and vocals / Ray White - rhythm
guitar and vocals / Bob Harris -
boy soprano and trumpet / Steve
Vai - guitar / Tommy Mars -
keyboards / Arthur Barrow -
bass / Ed Mann - percussion /
David Ocker - clarinet and bass
clarinet / Motorhead Sherwood -
tenor saxophone / Denny Walley -
slide guitar, vocals / David
Logeman - drums / Craig 'Twister'
Stewart - harmonica / Jimmy Carl
Black - vocals / Ahmet Zappa -
vocals / Moon Unit Zappa -
vocals / Mark Pinske - vocals

Producer: Frank Zappa at his
UMRK studio
Engineers: Mark Pinske,
Alan Sides
Re-mix engineer: Bob Stone

15 NOVEMBER
Painter's Mill Music Fair,
Baltimore, Md.

17 NOVEMBER
The Ritz, NYC.

19 NOVEMBER
Cleveland, Oh.

20 NOVEMBER
Cincinnati, Oh.

21 NOVEMBER
University of Illinois,
Champaign, Ill.

22 NOVEMBER
Bloomington, Ind.

24 NOVEMBER
Pittsburgh, Pa.

25 NOVEMBER
Cobo Hall, Detroit, Mi.

26 NOVEMBER
Cuyahoga Falls, Ohio.

27 - 29 NOVEMBER
Chicago, Ill.

1 DECEMBER
Milwaukee, Wi.

2 DECEMBER
De Kalb, Ill.

4 DECEMBER
Omaha, Nb.

5 DECEMBER
Kansas City, Ks.

6 DECEMBER
Boulder, Co.

7 DECEMBER
Salt Lake City, Utah.

10 DECEMBER
Community Center,
Berkeley, Ca.

11 DECEMBER
Civic Center, Santa Monica, Ca.

12 DECEMBER
Civic Center, San Diego, Ca.

20 DECEMBER
Community Center, Berkeley, Ca.

DECEMBER
Hollywood, Ca.

Many of the shows on this tour did
not sell out and Zappa's disappointment
was reflected in 1982 when he played
relatively few American concerts.

-1982-

LOOKING UP GRANNY'S DRESS
(Compilation) released.

6 - 20 APRIL
Studio recordings using same line-up at
Zappa's UMRK.

MAY
**SHIP ARRIVING TOO LATE TO SAVE
A DROWNING WITCH**
[Album 35] released.

5 MAY
Vejlby Risskov Hallen, Aarhus,
Denmark.

7 MAY
Isstadion, Stockholm, Sweden.

8 MAY
Drammenshallen, Oslo, Norway.

10 MAY
Scandinavium, Gothenburg, Sweden.

11 MAY
Brondby Hallen, Copenhagen, Denmark.

12 MAY
Deutschlandhalle, Berlin, Germany.

14 MAY
Voorst Nationaal Hal, Brussels, Belgium.

15 MAY
The Ahoy, Rotterdam, Holland.

17 – 19 MAY
Nouvel Hippodrome, Paris, France.

21 MAY
Sportshalle, Köln, Germany.

22 MAY
Philipshalle, Düsseldorf, Germany.

23 MAY
Ostseehalle, Kiel, Germany [The show ended after ten minutes after the audience threw objects at the band. Several subsequent German concerts were cancelled including Saarbrucken on the 25th and Offenburg on the 26th.]

28 MAY
Palais des Sports, St. Etienne, France.

29 MAY
Les Arenes, Fréjus, France.

30 MAY
Arenes, Cap d'Agde, France.

1 JUNE
Patinoire, Bordeaux, France.

2 JUNE
Salle Omnisports, Rennes, France.

3 JUNE
Palais des Sports, Dijon, France.

4 JUNE
Köln, Germany [may not have happened].

5 JUNE
Vechtewiese, Schuttdorf, Germany.

6 JUNE
Rhein Neckar Stadion, Mannheim, Germany. [very heavy rain stopped the concert after ten minutes].

8 JUNE
CCH, Hamburg, Germany.

9 JUNE
Stadthalle, Bremen, Germany.

10 JUNE
Grugahalle, Essen, Germany.

11 JUNE
Alte Opera, Frankfurt.

13 JUNE
Feste Marienburg, Würzburg, Germany.

15 JUNE
Centre Sportif, Differdange, Luxembourg.

17 JUNE
Foire de Lille, Lille, France [show cancelled after sound check.]

18 – 19 JUNE
Hammersmith Odeon, London, UK.

21 JUNE
The show in Strasbourg was cancelled.

22 JUNE
Parc des Expositions, Metz, France.

23 JUNE
Sporthalle, Boblingen, Germany.

24 JUNE
Hallenstadion, Zurich, Switzerland.

26 JUNE
Olympiahalle, Munich, Germany.

27 JUNE
Donauhalle, Ulm, Germany.

28 JUNE
Stadthalle, Vienna, Austria.

29 JUNE
Sporthalle, Linz, Austria.

30 JUNE
Patinoire des Vernets, Geneva, Switzerland. [The show ended after fifteen minutes after the audience threw objects at the band.]

31 JUNE
Bordeaux, France.

LOOKING UP GRANNY'S DRESS
(Compilation)
Rhino Records RNLP 804
Released 1982

Side 2, track 1 /Deseri

Line-up:
Ray Collins - lead vocals /
Frank Zappa - drums / Ronnie Williams - guitar
Recorded in 1962 at Studio PAL in Cucamonga, Ca

(The remaining tracks are all by various ex-members of The Mothers Of Invention)

SHIP ARRIVING TOO LATE TO SAVE A DROWNING WITCH
US Barking Pumpkin FW38066
Released May 1982
UK CBS 85804
Released May 1982
UK CD (w/Man From Utopia)
EMI CDP 7-90074-2
Re-issued as Zappa CDZAP 42
without Man From Utopia
Released 1991

Side 1:
1. No Not Now / 2. Valley Girl /
3. I Come From Nowhere.

Side 2:
1. Drowning Witch / 2. Envelopes /
3. Teen-age Prostitute

Line-up:
Frank Zappa - lead guitar, vocals / Steve Vai - guitar / Ray White - rhythm guitar, vocals / Tommy Mars - keyboards / Bobby Martin - keyboards, saxophone, vocals / Ed Mann - percussion / Scott Thunes - bass on Side 2 and on 'Valley Girl' / Arthur Barrow - bass on 'No Not Now' and first part of 'I Come From Nowhere' / Patrick O'Hearne - bass on 'I Come From Nowhere' / Chad Wackermann - drums / Roy Estrada - vocals / Ike Willis - vocals / Bob Harris - vocals / Lisa Popeil - vocal on 'Teen-age Prostitute' / Moon Unit Zappa - vocal on 'Valley Girls'

Producer: Frank Zappa
Engineer for basics and over-dubs: Mark Pinske
Engineer for over-dubs and remix: Bob Stone / Remote recordings done on the UMRK Mobile Overdubs and remix done at UMRK Central

2 JULY
Campo Sportivo, Turin, Italy.

3 JULY
Campo Communale, Bolzano, Italy.

4 JULY
Quartiere Fieristico, Bologna, Italy.

5 JULY
Campo Sportivo, Genoa, Italy.

6 JULY
Parco Redecessio, Milan, Italy.

7 JULY
Campo del Luga, Milan, Italy.

8 JULY
Stadio Municipale, Pistoia, Italy.

9 JULY
Grossetto, Italy.

10 JULY
Ex Mattatoio Do Testaccio, Rome, Italy.

11 – 12 JULY
Stadio St. Paolo, Naples, Italy.

14 JULY
Palermo, Sicily. The show was stopped after thirty minutes.
"I think three people got killed during our last show in Palermo in Sicily. We were playing a soccer stadium when for some unknown reason the cops started firing tear gas into the crowd. From what I could see from the stage, some of the kids

in the audience started shooting back at the cops. I didn't find out about the deaths until later.
"That was our last European tour. It's too expensive to play, too expensive to travel around, and with the anti-American sentiment around, it is hard to go onstage and do what you do with the emotional freight that is attendant to European attitudes toward American foreign policy." [Zappa: August 1982]

31 OCTOBER
Palladium, NYC Hallowe'en Concert.

–1983–

JANUARY
Four and a half days' rehearsal with the London Symphony Orchestra at Hammersmith Odeon, London, UK.

11 JANUARY
London Symphony Orchestra perform the music of Frank Zappa at the Barbican Centre, London.

12 – 14 JANUARY
Recording sessions with the London Symphony Orchestra at Twickenham Film Studios, London.

9 FEBRUARY
Zappa conducted the Edgard Varèse Memorial Concert to celebrate the 100th anniversary of the birth of Varèse at the San Francisco War Memorial Opera House, San Francisco, Ca.

MARCH
THE MAN FROM UTOPIA
[Album 36] released.

The sleeve was designed by Italian illustrator Tanino Liberatore whose work is seen in the Italian magazine *Frigidaire*. **"I saw his work in that and arranged through some frlends to meet him, he doesn't hardly speak any English. He's a great guy. The illustration will be understood better in Italy than any place else because the way he's painted me there is based on a character he uses in the Frigidaire magazine, a robot named Rank Xerox."** [Zappa: 1983]

MARCH
BABY SNAKES [Album 37]
(Movie soundtrack) (Picture disc) released.

THE LONDON SYMPHONY ORCHESTRA: ZAPPA VOLUME 1
[Album 38] released.

**"Kent Nagano came to one of our concerts when we were working in Berkeley, he conducts the Berkeley Symphony Orchestra and he had heard that I wrote music. Some friends of his brought him to the show and he came backstage afterwards. I said, 'Yeah, sure I write music, want to see some scores?' and he said 'Yeah' so I sent them to him and he flipped out... he loved them.
"That guy is a world class conductor and the orchestra really appreciated him. On the last day one of the guys brought a sign, something that you would find around dangerous electrical equipment. It said 'DANGER LIVE CONDUCTOR' and he had it hanging on his podium, and they gave him a big round of applause. They were really delighted to have worked with him. In fact I may even stick that part on the album. I mean he's fantastic. He's 31 years old, there are guys who've been conducting 50 years and can't do what he does.**
[Zappa: 1983]

"I originally didn't want to do a concert, I just came over here to make the record but doing the concert was part of the problem that every composer has in getting

a new piece played, for instance. If musicians have never seen the music before they have to rehearse it, they have to learn how to play it. If you're going to make a record there is no Union scale for rehearsing for a recording, if you're going to do a recording then the minute that the musician comes in you have to pay a recording salary which would make the cost of the project enormous. There is, however, a rehearsal scale for doing a concert, so what you do is rehearse at the rehearsal rate for a concert, play the concert and then do your recording at a higher rate, so that's why there was a concert.

"I'm glad people liked it but it wasn't a very accurate performance of the music. There were a lot of wrong notes in the show and the acoustics of the place were really shitty, if they liked it then the record will kill them because only on the record will you hear what the things are really supposed to be.

"The LSO has an air of professionalism about it that goes above and beyond most other orchestras that I've been associated with, which is not a lot, but I've been associated with a few. I like the attitude of the LSO and whatever the liabilities might be from some of the individual performers, or the attitude of some guys in the orchestra, the net result of working with them was really positive. They got into it, they took it seriously,

they did it like it was a professional job and some of them actually loved it. Then there were other people in the orchestra who couldn't care less because they're doing this as a job." "I think the audience should feel relaxed and happy when they go to see an orchestra play, because it's a miracle, it's a miracle that you can get a hundred people to do anything together, let alone play music. In spite of the fact that it wasn't as accurate as it should have been, that evening was a fantastic event, it was a miracle, people should appreciate that." [Zappa: 1983]

1 OCTOBER

Billboard reports that Zappa has acquired a Sony PCM-3324 digital recording system. He already owns a Sony PCM 1610 two-track digital audio mastering system. "Zappa is believed to be one of the few recording artists in the world to own a complete digital system… Zappa states that his decision to buy digital equipment was based on the astonishing difference between digital and analog."

OCTOBER

Zappa sues Warner Bros for $6M in damages. Zappa charges that Warner Bros Records has failed to account, provided misleading statements and thwarted his legal right to audit their accounts on his behalf. His suit asked $2.4M in actual damages, $600,000 in royalties due his Munchkin and Frank Zappa Music firms and $1M in exemplary and punitive damages.

THE MAN FROM UTOPIA
US Barking Pumpkin FW38403
Released March 1983

UK CBS 25251
Released March 1983
UK CD (w/Ship Arriving Too Late
To Save A Drowning Witch)
EMI CDP 7-90074-2
Re-issued by itself as
Fame CDP 790 0742
Released June 1988

Side 1:
1. Cocaine Decisions /
2. The Dangerous Kitchen /
3. Tink Walks Amok / 4. The
Radio Is Broken / 5. Moggio

Side 2:
1. The Man From Utopia Meets
Mary Lou / 2. Stick Together /
3. Sex / 4. The Jazz Discharge
Party Hats / 5. We Are Not Alone

Line-up:
Frank Zappa - lead guitar,
vocals / Steve Vai - guitar / Ray
White - rhythm guitar, vocals /
Tommy Mars - keyboards / Bobby
Martin - keyboards, saxophone,
vocals / Ed Mann - percussion /
Scott Thunes - bass / Chad
Wackerman - drums / Roy Estrada
- vocals / Ike Willis - vocals / Bob
Harris - vocals / Arthur Barrow -
keyboards, bass, micro-bass,
rhythm guitar / Vinnie Colaiuta -
drums on 'Dangerous Kitchen'
and 'Jazz Discharge' / Craig
Stewart - harmonica / Dick Fegy -
mandolin / Marty Krystall -
saxophones

Producer: Frank Zappa
Engineers: Bob Stone,
Mark Pinske, David Jerdan at
UMRK Central
All live material recorded using
the UMRK remote

BABY SNAKES
(Movie soundtrack) (Picture disc)
US Barking Pumpkin BPR 1115
Released March 1983
(originally as mail order only)
Digitally remixed and remastered
for commercial release as
Barking Pumpkin CD D2 74219.
Released 1988

UK CD Zappa CD ZAP 16
Released June 1989

Side 1:
1. Baby Snakes / 2. Titties 'n'
Beer / 3. The Black Page No.2 /
4. Jones Crusher / 5. Disco Boy

Side 2:
1. Dinah Moe Humm / 2. Punky's
Whips

Producer: Frank Zappa

**THE LONDON SYMPHONY
ORCHESTRA: ZAPPA
VOLUME 1**
US Barking Pumpkin FW38820
Released 9 June 1983
Rykodisc RCD 10022
Released 1986

UK Zappa CDZAP 34
Release date unknown

Side 1:
1. Sad Jane / 2. Pedro's Dowry
(large orchestra version) /
3. Envelopes

Side 2:
1. Mo 'n Herb's Vacation, First
Movement / 2. Mo 'n Herb's
Vacation, Second Movement /
3. Mo 'n Herb's Vacation, Third
Movement

Line-up:
David Ocker - solo clarinet /
Chad Wackermann - drum set /
Ed Man - featured percussionist.
The London Symphony Orchestra
of 102 players conducted by
Kent Nagano, Ashley Arbuckle -
concert master

Producer: Frank Zappa
Recorded at Twickenham Film
Studios, London 12-14 January
1983, using the Island Mobile
Engineer: Mark Pinske
Remixed at UMRK, 1983

Frank conducts the
London Symphony Orchestra,
January 1983

9 JANUARY

The "*Perfect Stranger*", commissioned by Pierre Boulez for his Ensemble InterContemporain, was given its première in Paris.

10 – 11 JANUARY

Boulez recorded his sections of the Perfect Stranger album in Paris. During the following three months Zappa recorded his synclavier parts for the Perfect Stranger album at his UMRK studio in Los Angeles.

April issue of Larry Flynt's Hustler magazine carried a 21-page colour pictorial photo fantasy directed by Zappa of still photographs based on his Broadway play Thing Fish. The pictures featured Annie Ample's eponymous anatomy.

4 – 8 APRIL

Nineteenth Annual Festival Conference of the American Society of University Composers held at Ohio State University, Columbus, Ohio. Keynote speaker Frank Zappa was present for performances of his "Naval Aviation In Art", "Black Page #2" and the "Perfect Stranger" played by Relâche, the Columbus Symphony and the Pro Musica Chamber Orchestra.

20 MAY

Zappa premièred his synclavier versions of the works of the 18th c Italian cellist and composer Francesco Zappa in the "Speaking Of Music" series at the sensory museum, the Exploratorium, San Francisco, Ca. Zappa also spoke about his composition "Herb 'n' Mo's Vacation."

15 – 16 JUNE

Zellerbach Auditorium, University of California, Berkeley, CA. "A Zappa Affair". The American première of Zappa's symphonic works performed by the Berkeley Symphony Orchestra. 111 players performed "Herb 'n' Mo's Vacation" as a ballet performed by the life-size puppets of the San Francisco Miniature Theater. An opening night party attended by Zappa was open to anyone prepared to pay $50 a head as a fund-raiser for the orchestra.

20 JUNE

The Berkeley Symphony Orchestra performed "A Zappa Affair" at the San José Center for Performing Arts, San José, Ca.

Frank Zappa June - December US, Canada and European tour line-up: Frank Zappa – guitar, vocals / Ike Willis – guitar, vocals / Ray White – guitar, vocals / Bobby Martin – keyboards, vocals / Napoleon Murphy Brock – saxophone, vocals [for the first week of the tour only] / Scott Thunes – bass / Chad Wackerman – drums / Alan Zevod – keyboards.

JUNE

Band rehearsals for "Twentieth Anniversary World Tour".

18 – 22 JULY

Palace Theater, Los Angeles, Ca.

24 JULY

State University, San Diego, Ca.

25 JULY

Civic Center, Santa Cruz, Ca.

27 JULY

Greek Theater, Berkeley, Ca.

29 JULY

Santa Barbara, Ca. Napoleon Murphy Brock leaves the band. On a TV interview Frank Zappa explained that Napoleon Murphy Brock was no longer with the tour band because…

"chemical alteration is not something that mixes well with precision performance."

31 JULY

Celebrity Theater, Phoenix, Az.

1 AUGUST

Paolo Soleri Amphitheater, Santa Fe, NM.

2 – 4 AUGUST

Turn of the Century Mardi Gras, Denver, Co.

5 AUGUST

Omaha, Na.

7 AUGUST

Civic Center, Des Moines, Iowa.

8 AUGUST

Minneapolis, Minn.

10 AUGUST

Milwaukee, Wi.

11 AUGUST

Oscar Meyer Theater, Madison, Wi.

12 AUGUST

Blossom Music Center, Cleveland, Ohio.

13 AUGUST
Garden State Arts Center, Holmdale, NJ.

15 AUGUST
Canadian National Grandstand, Toronto, Canada.

16 AUGUST
Jones Beach Theater, Wantagh, NY.

18 AUGUST
The Pavilion, Chicago, Ill.

19 AUGUST
Cincinnati, Ohio.

22 AUGUST
Vogue Theater, Indianapolis, Ind.

23 AUGUST
Meadowbrook, Rochester, NY.

**BOULEZ CONDUCTS ZAPPA:
THE PERFECT STRANGER**
[Album 39] released.

24 AUGUST
Detroit, Mi.

25 – 26 AUGUST
The Pier, NYC.

27 AUGUST
State Fairgrounds, Syracuse, NY.

29 AUGUST
Mid Hudson Civic Center, Poughkeepsie, NY.

30 AUGUST
Merriweather Post Pavilion, Columbia, Md.

31 AUGUST
Winter Island, Salem, Mass.

1 SEPTEMBER
Saratoga Performing Arts Center, Saratoga Springs, NY.

2 SEPTEMBER
Columbia, Tenn.

4 SEPTEMBER
Columbus, Ohio.

7 SEPTEMBER
Voorst Nationaal Hal, Brussels, Belgium.

8 SEPTEMBER
Motocross Stadion, Ahlen, Germany.

9 SEPTEMBER
Loreley-Freilichtbuhne, St. Goarshausen, Germany.

11 SEPTEMBER
Deutschlandhalle, Berlin, Germany.

12 SEPTEMBER
Lund, Norway.

13 SEPTEMBER
Drammenshallen, Oslo, Norway.

14 SEPTEMBER
Johanneshov Isstadion, Stockholm, Sweden.

16 SEPTEMBER
The Ahoy, Rotterdam, Holland.

17 SEPTEMBER
Palais Omnisports de Bercy, Paris, France.

19 SEPTEMBER
Palacio Municipal Desports, Barcelona, Spain.

20 SEPTEMBER
Velodrome Anoeta, San Sebastian, Spain.

21 SEPTEMBER
Palais des Sports, Toulouse, France.

22 SEPTEMBER
Palais de la Beaujoire, Nantes, France.

24 – 25 SEPTEMBER
Hammersmith Odeon, London.

27 SEPTEMBER
Luxembourg.

28 SEPTEMBER
Philipshalle, Düsseldorf, Germany.

29 SEPTEMBER
Lille, France.

30 SEPTEMBER
Espace Tony Carnier, Lyons, France.

Boulez Conducts Zappa *The Perfect Stranger* No 9 on Billboard Classical chart.

1 OCTOBER
Stuttgart, Germany.

2 OCTOBER
Sporthalle, Boblingen, Germany.

3 OCTOBER
Circus Krone, Munich, Germany.

4 OCTOBER
Stadthalle, Vienna, Austria.

6 OCTOBER
Le Stadium, Marseilles, France.

7 OCTOBER
Théâtre de Verdure, Nice, France.

8 OCTOBER
Palasport, Genoa, Italy.

9 OCTOBER
Teatro Nazionale, Milan, Italy.

10 OCTOBER
Viareggio, Italy.

11 OCTOBER
Venice, Italy.

12 OCTOBER
Teatro Tenda, Bologna, Italy.

13 OCTOBER
Palasport, Rome, Italy.

14 OCTOBER
Naples, Italy.

15 OCTOBER
Palazzo de la Sport, Padova, Italy.

20 OCTOBER
Coliseum, New Haven, Ct.

25 OCTOBER
E.M. Loews Theater, Worcester, Ma.

26 OCTOBER
The Civic Center, Providence, RI.

27 OCTOBER
Coliseum, New Haven, Ct.

28 OCTOBER
Fine Arts Center Concert Hall, Amherst College, Amherst, Mass.

**BOULEZ CONDUCTS
ZAPPA: THE PERFECT
STRANGER**
US Angel D5 38170
Released 23 August 1984

UK HMV CEC 747 125 2
Released January 1985
UK CD Zappa CDZAP 49

Side 1:
1. The Perfect Stranger /
2. Naval Aviation In Art? / 3. The Girl In The Magnesium Dress

Side 2:
Dupree's Paradise / 2. Love Story / 3. Outside Now Again / 4. Jonestown

Line-up:
Tracks 1, 2 and 4 performed by the Ensemble InterContemporain, conducted by and directed by Pierre Boulez and consisting of 29 players / Side 1 track 3 and Side 2 performed by the Barking Pumpkin Digital Gratification Consort

Producer: Frank Zappa
The Ensemble InterContemporain tracks were recorded at IRCAM in Paris on 10 and 11 January 1984 / The Barking Pumpkin Digital Gratification Consort tracks (Zappa on the synclavier) were recorded over the following three month period at Zappa's Utility Muffin Research Kitchen studio
Engineers: Didier Arditi at IRCAM: and Bob Stone at UMRK
Remixed at UMRK by Spencer Chrislu in 1992
Computer programmer for the UMRK material was David Ocker

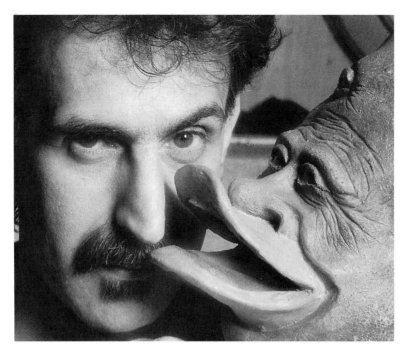

31 OCTOBER
Felt Forum, NYC. Hallowe'en show.

NOVEMBER
FRANCESCO ZAPPA [Album 40]
released.

Gail Zappa came across the listing for
the eighteenth century Italian composer
Francesco Zappa while looking up her
husband in volume 20 of the new edition
of The New Grove Dictionary Of Music And
Musicians, (MacMillan, 1980). They made
enquiries and Michael Keller, librarian at
the Music Library of the University of
California at Berkeley provided the Zappas
with copies of his predecessor's work.
It is easy to see why this is "His first
digital recording in over 200 years."

2 NOVEMBER
The Forum, Montreal, Canada.

3 NOVEMBER
State University of NY at Stoneybrook, NY.

4 NOVEMBER
Syracuse, NY.

6 NOVEMBER
Halifax, Nova Scotia, Canada.

8 NOVEMBER
Montreal, Quebec, Canada.

9 NOVEMBER
Orpheum Theater, Boston, Mass.

10 NOVEMBER
Tower Theater, Philadelphia, Pa.

11 NOVEMBER
Chrysler Arena, Norfolk, Va.

13 NOVEMBER
Constitution Hall, Washington DC.

14 NOVEMBER
Cleveland, Ohio.

16 NOVEMBER
Alumni Arena, State University of NY
at Buffalo, Buffalo, NY.

17 NOVEMBER
Syria Mosque, Pittsburgh, Pa.

18 NOVEMBER
Columbus, Ohio.

20 NOVEMBER
Louisville, Ky.

21 NOVEMBER
Royal Oak Music Hall, Detroit, Mi.

23 NOVEMBER
Bismarck Theater, Chicago, Ill.

24 NOVEMBER
Kiel Auditorium, St. Louis, Mo.

25 NOVEMBER
Fox Theater, Atlanta, Ga.

29 NOVEMBER
Orlando, Fl.

30 NOVEMBER
Sunrise Musical Theater,
Fort Lauderdale, Fl.

1 DECEMBER
The Bay Front Arena, St. Petersburg, Fl.

3 DECEMBER
McCalister Auditorium, New Orleans, L.A.

4 DECEMBER
Memphis, Tenn.

6 DECEMBER
Oklahoma City, Ok.

8 DECEMBER
Uptown Theater, Kansas City, Ks.

10 DECEMBER
Majestic Performing Arts Center,
San Antonio, Tx.

11 DECEMBER
Palmer Auditorium, Austin, Tx.

12 DECEMBER
Houston, Tx.

13 DECEMBER
Reunion Hall, State Fair Pavilion,
Dallas, Tx.

15 DECEMBER
Salt Lake City, Ut.

17 DECEMBER
Paramount Theater, Seattle, Wa.

18 DECEMBER
Queen Elizabeth Theater, Vancouver,
BC, Canada.

20 DECEMBER
Arlene Schwitzer Theater, Portland, Or.

21 DECEMBER
THEM OR US [Album 41].
(Double album) released.

The inclusion of Duane Allman's "Whippin'
Post" as an encore caused much surprise
among critics. Zappa explained…
**"I'll tell you how it happened.
We were playing Helsinki, Finland
about six or eight years ago, and in
the middle of this very quiet, nice
concert hall from the back of the
room a voice rings out, 'Whipping
Post.' And I thought, if we only knew
it we could blow this guy's socks off.
You know it would be great to just…
sure, fuck you, 'Whipping Post'…
all right, here it is. So, when we got
Bobbie Martin in the band I said, he
can sing the shit out of 'Whipping**

Post' and so let's go for it. The band said, 'God damn right, let's do it.' They love it. They enjoy playing it.

"I never listened to The Allman Brothers' music. I like 'Whippin' Post' though. In fact, I think they even premièred it when we were working together at this pop festival at the baseball stadium in Atlanta years and years and years ago. It was the first time I heard this song and I liked it then, thought it was really good but I am not an Allman Brothers consumer." [Zappa: 1982]

"My son Ahmet walked around the house one day singing a song that he made up called 'Frogs With Dirty Little Lips.' The words would change every day, and I'd always try to get him to sing it, you know, because I thought, what a great concept, 'Frogs With Dirty Little Lips.' But he kind of lost interest in it, so while I was in Detroit I had fifteen minutes before the soundcheck – got out a pen and finished that song. I wrote 'Frogs With Dirty Little Lips,' and I'm hoping we can get it ready in time to give him a surprise when we play L.A." [Zappa: 1982]

21 DECEMBER
THINGFISH [Album 42]
(Boxed set three albums) released.

"It's about a guy with a head like a potato and a face like a duck. Well, actually it's worse than that. The way he (the protagonist) gets turned into that is because the evil prince has invented a disease hoping to get rid of all unwanted

highly rhythmic individuals heretofore."

The prince plans to spread the disease through a men's cologne but tries it out first. The results make the subjects...
"so ugly they can't get normal work so they wind up on Broadway... It's weird stuff."

Though Zappa wrote Thing Fish as an original Broadway show, it is perhaps not surprising that it never opened on the Great White Way.

21 DECEMBER
Circle Star Theater, San Carlos, Ca.

22 DECEMBER
Fresno, Ca.

23 DECEMBER
Universal Amphitheater, Los Angeles, Ca.
This was to be the last tour until the ill-fated 1988 tour.

FRANCESCO ZAPPA
US Barking Pumpkin ST 74202
Released November 1984
(listed on CD as album 42 but in fact released before the two subsequent albums)
The Barking Pumpkin Digital Gratification Consort playing the music of Francesco Zappa (flourished 1763-1788)

Side 1:
Opus One:
1. 1st Movement Andante; 2nd Movement Allegro Con Brio / 2. 1st Movement Andantino; 2nd Movement Minuetto Grazioso / 3. 1st Movement Andante; 2nd Movement Presto / 4. 1st Movement Andante; 2nd Movement Allegro / 5. 2nd Movement Minuetto Grazioso / 6. 1st Movement Largo; 2nd Movement Minuet

Opus IV:
1. 1st Movement Andantino; 2nd Movement Allegro Assai/ 2. 2nd Movement Allegro Assai/ No. 3. 1st Movement Andante; 2nd Movement Tempo De Minuetto / 4. 1st Movement Minuetto

Line-up:
The Barking Pumpkin Digital Gratification Consort
(Zappa on the synclavier)
Recorded at UMRK Central
Engineers: Bob Stone and Mark Pinske, second engineer Tom Ehle
Synclavier document encryptation by David Ocker

THEM OR US
(double album)
US SVBO 742000
Released 21 December 1984
US CD Rykodisc RCD 40027
Released 1986

UK EMI EN 2402343
Released December 1984
UK CD Zappa CDZAP 30
Released 1990

Side 1:
1. The Closer You Are / 2. In France / 3. Ya Hozna / 4. Sharleena

Side 2:
1. Sinister Footwear II / 2. Truck Driver Divorce / 3. Stevie's Spanking

Side 3:
1. Baby, Take Your Teeth Out / 2. Marqueson's Chicken / 3. Planet Of My Dreams

Side 4:
1. Be In My Video / 2. Them Or Us / 3. Frogs With Dirty Little Lips

On CD release only addition final track: Whippin' Post

Line-up:
Frank Zappa - lead guitar, vocals / Steve Vai - guitar / Ray White - rhythm guitar, vocals / Tommy Mars - keyboards / Bobby Martin - keyboards, saxophone, vocals / Ed Mann - percussion / Scott Thunes - bass / Chad Wackerman - drums / Roy

Estrada - vocals / Ike Willis - vocals / Bob Harris - vocals / Arthur Barrow - keyboards, bass, micro-bass, rhythm guitar / Vinnie Colaiuta - drums

Producer: Frank Zappa
Recorded at UMRK
Engineers: Mark Pinske, Bob Stone. Digitally remixed at UMRK 1990 for CD release

THINGFISH
(boxed set three albums)
US SCKO 74201
Released 21 December 1984
US CD Rykodisc RCD 100/21
Released 1986

UK Capitol EX 24 0294 3
Released 1985
UK CD (double)
Zappa CDDZAP 21
Released 1990

Side 1:
1. Prologue / 2. The Mammy Nuns / 3. Harry & Rhonda / 4. Galoot Up-Date

Side 2:
1. The 'Torchum' Never Stops / 2. That Evil Prince / 3. You Are What You Is.

Side 3:
1. Mudd Club / 2. The Meek Shall Inherit Nothing / 3. Clowns On Velvet / 4. Harry-As-A-Boy / 5. He's So Gay

Side 4:
1. The Massive Improve'lence / 2. Artificial Rhonda / 3. The

Crab-Grass Baby / 4. The White Boy Troubles

Side 5:
1. No Not Now / 2. Briefcase Boogie / 3. Brown Moses.

Side 6:
1. Wistful Wit A Fist-Full / 2. Drop Dead / 3. Won Ton On

Line-up:
The cast: Ike Willis - Thing Fish / Terry Bozzio - Harry / Dale Bozzio - Rhonda / Napoleon Murphy Brock - Evil Prince / Bob Harris - Harry-as-a-boy / Johnny 'Guitar' Watson - Brown Moses / Ray White - Owl-Gonkwin-Jane Cowhoon
(The Zappa Records CD has a revised version of 'He's So Gay' with Johnny 'Guitar' Watson rapping)
The Musicians: Frank Zappa - guitar, synclavier / Steve Vai - guitar / Ray White - guitar / Tommy Mars - keyboards / Chuck Wild - Broadway piano / Arthur Barrow - bass / Scott Thunes - bass / Jay Anderson - string bass / Ed Mann - percussion / Chad Wackermann - drums / Steve De Furia - synclavier programmer / David Ocker - synclavier programmer

Producer: Frank Zappa
Recorded at UMRK
Digitally remixed 1989 for CD release
Engineers: Mark Pinske, Bob Stone

Above: Ahmet, Dweezil and Moon Unit Zappa

– 1985 –

19 APRIL
The Kronos Quartet play Zappa at
Schoenberg Hall, University of California
at Los Angeles.

THE OLD MASTERS
[Album 43] released.

OCTOBER
**FRANK ZAPPA MEETS THE MOTHERS
OF PREVENTION**
[Album 44] released.

– 1986 –

DOES HUMOR BELONG IN MUSIC
released.

Throughout 1985 and 1986, Zappa
was very actIve in counterattacking the
rock-censorshIp drIve sponsored by the
wives of Washington politicians, led by
Tipper Gore. Zappa sent out packages of
InformatIon and press clippIngs from the
BarkIng PumpkIn Records.
   **"I've spent up to $70,000 of
my own money that I've put into a
combination of my travel, printing
costs and phone bills just to keep
pressure on the other side. I've done
maybe 300 talk shows and interviews. And those Z-Pacs are still
going out the door. I will continue
to do it as long as people call up.
[Call 818-PUM-PKIN for information
on how to get one.]" [Zappa: 1986]**

25 OCTOBER
THE OLD MASTERS - BOX 2
[Album 45] (9 album boxed set) released.

15 NOVEMBER
JAZZ FROM HELL [Album 46] released.

– 1987 –

17 JUNE
JOE'S GARAGE ACTS 1, 2 & 3
(3 album boxed set) released.

17 SEPTEMBER
**THE LONDON SYMPHONY ORCHESTRA:
ZAPPA VOL 2**
[Album 47] released.

THE OLD MASTERS - BOX 3
(9 album boxed set) released.

THE OLD MASTERS - BOX 1
(7 album boxed set)
Barking Pumpkin BPR 7777
Released 19 April 1985

Records 1 and 2: Freak Out, double album / Record 3: Absolutely Free / Record 4: We're Only In It For The Money / Record 5: Lumpy Gravy / Record 6: Crusin' With Ruben And The Jets / Record 7: Mystery Disc / All records digitally 'refurbished' otherwise as originally issued, in original sleeves, with original inserts, except Mystery Disc which contains previously unreleased material and Freak Out has a bonus track: 'It Can't Happen Here' on Side 3

Mystery Disc

Side 1:
1. Theme From 'Run Home Slow' / 2. Original 'Duke Of Prunes' / 3. Opening Night Party at Studio 7 (collage) / 4. The Village Inn / 5. Steal Away / 6. I Was A Teenage Malt Shop / 7. The Birth Of Captain Beefheart / 8. Metal Man Has Won His Wings / 9. Power Trio Segment From The Saints 'N' Sinners / 10: Bossa Nova Pervertamento / 11. Excerpt From The Uncle Frankie Show / 12. Charva

Side 2:
1. Speed Freak Boogie / 2. Original Mothers At The Broadside (Pomona) / 3. Party Scene From Mondo Hollywood / 4. Original Mothers Rehearsal / 5. How Could I Be Such A Fool? / 6. Band Introductions At The Fillmore West / 7. Plastic People / 8. Original Mothers At The Fillmore East / 9. Why Don'tcha Do Me Right? / 10. Big Leg Emma

Producer: Frank Zappa. Assembled from a wide variety of sources

FRANK ZAPPA MEETS THE MOTHERS OF PREVENTION
US Barking Pumpkin
ST 74203
Released October 1985
US CD RCD
Rykodisc RCD 10023
Released 1986

UK EMI EMC 3507
Released February 1986
UK CD (w/Jazz From Hell)
EMI CDP 790 078 2

Released 1988
UK CD Zappa CDZAP 33
(Digitally remixed)
Released 1990

Tracks on US release:

Side 1:
1. We're Turning Again / 2. Alien Orifice / 3. Yo Cats

Side 2:
1. What's New In Baltimore? / 2. Little Beige Sambo / 3. Porn Wars / 4. Aerobics In Bondage

Tracks on UK release:

Side 1:
1. We're Turning Again / 2. Alien Orifice / 3. Yo Cats

Side 2:
1. What's New In Baltimore? / 2. I Don't Even Care / 3. One Man One Vote / 4. HR 2911 / 5. Little Beige Sambo / 6. Aerobics In Bondage (the 12 minute 'Porn Wars' was replaced as Zappa did not think it would make any sense in Britain)

CD release:
1. Porn Wars / 2. We're Turning Again / 3. Alien Orifice / 4. Aerobics In Bondage / 5. I Don't Even Care / 6. Little Beige Sambo / 7. What's New In Baltimore / 8. One Man One Vote / 9. HR 2911 / 10. Yo Cats

Line-up:
Frank Zappa - guitar, vocal and synclavier (most of Side 2) / Steve Vai - guitar / Ray White - guitar, vocal / Ike Willis - guitar, vocal / Tommy Mars - keyboards / Bobby Martin - keyboards, vocal / Scott Thunes - bass / Chad Wackermann - drums / Ed Mann - percussion / Moon Unit Zappa - voice / Dweezil Zappa - voice / Senator Danforth - voice / Senator Hollings - voice / Senator Trible - voice / Senator Hawkins - voice / Senator Exon - voice / Senator Gorton - voice / Senator Gore - voice / Tipper Gore - voice / Rev. Jeff Ling - voice / Spider Barbour - voice / All Nite John - voice / Unknown Girl In Piano - voice

Producer: Frank Zappa
Recorded at UMRK, 1985
Digitally remixed for CD at UMRK by Bob Stone, 1990
Engineer: Bob Stone
Computer assistant: Bob Rice

DOES HUMOR BELONG IN MUSIC
CD EMI CDP 7-46188-2
(UK and Germany only)
Released 1986

1. Zoot Allures / 2. Tinsel-Town Rebellion / 3. Trouble Every Day / 4. Penguin In Bondage / 5. Hot-Plate Heaven At The Green Hotel / 6. What's New In Baltimore? / 7. Cock-Suckers' Ball / 8. WPLJ / 9. Let's Move To Cleveland / 10. Whippin' Post

Line-up:
Frank Zappa - lead guitar, vocal / Ray White - guitar, vocal / Ike Willis - guitar, vocal / Bobby Martin - keyboards, vocal / Alan Zevod - keyboards / Scott Thunes - bass / Chad Wackermann - drums

---

Tracks differ from the EMI video of the same name and packaging / The CD was issued without Zappa's permission and was withdrawn

THE OLD MASTERS - BOX 2
(9 album boxed set)
Barking Pumpkin BPR 8888
Released 25 October 1986

Records 1 and 2: Uncle Meat, double album / Record 3: Hot Rats / Record 4: Burnt Weenie Sandwich / Record 5: Weasels Ripped My Flesh / Record 6: Chunga's Revenge / Record 7: Fillmore East '71 / Record 8: Just Another Band From L.A. / Record 9: Mystery Disc 2

All records digitally 'refurbished' otherwise as originally issued, in original sleeves, with original inserts, except Mystery Disc which contains previously unreleased material

Mystery Disc 2:

Side 1:
1. Harry You're A Beast / 2. Don Interrupts / 3. Piece One / 4. Jim / Roy / 5. Piece Two / 6. Agency Man

Side 2:
1. Agency Man, Studio Version,

Apostolic, NYC, 1967 / 2. Lecture / 3. Wedding Dress Song / The Handsome Cabin Boy, From The Uncle Meat Sessions, 1967 / 4. Skweezit, Skweezit, Skweezit, From The Ballroom, Hartford, CT / 5. The Story Of Willie The Pimp, With Annie Zannas & Cynthia Dobson / 6. Black Beauty, From Thee Image, Miami, 1968 / 7. Chucha, From Criteria, Miami, 1968 / 8. Mothers At KPFA / 9. Harmonica Fun

Producer: Frank Zappa
Side 1 and 'Lecture' recorded at the Festival Hall, London 1968

JAZZ FROM HELL
US Barking Pumpkin ST 74205
Released 15 November 1986
US CD Rykodisc RCD 10030
Released 1987

UK EMI EMC 3521
Released 1986
UK CD (w/Frank Zappa Meets The Mothers Of Prevention)
EMI CDP 790 078 2

Released 1988
UK CD Zappa CDZAP 32
(digitally remixed at UMRK)
Released 1990

Side 1:
1. Night School / 2. The Beltway Bandits / 3. While You Were Art II / 4. Jazz From Hell

Side 2:
1. G-Spot Tornado / 2. Damp Ankles / 3. St.Etienne / 4. Massaggio Galore

Line-up:
Frank Zappa - guitar / Steve Vai - rhythm guitar / Ray White - rhythm guitar / Tommy Mars - keyboards / Bobby Martin - keyboards / Scott Thunes - bass / Chad Wackermann - drums / Ed Mann - percussion

Producer: Frank Zappa
Recorded at UMRK, 1986
Engineer: Bob Stone
Computer assistant: Rob Rice

JOE'S GARAGE ACTS 1, 2 & 3
(3 album boxed set)
US Barking Pumpkin
SWCL 74206
Released 17 June 1987
Rykodisc RCD 10060/61
(double CD)
Released 17 June 1987

UK EMI FZAP 1
Released 1988
UK CD EMI CDS 790087-2
Released 1987

(Digitally remixed at UMRK and re-issued as Zappa CDDZAP 20-in January 1990)

THE LONDON SYMPHONY ORCHESTRA: ZAPPA VOLUME 2
US Barking Pumpkin SJ 74207
Released 17 September 1987
Side 1:
1. Bogus Pomp

Side 2:
1. Bob In Dacron
2. Strictly Genteel

Line-up:
Chad Wackermann - drum set / Ed Mann - featured percussionist / The London Symphony Orchestra of 102 players, conducted by Kent Nagano / Ashley Arbuckle - concert master /

Producer: Frank Zappa
Recorded at Twickenham Film Studios, London 12-14 January 1983, using the Island Mobile
Engineer: Mark Pinske
Remixed at UMRK

-1988-

Frank Zappa Jan - May "Broadway The Hard Way Tour" East Coast and European tour line-up: Frank Zappa - guitar, vocal / Scott Thunes - bass / Chad Wackermann - drums; Bobby Martin - keyboards, vocal / Ed Mann - percussion, vocal / Mike Keneally - guitar, keyboards, vocal / Bruce Fowler - trumpet / Walt Fowler - trumpet, flugelhorn, synthesizer / Albert Wing - tenor saxophone, flute / Paul Carmen - alto saxophone, baritone saxophone, flute / Kurt McGettrick - baritone saxophone, bass saxophone, clarinet.

JANUARY
Band rehearsals for the world tour held in Los Angeles.

2 FEBRUARY
Palace Theater, Albany, NY.

4-6 FEBRUARY
Beacon Theater, NYC.

8-10 FEBRUARY
Warner Theater, Washington, DC.

12-14 FEBRUARY
Tower Theater, Upper Darby, Philadelphia, Pa.

16-17 FEBRUARY
Bushnell Memorial Hall, Hartford, Ct.

19-20 FEBRUARY
Orpheum Theater, Boston, Mass.

23 FEBRUARY
Mid Hudson Civic Center, Poughkeepsie, NY.

25 FEBRUARY
Syria Mosque, Pittsburgh, Pa.

26-28 FEBRUARY
Royal Oak Theater, Troy, Detroit, Mi.

1 MARCH
Frauenthal Auditorium, Muskegon, Mi.

3-4 MARCH
Auditorium Theater, Chicago, Ill.

5 MARCH
Cleveland Music Hall, Cleveland, Ohio.

6 MARCH
Veterans' Memorial Hall, Columbus, Ohio.

8 MARCH
Syria Mosque, Pittsburgh, Pa.

9 MARCH
Shea's Theater, Buffalo, NY.

11 MARCH
War Memorial Auditorium, Rochester, NY.

12 MARCH
Memorial Auditorium, Burlington, Vt.

13 MARCH
Civic Center, Springfield, Mass.

15 MARCH
Cumberland County Civic Center, Portland, Mass.

16 MARCH
Civic Center, Providence, RI.

17 MARCH
Broome County Veterans Memorial Arena, Binghamton, NY.

19 MARCH
Memorial Hall, Muhlenburg College, Allentown, Pa.

20 MARCH
Rothman Center, Fairleigh Dickenson University, Teaneck, NJ.

21 MARCH
Landmark Theater, Syracuse, NY.

23 MARCH
Towson Center, Towson, Md.

24 MARCH
The Spectrum, Philadelphia, Pa.

25 MARCH
Nassau Veterans' Memorial Coliseum, Uniondale, NY.

APRIL
GUITAR [Album 48] (double CD) released.
The tour resumed in France:

9 APRIL
Le Stadium, Bourges.

10 APRIL
Sportpalais, Ghent, Belgium.

12 APRIL
Deutschlandhalle, Berlin, Germany.

13 APRIL
Stadthalle, Offenbach, Germany.

14 APRIL
Sporthalle, Köln, Germany.

16 APRIL
Brighton Conference Centre, Brighton, UK.

18-19 APRIL
Wembley Arena, London, UK.

20 APRIL
National Exhibition Centre, Birmingham, UK.

22 APRIL
Carl Diem Halle, Würzburg, Germany.

24 APRIL
Stadthalle, Bremen, Germany.

25 APRIL
Falkoner Theater, Copenhagen, Denmark.

26 APRIL
Olympen, Lund, Sweden.

27 APRIL
Skedsmohallen, Oslo, Norway.

29 APRIL
Isshalen, Helsinki, Finland.

1 MAY
Isstadion, Stockholm, Sweden.

3-4 MAY
The Ahoy, Rotterdam, Holland.

5 MAY
Westfallenhalle, Dortmund, Germany.

6 MAY
CCH, Hamburg, Germany.

8 MAY
Stadthalle, Vienna, Austria.

9 MAY
Rudi Sedlmeyer Halle, Munich, Germany.

11 MAY
Hallenstadion, Zurich, Switzerland.

13 MAY
Velodrome, Bilbao, Spain.

14 MAY
Palacio des Desportes, Madrid, Spain.

15 MAY
Prado de San Sebastian, Seville, Spain.

17 MAY
Palacio des Desportes, Barcelona, Spain.

18 MAY
Le Zenith, Montpellier, France.

19 MAY
Le Summun, Grenoble, France.

20-21 MAY
Le Zenith, Paris, France.

GUITAR
US CD (double CD)
Rykodisc RCD 10079/80
Released 1988
Barking Pumpkin (double album)
BPR 74212
Released April 1988

UK CD (double CD)
Zappa CDDZAP 6
Released 1988
ZAPPA 6 (double album)
Released 1988

CD 1:
1. Sexual Harassment In The Workplace / 2. Which One Is It? / 3. Republicans / 4. Do Not Pass Go / 5. Chalk Pie / 6. In-A-Gadda-Stravinsky / 7. That's Not Really Reggae / 8. When No One Was No One / 9. Once Again, Without The Net / 10. Outside Now (Original Solo) / 11. Jim & Tammy's Upper Room / 12. Were We Ever Really Safe In San Antonio? / 13. That Ol' G Minor Thing Again / 14. Hotel Atlanta Incidentals / 15. That's Not Really A Shuffle / 16. Move It or Park it / 17. Sunrise Redeemer

CD 2:
1. Variations On Sinister #3 / 2. Orrin Hatch On Skis / 3. But Who Was Fulcanelli? / 4. For Duane / 5. GOA / 6. Winos Do Not March / 7. Swans? What Swans? / 8. Too Ugly For Show Business / 9. Systems Of Edges / 10. Do Not Try This At Home / 11. Things That Look Like Meat / 12. Watermelon In Easter Hay / 13. Canadian Customs / 14. Is That All There Is? / 15. It Ain't Necessarily The Saint James Infirmary

The following tracks were not on the album release: 'Which One Is It?' 'Chalk Pie'; 'In-A-Gadda-Stravinsky' / 'Hotel Atlanta Incidentals' / 'That's Not Really A Shuffle' / 'Variations On Sinister #3' / 'Orrin Hatch On Skis' / 'Swans? What Swans?' / 'Too Ugly For Show Business' / 'Do Not Try This At Home' / 'Canadian Customs' / 'Is That All There Is?' and 'It Ain't Necessarily The Saint James Infirmary'

Recorded live using various line-ups: Frank Zappa - lead guitar / Ray White - rhythm guitar, except on CD 1 track 10 and CD 2 track 9 / Steve Vai - stunt guitar except CD 1 tracks 3, 6, 7, 9, 10, 12, 14 and 17, CD 2 tracks 1, 2, 4, 5, 6, 9, 12 and 13 / Tommy Mars - keyboards except CD 1 tracks 3, 6, 7, 9, 12, 14 and 17, CD 2 tracks 1, 2, 4, 5, 6, 11, 12 and 13 / Bobby Martin - keyboards except CD 1 track 10, CD 2 track 9 / Ed Mann - percussion except CD 1 tracks 3, 6, 7, 9, 12, 14 and 17, CD 2 tracks 1, 2, 4, 5, 6,12 and 13 / Scott Thunes - bass except CD 1 track 10, CD 2 track 9 / Chad Wackermann - drums except CD 1 track 10, CD 2 track 9 / Ike

Willis - rhythm guitar except on CD 1 tracks 1, 2, 4, 5, 8, 10, 11, 13, 15 and 16, CD 2 tracks 3, 7-11, 14 and 15 / Alan Zavod - keyboards except CD 1 tracks 1, 2, 4, 5, 8, 10, 11, 13, 15 and 16, CD 2 tracks 3, 7-11, 14 and 15; On 'Outside Now (Original Solo)' and 'Systems of Edges' / Denny Walley - slide guitar / Warren Cucurullo - rhythm guitar / Arthur Barrow - bass / Vinnie Colaiuta - drums

Recorded live at various locations:

CD 1:
1. Civic Center, San Diego, Ca, 12 December 1981, 2nd show / 2. Munich, Germany, June 1982 / 3. Tower Theater, Philadelphia, Pa, 10 November 1984, 2nd show / 4. Hammersmith Odeon, London, 19 June 1982 / 5.Salt Lake City, Utah, December 1981 / 6. Memphis, Tenn, 4 December 1984 / 7. Hammersmith Odeon, London, 25 September 1984 / 8. Sporthalle, Cologne, Germany, 21 May 1982 / 9. Portland, Or, 20 December 1984 / 10. Rudi-Sedlmayer-halle, Munich, 31 March 1979 - 2nd show / 11. Bordeaux, France, 31 June 1982 / 12. Majestic, San Antonio, Tx, 10 December 1984 / 13. Zurich, Switzerland, June 1982 / 14. Atlanta, Ga, November 1984 / 15. Dijon, France, June 1982 / 16. Alte Opera, Frankfurt, Germany, 11 June 1982 / 17. Sunrise Musical Theater, Fort Lauderdale, Fl, 30 November 1984

CD 2:
1. Madison, Wi, 11 August 1984 / 2. Fort Lauderdale, Fl, November 1984 / 3. Sporthalle, Cologne, Germany / 21 June 1982 / 4. Fox, Atlanta, Ga, 25 November 1984 / 5. Bismarck Theater, Chicago, Ill, 23 November 1984, 2nd show / 6. Fort Lauderdale, Fl, November 1984 / 7. San Diego, Ca, December 1981 / 8. Berkeley, Ca, December 1981 / 9. Rhein-Mainhalle, Wiesbaden, Germany, March 27, 1979, 2nd show / 10. Milan, Italy, July 1982 / 11. Salt Lake City, Utah, December 1981/ 12. Jones Beach Theater, NY, 16 August 1984 / 13. Vancouver, BC, 12 December 1984 / 14. Düsseldorf, Germany, 22 May 1982 / 15. Pistoia, Italy, July 1982

Producer: Frank Zappa
Engineer: Mark Pinske using the UMRK Remote except CD 1 tracks 7 and 10, CD 2 track 9
CD 1 track 7 is unknown
Klaus Wiedermann using a Scully Remote on CD 1 track 10 and CD 2 track 9
Remixed by Bob Stone at UMRK April 1988

one hour of material). From the begining we have been asking ourselves: 'How will we ever cram all this stuff into a normal vinyl release?' The only practical answer seems to be this double LP sampler. For those of you who don't own CD players yet, this release provides an 80-minute sneak preview of material from Volume One, as well as future You Can't Do That On Stage Anymore releases. We hope that you enjoy it, and that it provides some incentive for the acquisition of a CD player, and that eventually you get to hear the whole collection in the medium for which it was created."

1 JUNE
Palasport, Padova, Italy.

2 JUNE
Palatrussardi, Milan, Italy.

3 JUNE
Palasport, Turin, Italy.

5 JUNE
Palasport, Modena, Italy.

6 JUNE
Palasport, Florence, Italy.

7 JUNE
Palaeur, Rome, Italy.

9 JUNE
Palasport, Genova, Italy (final gig).

Frank was not very involved in the rehearsals for, or during, the tour and whenever he was unable to attend, Scott Thunes was appointed as rehearsal leader. In carrying out this role, he was apparently abrasive, blunt and rude to the other members of the band and eventually two factions developed: with Frank, Scott Thunes and Mike Keneally on one side, and the remaining nine members of the band on the other. The atmosphere was so bad that it seriously affected the music, particularly during the concerts in Italy.

Before leaving Europe, Zappa went to each member of the band and explained to them that there were ten more weeks of concerts booked in the USA and asked them…
"If Scott is in the band, will you do the tour?"
With the exception of Keneally, all the members of the band said "No." Rather

23 MAY
Hall Tivoli, Strasbourg, France.

24 MAY
Martin Schleyer Halle, Stuttgart, Germany.

25 MAY
Mozartsaal, Mannheim, Germany.

26 MAY
Stadthalle, Fürth, Germany.

27 MAY
Radio FFN, Germany Zappa special…
Zappa: "The Wall must come down and I proposed at a press conference in Berlin (4/11/88) a way to bring it down and I would like to see it come down. And a strange thing happened two days after I did that press conference in Berlin and talked about the Wall. Sixty metres of the Wall fell down all by itself. Did you hear about this? It just crumbled

down onto the West side. Power of suggestion!" [Zappa: 1988]

28 MAY
Sporthalle, Linz, Austria.

29 MAY
Liebenau, Graz, Austria.

30 MAY
Palasport, Udine, Italy.

MAY
YOU CAN'T DO THAT ON STAGE ANYMORE SAMPLER released.

The reason for the sampler was explained by Zappa in his sleeve notes…
"You Can't Do That On Stage Anymore in its complete form has a playing time of more than 13 hours. It was designed primarily for release on CD (six double sets, with each disc including more than

than replace Thunes, Zappa cancelled almost three months' worth of concerts and took a big loss on the tour. He never toured again.

OCTOBER

BROADWAY THE HARD WAY

[Album 49] released.

YOU CAN'T DO THAT ON STAGE ANYMORE VOLUME 1 [Album 50]

(double CD set) released 1988.

In a 1986 interview Zappa said…

"What's coming out in the next release is a double CD called 'You Can't Do That On Stage Anymore' that takes live performances going back as far as 1968. The basic idea of that album is that today in live performance there are very few bands that are actually playing anything. They go onstage with a freeze-dried show, and in many cases at least fifty percent of the show is coming out of a sequencer or is lip synced. Audiences have missed out on the golden age, when people went onstage and took a chance, which was probably the main forte of the bands that I had. One of the great recordings on that CD is from London in 1978. We were playing a matinée, doing 'St. Alphonzo's Pancake Breakfast' and 'Don't Eat

YOU CAN'T DO THAT ON STAGE ANYMORE SAMPLER
US Barking Pumpkin BPR 74313
Released May 1988

UK Zappa ZAP 7
Released June 1988

Side 1:
1. Plastic People / 2. The Torture Never Stops

Side 2:
1. Montana (Whipping Floss) / 2. The Evil Prince / 3. You Call That Music?

Side 3:
1. Sharlena / 2. Nanook Rubs It

Side 4:
1. The Florida Airport Tape / 2. Once Upon A Time / 3. King Kong / 4. Dickie's Such An Asshole / 5. Cosmic Debris

Various line-ups and locations - see the six double CDs of You Can't Do That On Stage Anymore for details

Producer: Frank Zappa (who also arranged, compiled and edited the albums) Engineering supervision for the entire series: Bob Stone at UMRK

BROADWAY THE HARD WAY
US CD Rykodisc RCD 40096
US Album Barking Pumpkin D 174218
Released October 1988

UK CD Zappa CD ZAP 14
UK Album Zappa ZAPPA 14
Released June 1989

1. Elvis Has Just Left The Building / 2. Planet Of The Baritone Women / 3. Any Kind Of Pain / 4. Dickie's Such An Asshole (The San Clemente Magnetic Deviation) / 5.When The Lie's So Big / 6. Rhymin' Man / 7. Promiscuous / 8. The Untouchables (monologue by Ike Willis) / 9. Why Don't You Like Me? / 10. Bacon Fat / 11. Stolen Moments / 12. Murder By Numbers / 13. Jezebel Boy / 14. Outside Now / 15. Hot Plate Heaven At The Green Hotel / 16. What Kind Of Girl? / 17. Jesus Thinks You're A Jerk

Album has less tracks in a different order:
Side 1:
1. Elvis Has Just Left The Building / 2. Planet Of The Baritone Women / 3. Any Kind Of Pain / 4. Jesus Thinks You're A Jerk

Side 2:
Dickie's Such An Asshole (The San Clemente Magnetic Deviation) /

2. When The Lie's So Big / 3. Rhymin' Man / 4. Promiscuous / 5. The Untouchables (monologue by Ike Willis)

Line-up:
Frank Zappa - lead guitar, vocal / Ike Willis - rhythm guitar, vocal / Mike Keneally - rhythm guitar, synthesizer, vocal / Bobby Martin - keyboards, vocal / Ed Mann - percussion / Walt Fowler - trumpet / Bruce Fowler - trombone / Paul Carman - tenor saxophone / Kurt McGettrick - baritone saxophone / Scott Thunes - bass / Chad Wackermann - drums / Eric Buxton - guest vocalist

Producer: Frank Zappa

Recorded in various locations during the European and east coast USA tour of 1988: Side 1, track 1. Opening recorded at Martin Schleyer Halle, Stuttgart, Germany, May 24th remainder from the final show of the tour at Palasport, Genoa, Italy on 9 June / 2. Opening from Cleveland Music Hall, Cleveland, Ohio, 5 March remainder from Tower Theater, Upper Darby, Philadelphia, Pa. 12 February and other unknown concerts / 3. From many sources beginning Tower Theater, Upper Darby, Philadelphia, Pa. 12 February. Different portions of the song are edited together from concerts at Washington, DC, 9 February, Cleveland Music Hall, Cleveland, Ohio, 5 March and Falkoner Theater, Copenhagen, Denmark, 25 April, switching back and forth / 4. Washington DC, 9 February, Tivoli, Strasbourg, France, 23 May, Washington DC 8 February, Broome County Arena, Binghamton, NY, 17 March , Olympen, Lund,

Sweden, 24 April, Cleveland Music Hall, Cleveland, Ohio, 5 March / 5. Washington DC, 9 February and other locations / 6. Rudi Sedlmayer Halle, Munich, Germany, 9 May / 7. Royal Oak Theater, Troy, Detroit, 26 February / 8. Civic Center, Providence, RI, 16 March / 9. Bushnell Auditorium, Hartford, Ct, 17 February, Syria Mosque, Pittsburgh, Pa, 25 February, Tower Theater, Upper Darby, Philadelphia, Pa, 13 February and Auditorium Theater, Chicago, Ill, 3 March / 10 and 11. Frauenthal Auditorium, Muskegon, Mi, 1 March except trumpet solo on 10 which is from Auditorium Theater, Chicago, Ill, 3 March / 12. Auditorium Theater, Chicago, Ill, 3 March / 13. Tower Theater, Upper Darby, Philadelphia, Pa, 13 February / 14. Wembley Arena, London, 19 April, ending from Palasport, Genoa, Italy, 9 June / 15. Stadthalle, Vienna, Austria, 8 May and Rudi Sedlmayer Halle, Munich, Germany, 9 May / 16. Frauenthal Auditorium, Muskegon, Mi, 1 March and Auditorium Theater, Chicago, Ill, 4 March / 17. Collaged from more than 20 tape portions including: Tower Theater, Upper Darby, Philadelphia, Pa, 13 and 14 February Royal Oak Theater, Troy, Detroit, 26 February, Cumberland County Civic Center, Portland, Ma, 15 March, Rothman Center, Fairleigh Dickenson University, Teaneck, NJ, 20 March, Civic Center, Providence, RI, 16 March, Nassau Coliseum, Uniondale, NY, 25 March, Washington DC, 9 February Wembley Arena, London, 19 April, Shea's Theater, Buffalo, NY, 9 March and War Memorial Auditorium, Rochester, NY. 11 March.

the Yellow Snow,' and there was this guy in the audience, completely out of his mind, who wanted to recite poetry. He came up to the stage and kept interrupting the songs. So we worked him into the set, and the result is very strange - mass-audience poetry reading."

OCTOBER

YOU CAN'T DO THAT ON STAGE ANYMORE VOLUME 2: THE HELSINKI CONCERT [Album 51] (double CD set and Boxed set 3 records) released.

Zappa commented in the sleeve notes... **"This concert... was fun, in spite of the fact that Napoleon Murphy Brock had pneumonia and that Coy Feather-stone, our lighting director, had been maced in the face by a guard at the Hotel Hesperia the night before. The repertoire is basically the same as the Roxy album. However, the ultra-fast tempos on the more difficult tunes demonstrate what happens when a band has played the material for a year, and is so comfortable with it they could probably perform it blindfolded. This band had a lot of skill (and miserable touring equipment - it was always breaking down, and full of hums and buzzes). In spite of this, it has remained one of the audiences' favourite ensembles, and so, for those of you who crave what they used to do, we present a full concert with a little bit of everything -including stuff that you can't do on stage anymore."**

—1989—

Zappa made several trips to Moscow to make arrangements for licensing of his own recordings, but as he met more people there he became interested in economic collaboration outside the sphere of music and began to discuss straightforward business deals to do with film distribution, mail order selling and the licensed manufacture of products. Zappa started Why Not?, an international licensing, consulting and social engineering company to handle these extra-curricular sides of his business..

YOU CAN'T DO THAT ON STAGE ANYMORE: VOLUME THREE
[Album 52] (double CD set) released.

12 NOVEMBER

Pro-choice rally in Los Angeles, at Rancho Park, on 12 November 1989. The rally was attended by at least 100,000 people including luminaries such as Jane Fonda, Richard Dreyfus, and Jesse "Rhymin' Man" Jackson. Frank was accompanied by his entire family, augmented by niece, Lala, and brother-in-law, Uncle Jay.

—1990—

Mid-Jan: Zappa visited Moscow on behalf of the Financial News Network to find potential partners to establish an international business channel.

"There is a potential in a lot of different areas in the Soviet Union, but unfortunately there is still a lot of prejudice among us Americans when it comes to working together with the Russians. Still I reckon the first ones into the USSR will get to pick up the best deals. In any case, it is in our interest to work in the USSR. It is an enormous market and the competition is not necessarily all that hard in every field."

One of Zappa's ideas was for a media centre mainly for Western journalists working in Moscow which would be fully fitted out with the latest in communications equipment.

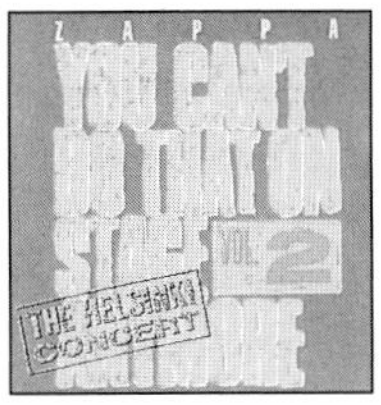

YOU CAN'T DO THAT ON STAGE ANYMORE VOLUME 1
(double CD set)
US Rykodisc RDC 10081/82
Released 1988

UK Zappa CDD ZAP 8
Released 1988

CD 1:
1. The Florida Airport Tape / 2. Once Upon A Time / 3. Sofa #1 / 4. The Mammy Anthem / 5. You Didn't Try To Call Me / 6. Diseases Of The Band / 7. Tryin' To Grow A Chin / 8. Let's Make The Water Turn Black / Harry You're A Beast / The Orange County Lumber Truck / 9. The Groupie Routine / 10. Ruthie-Ruthie / 11. Babbette / 12. I'm The Slime / 13. Big Swifty / 14. Don't Eat The Yellow Snow

CD 2:
1. Plastic People / 2. The Torture Never Stops / 3. Fine Girl / 4. Zomby Woof / 5. Sweet Leilani / 6. Oh No / 7. Be In My Video / 8. The Deathless Horsie / 9. The Dangerous Kitchen / 10. Dumb All Over / 11. Heavenly Bank Account / 12. Suicide Chump / 13. Tell Me You Love Me / 14. Sofa #2

Line-ups:
(Since virtually each track is by a different line-up, and is recorded at a different location, they are dealt with sequentially):

CD 1:
Track 1: Frank Zappa, Mark Volman, Howard Kaylan, Jeff Simmons, George Duke, Ian Underwood and Aynsley Dunbar in conversation
Recorded at an airport in Florida, April 1970
Track 2 and 3: Frank Zappa - guitar, vocal / Mark Volman - vocal / Howard Kaylan - vocal / Jim Pons - bass, vocal / Don Preston - keyboards, electronics / Ian Underwood - keyboards, alto saxophone / Aynsley Dunbar - drums
Recorded 10 December 1971, at the Rainbow Theatre, London
At the end of this concert Zappa was thrown from the stage by an irate fan
Track 4: Frank Zappa - guitar / Ray White - guitar / Steve Vai - guitar / Tommy Mars - keyboards / Bobby Martin - keyboards, saxophone / Ed Mann - percussion / Scott Thunes - bass; Chad Wackermann - drums
Recorded 12 July 1982 at the Stadio Communale, Palermo, Sicily / (The Palermo riot concert)
Track 5: Frank Zappa - guitar, vocal / Ike Willis - guitar, vocal / Ray White - guitar, vocal / Tommy Mars - keyboards / Arthur Barrow - keyboards, bass / David Logeman - drums
Recorded 3 July 1980 at the Olympia Hall, Munich, Germany
Track 6 and 7: Frank Zappa - guitar, vocal / Denny Walley - slide guitar, vocal / Ike Willis - lead vocal / Warren Cucurrullo - guitar / Tommy Mars - keyboards, vocal / Peter Wolf - keyboards / Ed Mann - percussion / Arthur Barrow - bass / Vinnie Colaiuta - drums.
Recorded 18 February 1979, at Hammersmith Odeon, London, UK
Track 8: Frank Zappa - guitar / Lowell George - guitar / Roy Estrada - bass / Don Preston - keyboards, electronics / Buzz Gardner - trumpet / Ian Underwood - alto saxophone / Bunk Gardner - tenor saxophone / Motorhead Sherwood - baritone saxophone / Jimmy Carl Black - drums / Arthur Dyer Tripp III - drums
Recorded February 1969 at The Ballroom, Stratford, CT
Track 9: Frank Zappa - guitar, vocal / Mark Volman - vocal / Howard Kaylan - vocal / Jim Pons - bass, vocal / Don Preston - keyboards, electronics / Ian Underwood - keyboards, alto saxophone / Aynsley Dunbar - drums
Recorded 7 July 1971 at the Pauley Pavilion, University of California, Los Angeles, CA
Track 10 and 11: Frank Zappa - guitar, vocal / Napoleon Murphy Brock - saxophone, vocal / George Duke - keyboards, vocal / Ruth Underwood - percussion / Tom Fowler - bass / Chester Thompson - drums. Recorded 18 November 1974 at the Capitol Theater, Passaic, NJ
Track 12 and 13: Frank Zappa - guitar, vocal / Napoleon Murphy Brock - saxophone, vocal / George Duke - keyboards, vocal / Ruth Underwood - percussion / Bruce Fowler - trombone / Tom Fowler - bass / Chester Thompson - drums / Ralph Humphrey - drums
Recorded 12 December 1973, at The Roxy, Hollywood, CA
Track 14: Frank Zappa - guitar, vocal / Denny Walley - slide guitar, vocal / Warren Cucurrullo - guitar / Tommy Mars - keyboards, vocal / Peter Wolf - keyboards / Ed Mann - percussion; Arthur Barrow - bass; Vinnie Colaiuta - drums. Recorded 18 February 1979 at the Hammersmith Odeon, London, UK

CD 2: Track 1: Frank Zappa - guitar, vocal / Lowell George - guitar, vocal / Roy Estrada - bass, vocal / Don Preston - keyboards, electronics / Buzz Gardner - trumpet / Ian Underwood - alto saxophone / Bunk Gardner - tenor saxophone / Motorhead Sherwood - baritone saxophone / Jimmy Carl Black - drums / Arthur Dyer Tripp III - drums
Recorded 13 February 1969 at The Factory, The Bronx, New York City, NY
Track 2: Frank Zappa - guitar, vocal / Adrian Belew - guitar, vocal / Tommy Mars - keyboards / Peter Wolf - keyboards / Ed Mann - percussion / Patrick O'Hearn - bass / Terry Bozzio - drums
Recorded 25 February 1978 at Hemmerleinhalle, Nürnberg, Germany
Tracks 3 and 4: Frank Zappa - guitar, vocal / Ray White - guitar, vocal / Steve Vai - guitar / Tommy Mars - keyboards, vocal / Bobby Martin - keyboards, saxophone, vocal / Ed Mann - percussion / Scott Thunes - bass / Chad Wackermann - drums
Recorded 6 July 1982 at the Parco Redecessio, Milan, Italy
Tracks 5 and 6: Frank Zappa - guitar, vocal / Lowell George - guitar, vocal / Roy Estrada - bass, vocal / Don Preston - keyboards, electronics / Buzz Gardner - trumpet / Ian Underwood - alto saxophone / Bunk Gardner - tenor saxophone / Motorhead Sherwood - baritone saxophone / Jimmy Carl Black - drums / Arthur Dyer Tripp III - drums
Recorded February 1969, The Ballroom, Stratford, CT
Tracks 7, 8 and 9: Frank Zappa - guitar, vocal / Ike Willis - guitar, vocal / Ray White - guitar, vocal / Bobby Martin - keyboards, saxophone, vocal / Alan Zavod - keyboards / Scott Thunes - bass / Chad Wackermann - drums
Recorded 26 August 1984, at the Pier, New York City, NY
The short intro was recorded backstage c.1970
Tracks 10, 11, 12, 13 and14: Frank Zappa - guitar, vocal / Ray White - guitar, vocal / Steve Vai - guitar / Tommy Mars - keyboards, vocal / Bobby Martin - keyboards, saxophone, vocal / Ed Mann - percussion / Scott Thunes - bass / Chad Wackermann - drums
Tracks 10, 11 and 12 recorded 31 October 1981 at The Palladium, New York City, NY and (amazingly) broadcast live as part of an early MTV special
Tracks 13 and 14 were recorded 7 July 1982, at the Soccer Stadium, Genoa, Italy

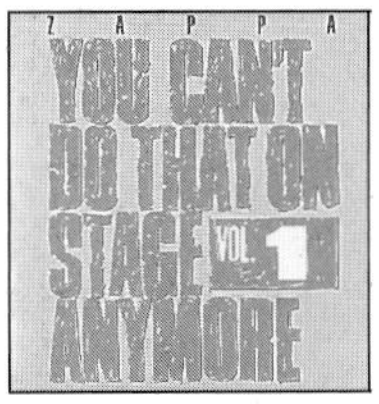

YOU CAN'T DO THAT ON STAGE ANYMORE VOLUME 2: THE HELSINKI CONCERT
(double CD set and Boxed set 3 records)
US Rykodisc RDC 10083/84
Released October 1988
US Album set
Barking Pumpkin BPR 74217

UK Zappa CDD ZAP 9
Released 1988

CD 1:
1. Tush Tush Tush (A Token Of My Extreme) / 2. Stinkfoot / 3. Inca Roads / 4. RDNZL / 5. Village Of The Sun / 6. Echidna's Arf (Of You) / 7. Don't You Ever Wash That Thing? / 8. Pygmy Twylyte / 9. Room Service / 10. The Idiot Bastard Son / 11. Cheepnis.

CD 2:
1. Approximate / 2. Dupree's Paradise / 3. Satumaa (Finnish Tango) / 4. T'Mershi Duween / 5. The Dog Breath Variations / 6. Uncle Meat / 7. Building A Girl / 8. Montana (Whipping Floss) / 9. Big Swifty

The three-record box set does not have the following tracks: 'Echidna's Arf (Of You)' / 'Room Service' and replaces 'The Dog Breath Variations', 'Uncle Meat' and 'Building A Girl' with 'Dog/Meat'

Line-up:
Frank Zappa - lead guitar, vocal / Napoleon Murphy Brock - saxophone, vocal / George Duke - keyboards, vocal / Ruth Underwood - percussion / Tom Fowler - bass / Chester Thompson - drums

Producer: Frank Zappa
Engineer: unknown
Recorded live in Helsinki, Finland, on 22 September 1974
Re-mix engineer: Bob Stone at UMRK

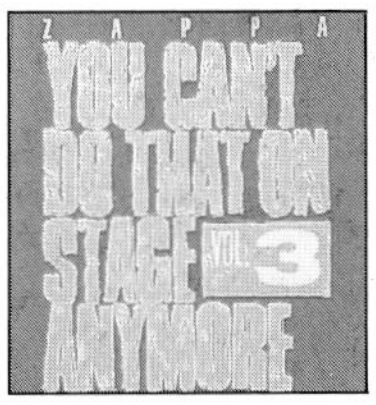

YOU CAN'T DO THAT ON STAGE ANYMORE: VOLUME 3
(double CD set)
US Rykodisc RCD10085/86
Released 1989
UK Zappa CDD ZAP 17
Released 1989

CD 1:
1. Sharleena / 2. Bamboozled By Love / 3. Lucille Has Messed My Mind Up / 4. Advance Romance (1984) / 5. Bobby Brown Goes Down / 6. Keep It Greasy / 7. Honey, Don't You Want A Man Like Me? / 8. In France / 9. Drowning Witch / 10. Ride My Face To Chicago / 11. Carol, You Fool / 12. Chana In De Bushwop / 13. Joe's Garage / 14. Why Does It Hurt When I Pee?

CD 2:
Dickie's Such An Asshole / 2. Hands With A Hammer / 3. Zoot Allures / 4. Society Pages / 5. I'm A Beautiful Guy / 6. Beauty Knows No Pain / 7. Charlie's Enormous Mouth / 8. Cocaine Decisions / 9. Nig Biz / 10. King Kong / 11. Cosmik Debris

Line-up: Frank Zappa - lead guitar, vocal / Ike Willis - rhythm guitar, vocal / Ray White - rhythm guitar, vocal / Bobby Martin - keyboards, vocal / Alan Zavod - keyboards; Scott Thunes - bass / Chad Wackermann

Producer: Frank Zappa
Engineer: Mark Pinske with the UMRK Remote facility
Remix engineer Bob Stone
Recorded, various dates and locations as follows:

CD 1:
Track 1 recorded on 23 December 1984 at the Universal Amphitheater, Los Angeles, Ca, with Zappa's 15-year old son, Dweezil appearing on stage and playing guitar with his father for the first time
Tracks 2, 3, 4, 8, 10, 11, 12, 13 and 14 recorded 23 November 1984 at the Bismarck Hotel, Chicago, Il
Tracks 5, 6 and CD 2, track 11 recorded 17 December 1984 at Paramount Theater, Seattle, Wa
Track 7 recorded July 1984 at The Pier, New York City, NY
Track 9 recorded 17 December 1984 at the Paramount Theater, Seattle, WA added to which is a version from July 1982 at the Soccer Stadium, Bolzano, Italy with the following line-up: Frank Zappa - lead guitar / Ray White - rhythm guitar / Steve Vai - stunt guitar / Tommy Mars - keyboards / Bobby Martin - keyboards / Ed Mann - percussion / Scott Thunes - bass / Chad Wackermann - drums
The track is edited to collate the best performance of both groups
CD 2, track 1 recorded 12 December 1973 at The Roxy, Hollywood, Ca with the following line-up: Frank Zappa - lead guitar, vocal / Napoleon Murphy Brock - saxophone, vocal / George Duke - keyboard, vocal / Ruth Underwood - percussion / Bruce Fowler - trombone / Tom Fowler - bass / Chester Thompson - drums / Ralph Humphrey - drums
Track 2 is a drum solo by Terry Bozzio recorded 31 October 1977 in the dressing room of the Palladium, New York City, NY, and in 1975 in Tokyo, Japan, edited to form a seamless performance.
Track 3: Recorded 30 May 1982 at the Bullfight Arena, Cap d'Agde, France and 1975 (month unknown) in Tokyo, Japan

1975 line-up:
Frank Zappa - lead guitar / Napoleon Murphy Brock - saxophone / André Lewis - keyboards / Roy Estrada - bass / Terry Bozzio - drums
1982 line-up: Frank Zappa - lead guitar / Ray White - rhythm guitar; Steve Vai - stunt guitar / Tommy Mars - keyboards / Bobby Martin - keyboards / Ed Mann - percussion / Scott Thunes - bass / Chad Wackermann - drums

Tracks 4, 5, 6 and 7 recorded 31 October 1981 at the Palladium, NY

Line-up:
Frank Zappa - lead guitar / Ray White - rhythm guitar / Steve Vai - stunt guitar / Tommy Mars - keyboards / Bobby Martin - keyboards / Ed Mann - percussion / Scott Thunes - bass / Chad Wackermann - drums

Track 8: Recorded 23 November 1984 at the Bismarck Hotel, Chicago, Ill
Line-up: Frank Zappa - lead guitar, vocal / Ike Willis - rhythm guitar, vocal / Ray White - rhythm guitar, vocal / Bobby Martin - keyboards, vocal / Alan Zavod - keyboards; Scott Thunes - bass / Chad Wackermann

The track is edited to the beginning of the riot in Palermo, Sicily, during the 14 July 1982 concert. 'You can hear a loud 'crack' as the first tear gas grenade is launched, causing all of us to fumble in confusion momentarily. We couldn't see what was going on out in the middle of the soccer field. The Army and the local Police (who didn't like each other, and who were completely uncoordinated) began a random process of blasting these little presents into the crowd. We could see fires in the distant bleachers. Tear gas seeped onto the stage. We continued the show in spite of this' (Zappa's sleeve notes)
Track 9: Recorded at the actual Palermo concert, 14 July 1982 at the Stadio Communale, Palermo, Sicily. This was the last show the 1982 line-up ever played
Track 10: Recorded on 22 June 1982 at the Parc des Expositions, Metz, France / June 18th or 19th at Hammersmith Odeon, London, UK / 3 June Palais des Sports, Dijon, France / 10 December 1971 at the Rainbow Theatre, London, UK
The 1982 line-up as track 9
The Rainbow concert line-up was Frank Zappa - guitar, vocal / Mark Volman - vocal / Howard Kaylan - vocal / Jim Pons - bass, vocal / Don Preston - keyboards, electronics / Ian Underwood - keyboards, alto saxophone / Aynsley Dunbar - drums

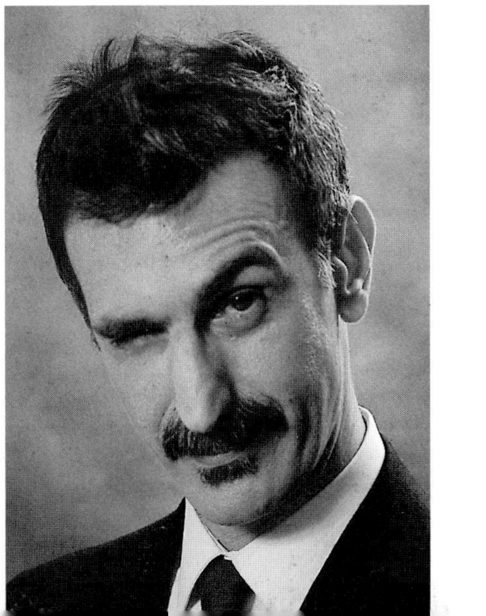

"There's a definite need for this kind of centre. I have talked it over with a lot of Moscow correspondents and many of them are crying out for better facilities, so what I have in mind would be a definite improvement."

Zappa signed a preliminary agreement with a Soviet partner but the deal appears not to have gone through.

JANUARY

Zappa stopped off in Prague on his way back to the States and met the then president Vaclav Havel…

"I called Michael Kocab, who is both a famous Czechoslovak rock-and-roll musician and – now here's progress – a member of Parliament. We had met in Los Angeles last year, and now all of a sudden he's in the middle of a democratic revolution. 'Could I possibly have an interview with Haval?' I asked. 'No problem', he said. Thousands of fans greeted me when I arrived in Prague with my video crew. For twenty years, my albums have been smuggled into the country." [Zappa: 1990]

"When I arrived at the airport, there were approximately five thousand people piled on top of the airport waiting for me when I got off the Aeroflot flight. It was unbelievable! Never in my 25 years in the rock and roll business have I gotten off an airplane and seen anything like that. They were totally unprepared for the situation, there was no security, but the people were just wonderful! When I managed to inch my way through the airport, and once we got out the front door of the airport, it took about a half an hour to go forty feet from the curb to the bus because of the people that were just piling on top of us. It was unbelievable!" [Zappa: 1990]

"After spending a day or so just looking about at life in Czechoslovakia, I went to Hradcany Castle to meet President Havel - The President told me he especially likes my early records with The Mothers of Invention and the 'Bongo Fury' album I made with Captain Beefheart. He asked me to play at a concert honouring him during his State visit to the United States. He was hoping that The Rolling Stones and Joan Baez would also perform. [The line-up was in fact Paul Simon, James Taylor and Dizzy Gillespie.]

"I started to talk to him on behalf of FNN. 'What sort of foreign investment is Czechoslovakia looking for? Why should foreign investors put their money into Czechslovakia?' These questions, Havel said, should be addressed to his financial ministers. Then at a small lunch with Havel, his wife, Olga, Richard Wagner, Vice Minister and adviser for economy and ecology, and Valtr Komarek, a deputy prime minister and leader of their new economic team, we discussed how the country could increase its income, and the conversation continued later that day at dinner in a villa near the castle. At my request, Milan Lukes, the Czech Minister of Culture, was present. Havel and his ministers know they need some Western investment, but they don't want all the ugliness that often invades a country with Western investment. The easiest way to keep the lid on that is to have someone involved whose primary concern is culture, who can reject or modify a project if it is going to have a negative impact on society. Hence my request for the involvement of the Minister of Culture. After dinner, Lukes went on television and announced that I would be representing Czechoslovakia on trade, tourism and cultural matters."

The letter was signed by Valter Lomarek, a government financial adviser and read:

"Dear Sir: I entrust you with leading negotiations with foreign partners for preparation of preliminary projects, possibly drafts of trade agreements directed to participation of foreign firms. It concerns tourist, agricultural and other enterprises in Czechoslovakia. I am very obliged to you for the help offered in this respect and I am looking to further cooperation.."

"So I had my lawyer fill out papers to have me registered in the US as an agent of a foreign country. Suddenly it looks like I have a new job." [Zappa: 1990]

His company, Why Not? represented Czechoslovakia for one year.

26 FEBRUARY

Zappa produced and appeared in a number of business news shorts called "Frank Zappa's Wild Wild East" that aired on FNN. In late Feb, early March: Zappa was a guest host on "FNN: Focus" for three days.

MAY

Zappa in Amsterdam as a keynote speaker at the Music Media Exhibition

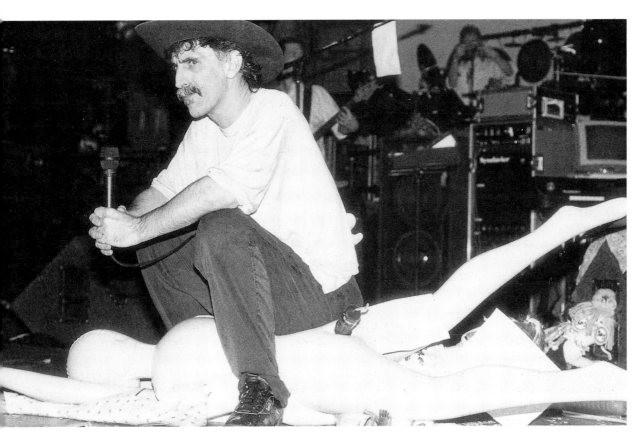

–1991–

MARCH

THE BEST BAND YOU NEVER HEARD IN YOUR LIFE [Album 53] (double CD) released.

"The 1988 road band self-destructed before U.S. audiences in the South, Midwest and West could hear it perform. It was, however, heard and appreciated by East Coast and European audiences during its brief existence (four months of rehearsal in 1987/8, followed by a tour, February through June, 1988), and it is from those performances that this compilation has been made. The collection features big-band arrangements of concert favourites and obscure album cuts, along with deranged versions of cover tunes and a few première recordings." [Zappa: sleeve notes]

MAKE A JAZZ NOISE HERE [Album 54] (double CD) released.

YOU CAN'T DO THAT ON STAGE ANYMORE: VOLUME FOUR [Album 55] (double CD set) released.

15 APRIL

Frank Zappa announces on KPFA-FM Berkeley Ca that he is researching the idea of running for President

THE BEST BAND YOU NEVER HEARD IN YOUR LIFE
(double CD)
UK CD Zappa CDDZAP 38
Released March 1991

CD 1:
1. Heavy Duty Judy / 2. Ring Of Fire / 3. Cosmik Debris / 4. Find Her Finer / 5. Who Needs The Peace Corps? / 6. I Left My Heart In San Francisco / 7. Zomby Woof / 8. Bolero / 9. Zoot Allures / 10. Mr. Green Genes / 11. Florentine Pogen / 12. Andy / 13. Inca Roads / 14. Sofa #1

CD 2:
1. Purple Haze / 2. Sunshine Of Your Love / 3. Let's Move To Cleveland / 4. When Irish Eyes Are Smiling / 5. 'Godfather Part II' Theme / 6. A Few Moments With Brother A West / 7. The Torture Never Stops Part One / 8. Theme From 'Bonanza' / 9. Lonesome Cowboy Burt (Swaggart version) / 10. The Torture Never Stops Part Two / 11. More Trouble Every Day (Swaggart Version) / 12. Penguin In Bondage (Swaggart Version) / 13. The Eric Dolphy Memorial Barbecue / 14. Stairway To Heaven

Line-up:
Frank Zappa - lead guitar, vocal, computer-synthesizer / Ike Willis - rhythm guitar, synthesizer, vocal / Mike Keneally - rhythm guitar, synthesizer, vocal / Bobby Martin - keyboards, vocal / Ed Mann - vibes, marimba, electronic percussion / Walt Fowler - trumpet, flugelhorn, synthesizer / Bruce Fowler - trombone / Paul Carman - alto saxophone, soprano saxophone, baritone saxophone / Albert Wing - tenor saxophone / Kurt McGettrick - baritone saxophone, bass saxophone, contrabass clarinet / Scott Thunes - electric bass, mini-moog / Chad Wackermann - drums, electronic percussion

Producer: Frank Zappa
Recorded in various locations during the European and east coast USA tour of 1988:

CD 1:
Track 1: Carl Diem Halle, Würzburg, Germany, 22 April and The Ahoy, Rotterdam, 3 May / 2, 3 and 6 Carl Diem Halle, Würzburg, Germany, 22 April / 4. Rudi Sedlmayer Halle, Munich, 9 May / 5. Intro from Munich, rest from Würzburg / 7. Munich and Memorial Hall, Muhlenburg College, Allentown, Pa, 19 March / 8. The Ahoy, Rotterdam, 3 May / 9. Brighton Centre, Brighton, Sussex, 16 April / 10 and 11 / Tivoli, Strasbourg, France, 23 May / 12. The record says this track was recorded at Allentown, Pa and Binghamton, NY but Zappa scholars dispute this / 13. Guitar solo from Stadthalle, Vienna, Austria, 8 May another part is from Würzburg, rest unknown / 14. Martin Schleyer Halle, Stuttgart, 24 May CD 2. tracks 1 and 2 from soundcheck at Sporthalle, Linz, Austria, 28 May / 3. Palasport, Modena, Italy, 5 June and Le Zenith, Montpellier, France, 18 May / 4 and 5. Broome County Arena, Binghamton, NY, March 17th / 6. Tower Theater, Upper Darby, Philadelphia, Pa, 14 February / 7. Wembley Arena, London, 19 April and Carl Diem Halle, Würzburg, Germany, 22 April / 8. Wembley Arena, London, 19 April / 9. Syria Mosque, Pittsburgh, Pa, 25 February / 10. Rothman Center, Fairleigh Dickenson University, Teaneck, NJ, 20 March / 11 and 12. Mid Hudson Civic Center, Poughkeepsie, NY, 23 February / 13. Landmark Theater, Syracuse, NY, 21 March, Royal Oak Theater, Troy, Detroit, Mi, 28 February and Stadthalle, Vienna, Austria, 8 May / 14. Stadthalle, Vienna, Austria, 8 May Wembley Arena, London, 18 April and Palasport, Firenzi, Italy, 6 June

Producer: Frank Zappa
Engineer: Bob Stone at UMRK

MAKE A JAZZ NOISE HERE
(double CD)
UK CD Zappa CDDZAP 41.
Released May1991

CD 1:
Track 1. Stinkfoot / 2. When Yuppies Go To Hell / 3. Fire And Chains / 4. Let's Make The Water Turn Black / 5. Harry You're A Beast / 6. The Orange County Lumber Truck / 7. Oh No / 8. Theme From Lumpy Gravy / 9. Eat That Question / 10. Black Napkins / 11. Big Swifty / 12. King Kong / 13. Star Wars Won't Work

CD 2:
Track 1. The Black Page (New Age version) / 2. T'Mershi Duween / 3. Dupree's Paradise / 4. City Of Tiny Lights / 5. Royal March From 'L'Histoire Du Soldat' (Stravinsky) / 6. Theme From The Bartók Piano Concerto #3 / 7. Sinister Footwear 2nd Movement / 8. Stevie's Spanking / 9. Alien Orifice / 10. Cruisin' For Burgers / 11. Advance Romance / 12. Strictly Genteel
Line-up: Frank Zappa - lead guitar, vocal, synthesizer / Ike Willis - rhythm guitar, synthesizer, vocal / Mike Keneally - rhythm guitar, synthesizer, vocal / Bobby Martin - keyboards, vocal / Ed Mann - vibes, marimba, electronic percussion / Walt Fowler - trumpet, flugelhorn, synthesizer / Bruce Fowler - trombone / Paul Carman - alto saxophone, soprano saxophone, baritone saxophone / Albert Wing - tenor saxophone / Kurt McGettrick - baritone saxophone, contrabass clarinet / Scott Thunes - electric bass, mini-moog / Chad Wackermann - drums, electronic percussion

Producer: Frank Zappa
Recorded in various locations during the European and east coast USA tour of 1988:

CD 1:
Track 1. Boston, Mass and Mid Hudson Civic Center, Poughkeepsie, NY. 23 February / 2. Sporthalle, Linz, Austria, 28 May, Brighton Centre, Brighton, Sussex, 16 April, Memorial Auditorium, Burlington, Vt, 12 March, Warner Theater, Washington, DC, 8 or 9 February/ 3. Warner Theater, Washington, DC, 8 or 9 February / 4, 5, 6 and 8 The Ahoy, Rotterdam, Holland, 3 May / 7. Wembley Arena, London, 18 or 19 April / 9. Rome / 10. Stadthalle, Vienna, Austria, 8 May / 11. Rudi Sedlmayer Halle, Munich, Germany, 9 May / 12. Munich and Cleveland Music Hall, Cleveland, Ohio, 5 March / 13. Martin Schleyer Halle, Stuttgart, Germany, 24 May

CD 2:
Track 1. Tower Theater, Upper Darby, Philadelphia, Pa February, Palasport, Modena, Italy, 5 June / 2 and 3. Mannheim, Germany / 4. Palasport, Modena, Italy, 5 June / 5. Syria Mosque, Pittsburgh, Pa. 25 February / 6. Springfield, Mass / 7 and 8. Memorial Hall, Muhlenburg College, Allentown, Pa 19 March / 9. Palasport, Firenzi, Italy, 6 June / 10. Olympen, Lund, Sweden, 24 April / 11. Palasport, Firenzi, Italy, 6 June / 12. Seville, Spain

Producer: Frank Zappa
Engineer: Bob Stone at UMRK

7-10 NOVEMBER

A four day appreciation of Zappa's work was held at the Roxy, New York City. Zappa was scheduled to attend but didn't make it. There had been rumours about Zappa's ill-health for some time, but his inability to attend the concerts meant that his family had to finally make a statement to the press. Moon Unit, flanked by Dweezil Zappa, Zappa's publicist Sean Mahoney and the promoter John Scher, stood before a battery of microphones, video cameras and assembled reporters and read a prepared statement:

"We're here to make a statement on behalf of our family. Although Frank was looking forward to being here and really intended to be here, unfortunately he's not here. As many of you know, he's been diagnosed by journalists as having cancer. We'd like you to know his doctors have diagnosed prostate cancer which he's been fighting successfully and he has been feeling well and working too hard and planned to attend. Up until the last minute we were still hoping he would feel well enough to get on a plane and come here. There are occasional periods where he's not feeling as well and it's really unfortunate it happened to coincide with this event. He's thrilled people are performing his music. The more the merrier. And we're thrilled. And we're here to participate in this event…
We thank you for your attention."

—1992—

JULY
YOU CAN'T DO THAT ON STAGE ANYMORE: VOLUME FIVE
[Album 56] (double CD set) released.

JULY
YOU CAN'T DO THAT ON STAGE ANYMORE: VOLUME SIX
[Album 57] (double CD set) released.

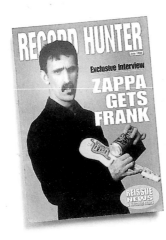

Frank and Moon

YOU CAN'T DO THAT ON STAGE ANYMORE: VOLUME 4
(double CD set)
UK Zappa CDD ZAP 40
Released 1991

CD 1:
1, Little Rubber Girl /
2, Stick Together / 3. My Guitar
Wants To Kill Your Mama / 4.
Willie The Pimp / 5. Montana /
6. Brown Moses / 7. The Evil
Prince / 8. Approximate / 9. Love
Of My Life: Mudd Club version /
10. Let's Move To Cleveland -
Solos (1984) / 11. You Call That
Music / 12. Pound For A Brown -
Solos (1978) / 13. The Black
Page (1984) / 14. Take Me Out
To The Ball Game / 15. Filthy
Habits / 16. The Torture Never
Stops: Original Version.

CD 2:
1. Church Chat / 2. Stevie's
Spanking / 3. Outside Now /
4. Disco Boy / 5. Teen-Age Wind /
6. Truck Driver Divorce /
7. Florentine Pogen / 8. Tiny Sick
Tears / 9. Smell My Beard /
10. The Booger Man /
11. Carolina Hard Core Ecstasy /
12. Are You Upset? / 13. Little
Girl Of Mine / 14. The Closer You
Are / 15. Johnny Darling / 16. No,
No Cherry / 17. The Man From
Utopia / 18. Mary Lou

Line-ups: (Since virtually each
track is by a different line-up, and
is recorded at a different
location, they are dealt with
sequentially):

CD 1:
Tracks 1 and 12:
Recorded 31 October 1979 at
The Palladium, NYC

Line-up:
Frank Zappa - guitar, vocal /
Denny Walley - vocal / Tommy
Mars - keyboards / Peter Wolf -
keyboards / Ed Mann -
percussion / Patrick O'Hearn -
bass / Arthur Barrow - bass /
Vinnie Colaiuta - drums
Tracks 2 and 13 recorded
November 1984, in Vancouver,
BC, Canada (more likely 18
December, Queen Elizabeth
Theater, Vancouver, BC, Canada)
Line-up: Frank Zappa - vocal,
guitar / Ike Willis - guitar, vocal /
Ray White - guitar, vocal / Bobby
Martin - keyboards, saxophone,
vocal / Alan Zevod - keyboards;
Scott Thunes - bass / Chad
Wackermann - drums
Tracks 3, 4, and 6: Recorded
23 December 1984 at the
Universal Amphitheater,
Hollywood, CA
Same line-up as track 2
Track 5: Recorded November
1973 at The Roxy, Hollywood, CA
and 23 December 1984 at the
Universal Amphitheater,
Hollywood, CA

Line-up 1973:
Frank Zappa - guitar, vocal /

Napoleon Murphy Brock -
saxophone, vocal / George Duke -
keyboards, vocal / Ruth
Underwood - percussion / Bruce
Fowler - trombone / Tom Fowler -
bass / Chester Thompson -
drums / Ralph Humphrey - drums
1984 line-up same as track 2
Track 7. Recorded 24 or 25
September 1984, Hammersmith
Odeon, London, UK

Same line-up as track 2
Track 8 and CD 2, tracks
17 and 18 recorded 8 July 1982:
Stadio Municipale, Pistoia, Italy

Line-up: Frank Zappa - guitar,
vocal / Ray White - guitar, vocal /
Steve Vai - stunt guitar / Tommy
Mars - keyboards, vocal / Bobby
Martin - keyboards, saxophone,
vocal / Ed Mann - percussion /
Scott Thunes - bass / Chad
Wackermann - drums
Track 9. Recorded at The Mudd
Club, NYC, NY 1980
Line-up: Frank Zappa - guitar,
vocal / Ike Willis - guitar, vocal /
Ray White - guitar, vocal /
Tommy Mars - keyboards / Arthur
Barrow - keyboards, bass / David
Logeman - drums
Track 10: Recorded 28 October
1984: Fine Arts Center Concert
Hall, Amherst College, Amherst,
MA

Line-up same as track 2 plus
Archie Shepp - tenor saxophone
Track 11: Recorded during the
Spring tour of 1969 at Columbia
University, NYC, NY

Line-up: Frank Zappa - guitar,
vocal / Roy Estrada, bass, vocal /
Don Preston - keyboards,
electronics / Buzz Gardner -
trumpet / Ian Underwood -
clarinet / Bunk Gardner - tenor
saxophone / Motorhead
Sherwood - baritone saxophone /
Jimmy Carl Black - drums /
Arthur Dyer Tripp III - drums /
Dave Samuels - guest soloist
on vibes.
Track 14: Recorded 13 May
1988: Velodrome, Bilbao, Spain

Line-up: Frank Zappa - guitar,
vocal / Ike Willis - vocal / Mike
Keneally - guitar, synthesizer /
Bobby Martin - keyboards /
Ed Mann - percussion / Walt
Fowler - trumpet, vocal / Bruce
Fowler - trombone / Paul Carman -
alto saxophone / Albert Wing -
tenor saxophone / Kurt
McGettrick - baritone saxophone /
Scott Thunes - bass / Chad
Wackermann - drums
Track 15: Same as track 14
except it is edited together
with the concert of 19 May,
Le Summun, Grenoble, France
Track 16: Recorded 1976
(1975?) at the Armadillo World
Headquarters, Austin, Texas

Line-up:
Frank Zappa - guitar, vocal /
Captain Beefheart - harmonica,
vocal / Napoleon Murphy Brock -
saxophone / Bruce Fowler -
trombone / Denny Walley - slide
guitar / George Duke -
keyboards / Tom Fowler - bass /
Terry Bozzio - drums.

CD 2:
Track 1. Recorded 22 June 1982
at Parc des Expositions, Metz,
France

Line-up same as CD 1, Track 8
Track 2: Recorded 10 July 1982
at Ex Mattatoio Do Testaccio,
Rome, Italy

Line-up same as CD 1, Track 8
Track 3. Recorded 10 November
1984 at the Tower Theater,
Philadelphia, PA

Line-up same as CD 1, Track 2
Tracks 4 and 5. Recorded 3
October 1984: Circus Krone,
Munich, Germany

Line-up same as CD 1, Track 8
Track 6. Recorded November
1984 at Paramount Theater,
Portland, Or (17 December 1984,
Seattle, Wa) and either
24 or 25 September 1984,
Hammersmith Odeon,
London, UK

Line-up same as CD 1, Track 2
Track 7. Recorded 18 February
1979 at the Hammersmith
Odeon, London, UK

Line-up: Frank Zappa - guitar,
vocal / Ike Willis - lead vocal /
Denny Walley - slide guitar,
vocal / Warren Cucurullo - guitar /
Tommy Mars - keyboards, vocal /
Peter Wolf - keyboards / Ed
Mann - percussion / Arthur
Barrow - bass / Vinnie Colaiuta -
drums
Track 8: Recorded during
Spring tour 1969 at The Factory,
The Bronx, NY

Line-up same as CD 1, Track 11
minus guest
Tracks 9 and 10: Recorded
Winter 1974 somewhere in
New Jersey

Line-up: Frank Zappa - guitar,
vocal / Napoleon Murphy Brock -
saxophone, vocal / George Duke -
keyboards, vocal / Ruth
Underwood - percussion /
Tom Fowler - bass /
Chester Thompson - drums
Track 11: Recorded November
1984 at Paramount Theater,
Portland, Or (17 December 1984,
Seattle, Wa)

Line-up same as CD 1, Track 2
Track 12: Recorded on the
Spring tour 1969 at the Fillmore
East, NYC. NY

Line-up same as CD 1, Track 11
minus guest Tracks 13, 14, 15
and 16

Line-up same as CD 1, track 2

Produced, arranged, compiled
and edited by Frank Zappa
Engineering supervision:
Bob Stone at UMRK

YOU CAN'T DO THAT ON STAGE ANYMORE: VOLUME 5
(double CD set)
UK Zappa CDD ZAP 46
Released August 1992

CD 1:
1. The Downtown Talent Scout /
2. Charles Ives / 3. Here Lies
Love / 4. Piano/Drum Duet /
5. Mozart Ballet / 6. Chocolate
Halvah / 7. JCB & Kansas On The
Bus #1 / 8. Run Home Slow /
Main Title Theme / 9. The Little
March / 10. Right There /
11. Where Is Johnny Velvet? /
12. Return Of The Hunch-Back
Duke / 13. Trouble Every Day /
14. Proto-Minimalism / 15. JCB &
Kansas On The Bus #2 / 16. My
Head? / 17. Meow / 18. Baked-
Bean Boogie / 19. Where's Our
Equipment? 20. FZ/JCB Drum
Duet / 21. No Waiting For
The Peanuts To Dissolve /
22. A Game Of Cards /
23. Underground Freak-Out
Music / 24. German Lunch /
25. My Guitar Wants To Kill
Your Mama

CD 2:
1. Easy Meat / 2. Dead Girls Of
London / 3. Shall We Take
Ourselves Seriously? / 4. What's
New In Baltimore? 5. Maggie /
6. Dancin' Fool / 7. RDNZL /
8. Advance Romance / 9. City Of
Tiny Lites / 10. A Pound For A
Brown (On The Bus) /
11. Doreen / 12. The Black
Page / 13. Geneva Farewell

Line-ups:
(Since virtually each track is by a
different line-up, and is recorded
at a different location, they are
dealt with sequentially)

CD 1:
Track 1 recorded in 1965 at The
Fillmore West, San Francisco, Ca

Line-up:
Frank Zappa - guitar, vocal /
Elliot Ingber - rhythm guitar /
Roy Estrada - bass / Jimmy Carl
Black - drums / Ray Collins -
tambourine

Track 2, 3, 8, 9 and 14 recorded
in 1969 at Columbia University,
NYC. NY. Line-up: Frank Zappa -
guitar, vocal / Lowell George -
guitar, vocal / Roy Estrada -
bass, vocal / Don Preston -
keyboards, electronics / Buzz
Gardner - trumpet / Ian
Underwood - alto saxophone,
clarinet / Bunk Gardner - tenor
saxophone / Motorhead
Sherwood - baritone saxophone /
Jimmy Carl Black - drums / Arthur
Dyer Tripp III - drums

Track 4 recorded in 1969 at The
Ark, Boston, Mass. Piano / drum
duet between Ian Underwood on
piano and Arthur Dyer Tripp III on
drums

Track 5 recorded on 6 June
1969 at The Royal Albert Hall,
London, UK

Line-up:
Frank Zappa - conductor, vocal /
Noel Redding - dance stylings /
Dick Barber - rubber chicken
strangulation / Kanzus J. Kanzus -
biological masterpiece / Roy
Estrada - bass, asthmatic
laughter / Don Preston -
electronics, injured chicken
noises / Buzz Gardner - trumpet /
Ian Underwood - acoustic piano
solo / Bunk Gardner - tenor
saxophone / Motorhead
Sherwood - victim of evil

experiments / Jimmy Carl Black -
drums / Arthur Dyer Tripp III -
drums

Tracks 6, 21 and 23 recorded in
1969 at Thee Image, Miami, Fl

Line-up same as track 2

Tracks 7 and 15 recorded in
1969 in The Mothers' Greyhound
tour bus: Jimmy Carl Black,
Kanzus J. Kanzus, Dick Kunc,
Dick Barber in conversation.
Track 10 recorded in 1969 on
stage in Miami and at Criteria
Studios, Miami, Fl

Line-up same as track 2

Tracks 11, 12 and 13 recorded
on February 13, 1969 at The
Factory, The Bronx, NY

Line-up same as track 2

Track 16 recorded in 1969 at
Sunset Sound Studios,
Hollywood, CA. Partytime with
Roy Estrada, Don Preston, Ian
Underwood, Bunk Gardner,
Motorhead Sherwood, Jimmy Carl
Black and Arthur Dyer Tripp III on
the occasion of Art Tripp's
birthday.

Track 17 recorded in 1968 at
The Whisky-A-Go-Go, Hollywood,
CA

Line-up:
Frank Zappa - guitar, vocal /
Ray Collins - tambourine, vocal /
Roy Estrada - bass, vocal /
Don Preston - keyboards,
electronics / Ian Underwood - alto
saxophone, clarinet / Bunk
Gardner - tenor saxophone /
Motorhead Sherwood - baritone
saxophone / Jimmy Carl Black -
drums / Arthur Dyer Tripp III -
drums

Track 18 recorded in 1969 at
The Ark, Boston, MA

Line-up same as track 2

Track 19 recorded in 1967 at
The Falkoner Centre,
Copenhagen, Denmark

Line-up:
Frank Zappa - conductor / Ray
Collins - tambourine / Roy
Estrada - bass / Don Preston -
piano / Ian Underwood - alto
saxophone / Bunk Gardner - tenor
saxophone / Motorhead
Sherwood - baritone saxophone /
Jimmy Carl Black - drums /
Billy Mundi - drums

Track 20 recorded in 1969 at
Columbia University, NYC, NY

Line-up:
Frank Zappa - drums / Jimmy
Carl Black - rhythm drums /
Arthur Dyer Tripp III - drums

Track 22 recorded in 1969
in a backstage dressing room,
Providence, RI

Voices by Frank Zappa,
Motorhead Sherwood, Arthur
Dyer Tripp III and Ian Underwood.
Track 24 recorded in 1969 at
Criteria Studios, Miami, Fl

The Mothers acting out German
Customs: Lowell George as main

Customs Officer
Voices: Jimmy Carl Black, Roy
Estrada, Bunk Gardner, Don
Preston, Motorhead Sherwood,
Ian Underwood, Arthur Dyer Tripp
III, Buzz Gardner, Frank Zappa

Track 25 recorded in 1969 at A
& R Studios, NYC, NY

Line-up:
Frank Zappa - lead guitar,
vocal / Roy Estrada - bass /
Don Preston - keyboards,
electronics / Ian Underwood -
alto saxophone / Bunk Gardner -
tenor saxophone / Motorhead
Sherwood - baritone saxophone /
Jimmy Carl Black - drums /
Arthur Dyer Tripp III - drums

CD 2:
Tracks 1 - 13 recorded on
11 June 1982 at Alte Opera,
Frankfurt / 30 June 1982 at
Patinoire des Vernets, Geneva,
Switzerland / 3 July 1982 at
Campo Communale, Bolzano,
Italy and 26 June 1982 at
Olympiahalle, Munich, Germany

Line-up:
Frank Zappa - lead guitar, vocal /
Ray White - guitar, vocal / Steve
Vai - stunt guitar / Tommy Mars -
keyboards, vocal / Bobby Martin -
keyboards, saxophone, vocal /
Ed Mann - percussion / Scott
Thunes - bass / Chad
Wackermann - drums

Produced, arranged, compiled
and edited by Frank Zappa

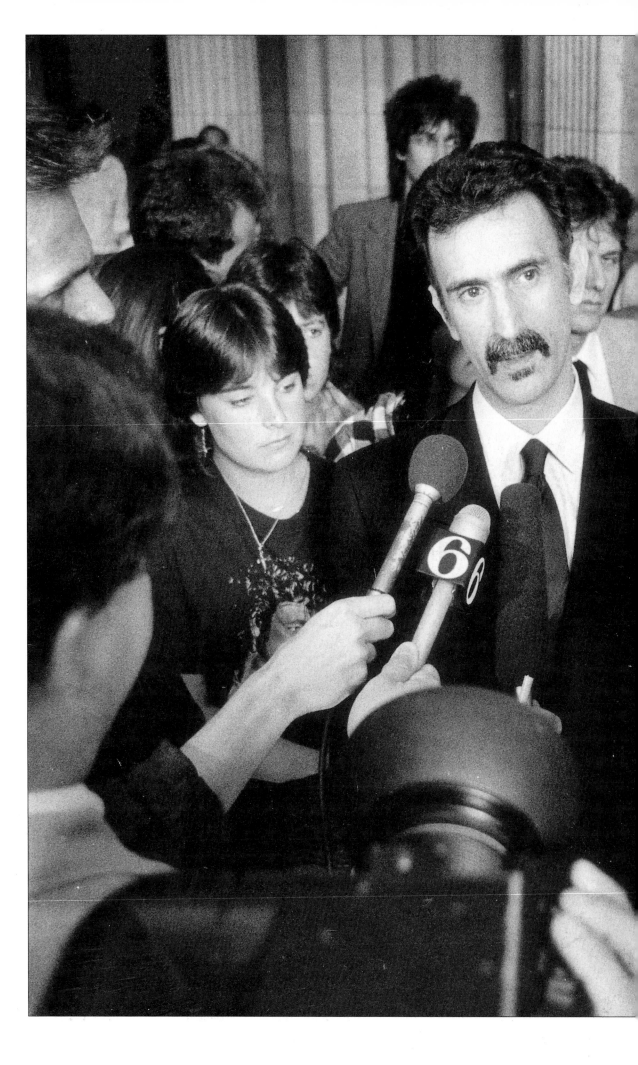

1967

Frank being interviewed after
his appearance at the Senate
obscenity hearings

YOU CAN'T DO THAT ON STAGE ANYMORE: VOLUME 6
(double CD set)
UK CD Zappa CDDZAP 47
Released August 1992

CD 1:
1. The M.O.I. Anti-Smut Loyalty Oath / 2. The Poodle Lecture / 3. Dirty Love / 4. Magic Fingers / 5. The Madison Panty-Sniffing Festival / 6. Honey, Don't You Want A Man Like Me? / 7. Father O'Blivion / 8. Is That Guy Kidding Or What? / 9. I'm So Cute / 10. White Person / 11. Lonely Person Devices / 12. Ms. Pinky / 13. Shove It Right In / 14. Wind Up Working In A Gas Station / 15. Make A Sex Noise / 16. Tracy Is A Snob / 17. I Have Been In You / 18. Emperor Of Ohio / 19. Dinah-Moe Humm / 20. He's So Gay / 21. Camarillo Brillo / 22. Muffin Man.

CD 2:
NYC Hallowe'en Audience / 2. The Illinois Enema Bandit / 3. Thirteen / 4. Lobster Girl / 5. Black Napkins / 6. We're Turning Again / 7. Alien Orifice / 8. Catholic Girls / 9. Crew Slut / 10. Tryin' To Grow A Chin / 11. Take Your Clothes Off When You Dance / 12. Lisa's Life Story / 13. Lonesome Cowboy Nando / 14. 200 Motels Finale / 15. Strictly Genteel

Line-ups:
(Since virtually each track is by a different line-up, and is recorded at a different location, they are dealt with sequentially):

CD 1:
Track 1 recorded September 1970 in Florida

Line-up: Frank Zappa - guitar, vocal / Mark Volman - vocal / Howard Kaylan - vocal / Jeff Simmons - bass / George Duke - keyboards / Ian Underwood - keyboards, alto saxophone / Aynsley Dunbar - drums

Tracks 2 and 8 and CD two-track 10 recorded 31 October 1977 at The Palladium, NYC NY

Line-up:
Frank Zappa - guitar, vocal / Adrian Belew - guitar, vocal / Tommy Mars - keyboards / Peter Wolf - keyboards / Ed Mann - percussion / Patrick O'Hearn - bass / Terry Bozzio - drums

Track 3 recorded 18 February 1979 at the Hammersmith Odeon, London, UK

Line-up:
Frank Zappa - guitar, vocal / Ike Willis - guitar, vocal / Denny Walley - slide guitar, vocal / Warren Cucurullo - guitar / Tommy Mars - keyboards, vocal / Peter Wolf - keyboards / Ed Mann - percussion / Arthur

Barrow - bass / Vinnie Colaiuta - drums

Tracks 4, 9 and 12 and CD two track 12 recorded 11 December 1980 at the Santa Monica Civic Auditorium, Santa Monica, Ca

Line-up:
Frank Zappa - guitar, vocal / Ike Willis - guitar, vocal / Ray White - guitar, vocal / Steve Vai - stunt guitar / Tommy Mars - keyboards, vocal / Bob Harris - keyboards, vocal / Scott Thunes - bass / Chad Wackermann - drums

Track 5 recorded 16 November 1980 in Madison, Wi

Line-up:
Same as track 4

Tracks 6, 15 and CD two track 6 recorded 23 March 1988 in Towson, Md

Line-up:
Frank Zappa - guitar, vocal / Ike Willis - guitar, vocal / Mike Keneally - rhythm guitar, synthesizer, vocal / Bobby Martin - keyboards, vocal / Ed Mann - vibes, marimba, electronic percussion / Walt Fowler - trumpet, flugelhorn, synthesizer / Bruce Fowler - trombone / Paul Carman - alto saxophone, soprano saxophone, baritone saxophone / Albert Wing - tenor saxophone / Kurt McGettrick - baritone saxophone, bass saxophone, contrabass clarinet / Scott Thunes - electric bass, mini-moog / Chad Wackerman - drums, electronic percussion

Track 7 recorded in 1972 in Sydney, Australia (June or July 1973)

Line-up:
Frank Zappa - guitar, vocal / Jean-Luc Ponty - violin / George Duke - keyboards / Ian Underwood - woodwinds / Ruth Underwood - percussion / Bruce Fowler - trombone / Tom Fowler - bass / Ralph Humphrey - drums

Track 10 recorded on 25 January 1977 at the Hemmerleinhalle, Nürnberg, Germany

Line-up:
Same as track 2

Track 11 recorded in February 1975 at the Tivoli Gardens, Copenhagen, Denmark

Line-up:
Frank Zappa - guitar, vocal / Napoleon Murphy Brock - saxophone, vocal / André Lewis - keyboards / Roy Estrada - bass / Terry Bozzio - drums

Track 13 recorded on June 5 or 6,1971 at the Fillmore East, 1971. Line-up: Frank Zappa - guitar, vocal / Mark Volman - vocal / Howard Kaylan - vocal / Jim Pons - bass, vocal / Bob Harris - keyboards / Ian Underwood - keyboards, alto saxophone / Aynsley Dunbar - drums

Track 14 recorded on November 3,1975 at The Spectrum, Philadelphia, PA

Line-up:
Frank Zappa - guitar, vocal / Ray White - guitar, vocal / Bianca Odin - keyboards, vocal / Patrick O'Hearn - bass / Terry Bozzio - drums

Tracks 16 and 18 recorded on 3 December 1980 in Salt Lake City, Utah

Line-up:
Same as track 4

Track 17 and CD 2, tracks 3 and 11 recorded on 31 October 1978 at the Palladium, NYC, NY

Line-up:
Frank Zappa - guitar, vocal / Denny Walley - slide guitar, vocal / Tommy Mars - keyboards, vocal / Peter Wolf - keyboards / Ed Mann - percussion / Arthur Barrow - bass / Patrick O'Hearn - bass / Vinnie Colaiuta - drums

Tracks 19, 21 and 22 recorded on 23 November 1984 at the Bismarck Theater, Chicago, Ill

Line-up:
Frank Zappa - guitar, vocal / Ike Willis - guitar, vocal / Ray White - guitar, vocal / Bobby Martin - keyboards, saxophone, vocal / Alan Zavod - keyboards / Scott Thunes - bass / Chad Wackerman - drums

Track 20 recorded 25 or 26 August 1984 at The Pier, New York City, NY
Line-up:
Same as track 19

CD two: Track 1 recorded 31 October (no year given) in New York
Tape of audience

Track 2 recorded on 23 December 1984 at the Universal Amphitheater, Los Angeles, Ca

Line-up: same as CD 1, track 19

Track 4 recorded 31 December 1978 at the Palladium, New York City, NY

Line-up: Patrick O'Hearn - bass solo, vocal / Vinnie Colaiuta - drums

Track 5 recorded 29 December 1976 at the Palladium, New York City, NY

Line-up:
Frank Zappa - guitar, vocal / Ray White - guitar, vocal / Eddy Jobson - keyboards / Ruth Underwood - percussion / Patrick O'Hearn - bass / Terry Bozzio - drums / Michael Brecker - tenor saxophone solo / Randy Brecker - trumpet / Lou Marini - alto saxophone / Ronnie Kuber - baritone saxophone / Tom Malone - trombone

Tracks 7 and 15 recorded 31 October 1981 at the Palladium, New York City, NY

Line-up:
Frank Zappa - guitar, vocal / Ray White - guitar, vocal / Steve Vai - stunt guitar / Tommy Mars - keyboards, vocal / Bobby Martin - keyboards, saxophone, vocal /

Ed Mann - percussion / Scott Thunes - bass / Chad Wackermann - drums

Track 8 recorded 12, 13 or 14 February 1988 at Tower Theater, Upper Darby, Philadelphia, Pa

Line-up:
same as CD 1 track 6

Track 9 recorded 3 or 4 March 1988 at Auditorium Theater, Chicago, Ill

Line-up:
Same as CD 1 track 6
Track 13 recorded 9 June 1988 at the Palasport, Genoa, Italy and on 7 August 1971 at the Pauley Pavilion, University Of California, Los Angeles, Ca

Line-up:
1988 same as CD 1 track 6

1971 line-up:
Frank Zappa - guitar, vocal / Jimmy Carl Black - vocal / Mark Volman - vocal / Howard Kaylan - vocal / Jim Pons - bass, vocal / Don Preston - keyboards, electronics / Ian Underwood - keyboards, alto saxophone / Aynsley Dunbar - drums

Track 14 recorded on 7 August 1971 at the Pauley Pavilion, University of California, Los Angeles, Ca

Line-up:
Same as CD 2 track 13

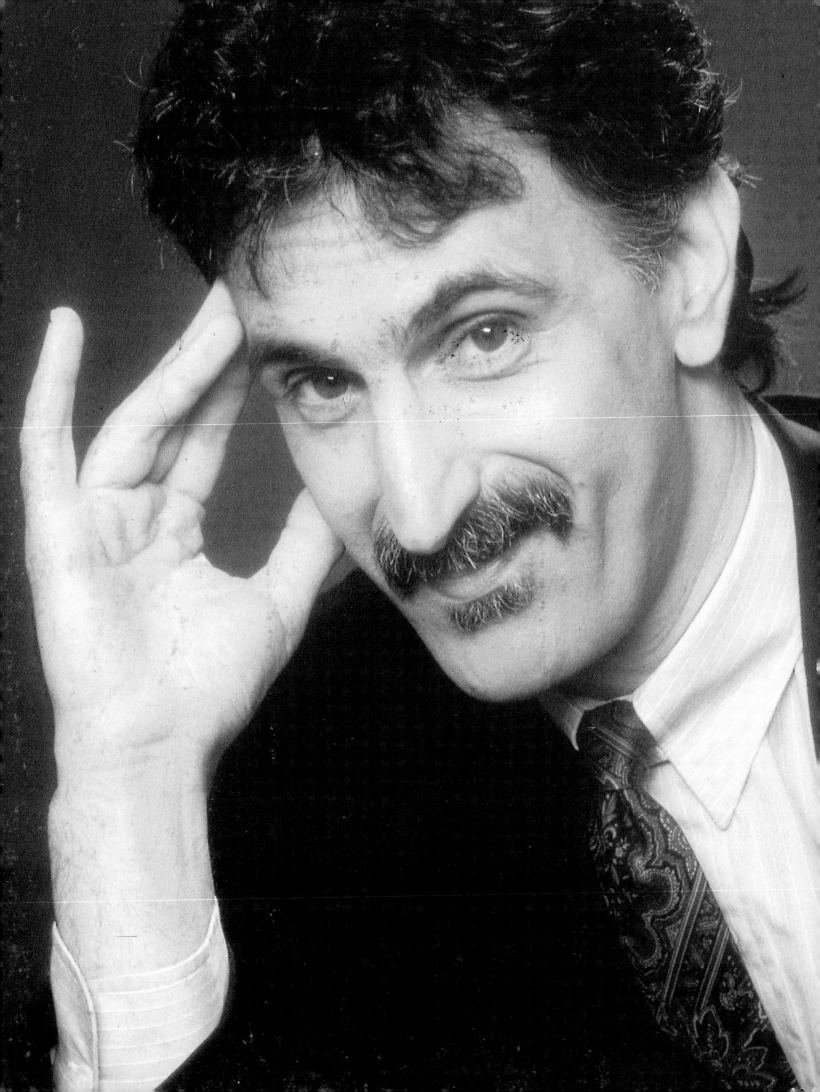